The Hawk's Done Gone

The Hawk's Done Gone

AND OTHER STORIES

Mildred Haun

Edited by
HERSCHEL GOWER

Vanderbilt University Press 1968

"For Lead" and portions of the Introduction were first published
in the *Tennessee Folklore Society Bulletin*, Volume XXXIII, Number 3 (September 1967)
"The Turkey's Feather" was first published in the *Georgia Review*,
Volume VI, Number 4 (Winter 1952)

Composed by Western Typesetting Company
Kansas City, Missouri

Library of Congress Catalogue Card Number 68-20546
PRINTED IN THE UNITED STATES OF AMERICA

CONTENTS

MILDRED HAUN, STORYTELLER

EXCEPT for the brief introduction she wrote to her collection of Cocke County ballads, Mildred Haun committed very little about herself to paper. Although she was not evasive about her personal history, she was characteristically quiet and reserved. She left no autobiographical notes that answer the kind of questions which the reader of the stories in this volume will be obliged to ask. Even to discover the milieu of the young woman who wrote most of these tales before she was thirty, one must go back to the early decades of this century and understand that part of East Tennessee where the French Broad River flows through the center of Cocke County and the Smoky Mountains rise with heavy timber in a series of alternating high hills and narrow coves. After such an exploration, one must move almost directly to the stories, for Mildred Haun confronted herself and her personal world almost entirely in fiction.

In the footlocker of papers that she willed to Vanderbilt University, the bare biographical details can be assembled almost by chance. The daughter of James Enzor Haun and his wife Margaret Ellen, Mildred Eunice Haun was born on January 6, 1911. "My mother was a Cocke County Haun and married a Hamblen County Haun," she wrote in 1937 in the preface to her ballad collection. In that same sketch she recorded that she was born in Cocke County. Some years later she learned that she had actually seen her "first daylight" at her paternal grandmother's home in Hamblen County. Yet it was at the head of Haun Hollow, Hoot Owl District, Cocke County, that she grew up and reached an awareness of people and the ways of the world. During her childhood she was accustomed to a big family of hardy, independent mountain kin, most of them hillside farmers, whose inherited code and typical attitudes are characterized, one strongly suspects, by such inflexible protagonists as Pharis in "God-Almighty and the Government," Wilbur in "Square Bread," and Claude in "The Picture Frame." Miss Haun always insisted, however, that except for her narrator, Mary Dorthula White, whom she acknowledged as an actual acquaintance, all the characters in her stories were imaginary.

She took a child's delight in the Saturday night gatherings when neighbors came in to hear music, sing songs, and tell tales. "My foreparents have lived, farmed, and sung the old songs since the county was formed in 1779." Some of the stories were old and handed down; some were made by the teller. Her mother played the accordion for the company, one brother played the dulcimer and guitar, another the melodeon. Mrs. Haun sang the ballads and a lot of other songs on these occasions, as did the sons Fred and Greeley. More often than not they sang unaccompanied, because many of the older tunes were not meant to go with an instrument put together at home or brought in from New Port or Morristown.

Mildred Haun also grew up hearing the old proverbs on the tongues of the community and soon learned to reckon that "One sorrow never comes but what two more follow it," or "Bad rumor flies as fast as a hornet," or "A crow's egg don't hatch an eagle." She was taught to read the accepted "signs" that nature discloses to the wary and discerning eye—at times harshly, always gratuitously: "A dove sitting on top of the house hollering means that one member of the family will die within a year. A honeybee or newsbee flying around one's head means good luck. If a man sees two snakes fighting, he will win the next fight he gets into. If, the night before the first morning in May, a girl catches a snail and puts it under a plate, it will write in silver letters the initials of her future husband."[1]

Because the inscrutable world of nature was always close at hand, the capricious world of spirits, spells, witches, and charms was inevitably as close. From a grandmother, Mildred heard that "hogs still get bewitched, and the only thing that will cure them is to slice up a silver dollar and put it in their slop. . . . When a witch dies her cow gives bloody milk out of three tits for three days. Silver bullets are the only things that will kill witches. A man can cast off a witch's spell by standing in a stream of water up to his knees. He must stick his arms down in the water up to his elbows and pray to the Lord to the top of his voice. Witches also have the power to charm land so it will not produce anything. But an ordinary person has the power to uncharm it if he follows the right rituals. . . . And if there is a crowd sitting around a fire and the sparks keep popping out and going toward one person, that person is a witch. Any woman can have this power transferred to her if she will go to a witch and ask to be taught the witch's prayer. She must learn this, go to a spring, turn her back to it, lean over backwards as far as possible, and repeat the prayer to the devil and all evil spirits nine times."

There was talk of this kind commingled with practical talk: the right phase of the moon for planting potatoes; the best homemade cures for farm animals; the market price which chickens and turkeys were bringing; the building of a bigger lean-to or putting a new roof on the house. Obviously the family's economic code, like that of their neighbors before World War I, was a kind of inheritance. Most of the community agreed that "it is easier to make the things one needs

---

1. These and other quotations are from "Cocke County Ballads and Songs," the unpublished M. A. thesis, signed by Donald Davidson and John Crowe Ransom, Vanderbilt University, 1937.

than to make the money to buy them . . . storekeepers have heisted things up out of sight. It's got to the place it takes a whole dozen eggs to buy one yard of gingham. And that store-bought cloth never was very lasty anyhow."

In this nearly independent Appalachian community where the Hauns had looked after themselves for a century and a half and had fared pretty well by their own standards, it is significant that Mildred took more to school and books than did Fred and Greeley. Although books were only another kind of learning, she hit on the notion of someday going to high school and then on to college to study medicine. At age fourteen she decided she would like to come back to Cocke County as an educated granny-woman with a black case so she could doctor the sick, deliver babies safely, and care for the mothers. Trained doctors were scarce; the midwives of Cocke County had begun to get old at the job; the granny-woman whom Mildred knew best, who had brought her and her brothers into the world, was hard pressed to look after the needs of the women and children in the Hoot Owl District. It was time somebody went away, the girl concluded, and learned enough to set about the job with a skilled hand. So in 1927, at age sixteen, Miss Haun was able to start to high school after leaving home and crossing half the width of Tennessee to live with an uncle and aunt at Franklin, Mr. and Mrs. A. J. Haun. There, as the high school transcript shows, she took four years of Latin, four of English, and introductory courses in biology, chemistry, and physics in preparation for medicine. Her uncle's shelter for the next dozen years was testimony of her promise.

After graduation from the Franklin High School in 1931, she applied for entrance to Vanderbilt. During the four years she was an undergraduate she made the journey to Nashville each day on the electric interurban as far as Douglas Corner. That was the point which marked the city limits—the stop where an extra fare was collected from passengers who crossed the line. So from Douglas Corner Miss Haun walked to the Vanderbilt Campus—a matter of two miles twice a day—for classes with Elizabeth Harris McDavid, Edwin Mims, Fred Santee, John Donald Wade, and Robert Penn Warren.

It was during her final year, 1934-35, that she enrolled in John Crowe Ransom's English 9, a course listed in the catalogue as Advanced Composition. Inspiring good work in his unassertive way, Ransom assigned the small class, quarter by quarter, (a) the article or essay; (b) the short story; (c) verse. Because Miss Haun had failed German and trigonometry earlier and needed to make up credits for graduation, she entered the composition class at the middle of the year as a desperate last-minute measure. Although she had given up on the sciences and medicine by this time, in the back of her head—as the "matter" of the stories she began to write for Ransom—there were mid-wifery, witchcraft, and a long-recollected granny-woman in the Hoot Owl District of Cocke County. "It is my place, seems like, to doctor sick folks and bring babies into the world, and lay out the dead," says Mary Dorthula White in *The Hawk's Done Gone*. She was born on January 6, 1847. Miss Haun was born on the same day in 1911. As mountain people know, the sixth day of January is Old Christmas, and Miss Haun has her narrator comment on the date:

> *The cows all kneel at midnight on Old Christmas to pray for any youngon born then. They pray that the youngon won't ever die. And it never will. Or so folks say. The breath may go out sometime. But the body goes on doing the same thing it did while it was breathing. Letitia Edes was born on Old Christmas. That's the reason [the mountain] keeps on growing. And will always.*

Letitia Edes, Mary Dorthula White, and Mildred Haun: one can only wonder about the coincidence of birthdays.

As the winter quarter was drawing to a close, Ransom saw enough originality in her work to encourage her to keep on writing until she had a full book of stories. "I promised him

I'd stay in the class for the spring quarter if I wouldn't have to write poetry," she later recalled. And with this request Ransom gave her a dispensation. While the rest of the class wrote verse, the shy senior sat in the back of the room and kept on with her prose ballads of Cocke County.

Other stories followed in the months after graduation—while Miss Haun was teaching at the high school in Franklin and working part-time on the M.A. in English. When Ransom left Nashville in 1937, he turned her stories over to his Vanderbilt colleague Donald Davidson, under whose direction she had collected and edited "Cocke County Ballads and Songs," the M.A. thesis of 440 pages containing some of the most valuable ballad texts recorded in the South. Davidson's interest in song lore, folk tales, and Tennessee history—written and unwritten—brought her to a full awareness of the East Tennessee heritage she was to go on dramatizing in the stories.

It is not too much to say that her ear for dialect and the rhythms of mountain speech was sharpened against the foreign clamor of urban Nashville. As a graduate student living in a rooming house at Broadway and Twenty-first Avenue, she was confronted with the din of city traffic just outside her window. Late at night across the hall a student with a gramophone played Cole Porter: "Like the beat, beat, beat of the tom-tom. . . ." Miss Haun once recalled—years later—that it was under these conditions she began writing the story "Barshia's Horse He Made, It Flew." Inside her head she first heard the rhythm of Barshia's foot beating against the planks of the porch at home. The voices of Barshia, Amy, Teelie Edes, and the others rose and fell and became more distinct. Gradually the accents of home drowned out the noises of the city, and the next day she took a first draft of the story to Donald Davidson in his office at Calhoun Hall.

After a second post-graduate year at Vanderbilt and a writing fellowship with Wilbur Schramm at the University of Iowa, Miss Haun had a book of stories that fit together as a fictionized chronicle of Cocke County. Her manuscript was accepted by Bobbs-Merrill early in 1940 and published as *The Hawk's Done Gone* on October 10 of that year. No other dialect collection from the South has been as close to the oral tradition or has achieved the same distinctive flavor and natural tonal qualities. As Amy Kanipe, the Granny-woman's daughter, looks at the pages of Births, Marriages, and Deaths in the family Bible, she makes a point of saying, "My writing looks as different from Ma's as a cow's path does from a guinea's path." And just as distinct are Miss Haun's stories—as distinct as those of Robert Penn Warren, Jesse Stuart, Peter Taylor, and Elizabeth Spencer—all of whom sat under the guidance of Ransom and Davidson.

From 1942 to 1943 Miss Haun worked as book review editor for the Nashville *Tennessean*; from 1944 to 1946 she was an editorial assistant to Allen Tate on the *Sewanee Review*. When her brother Greeley went into service during World War II, she returned to the Haun homestead from time to time to do the farm work and care for her mother. The fiction she wrote during this decade, excepting "The Turkey's Feather," has remained in manuscript till now. She also worked on a novel, "Runner Girl," which was never published.

In 1950 she continued to support herself and her mother with professional writing of another kind—as an editorial and information specialist at the Arnold Engineering Development Center in Tullahoma. Her publications for the next thirteen years—while she was living in Memphis and Washington—included news releases, speeches, correspondence courses on engineering and technical subjects for military personnel, training manuals, and a number of feature articles for the Department of Agriculture. In 1965 she was sent to Europe and the Near East to interview the directors of agricultural development programs sponsored by the United States and to report on several international co-operative projects under American foreign aid.

During a severe illness at the end of 1965, Mildred Haun

returned to Nashville for hospitalization and treatment. Part of the time she was nursed by her old friends Frances and Brainard Cheney at their home in Smyrna. She came to Vanderbilt one mid-morning in January of 1966 and talked informally to a new generation of students about the songs she had collected thirty years before from her kin and neighbors at home. In her quiet East Tennessee voice—soft, properly flat, and a little nasal—she read "Barshia's Horse He Made, It Flew." The awed students could not help noting the incongruity between the frail, diminutive figure in front of them and the story she told of cruelty and revenge.

After further months of hospitalization, Miss Haun died on December 20, 1966, at the age of 55, in Washington. She was buried a few days later beside her mother in the Haun family plot at Morristown, Tennessee.

One wishes the external, biographical facts could provide ready answers to the kind of questions we ponder after we have read the stories. What was the strange, powerful combination of heart, psyche, and hand which brought these remarkable tales to completion more than a quarter century ago? How does one account for the intense absorption in somber, discomfiting themes—witchcraft, incest, miscegenation, infanticide—by an "ingenuous" Vanderbilt coed not long removed from the "idyllic" scenes of East Tennessee? Did the stories, once written and set aside, mark the end of a private confrontation and somehow resolve a personal crisis?

We discover in Miss Haun's work an almost comprehensive treatment of superstition in the Southern Appalachians; it dramatizes the same attitudes toward the supernatural that we find in the traditional ballads and folk tales. Attesting to an unbroken folk tradition, the stories commingle modern realism and ancient metaphysical beliefs. As in the tales commonly associated with heroic and epic poetry, here is the shadowy world of dimly glimpsed magic—a world with its own set of rules and its only partially revealed *modus operandi*.

The manifestations of that world crop up at every turn: the souls of the dead live on in goats; a woman continues to grow after death and becomes the mountain which later bears her name; chains rattle in a cave and betoken the unquiet spirit of a dead son; a witch made angry persecutes and destroys her enemies; a husband unfaithful to his wife is haunted by her spirit when he lies in bed with another woman. All the supernatural events, in combination, suggest a theory of man's relationship to nature and point to a philosophical view of the world's phenomena.

This is how the narrator of "Apple Tree" records her convictions about spirits and the transmigration of souls:

> *And Buck set enough store by Pairlee to make up for anything else. Pairlee set a heap a store by him too, of course. She always looked like a little fairy. Some folks think she was Dunk's Spirit. They think the soul went out from Dunk and lived on in Pairlee. But common sense would tell a body that is not so. Spirits don't do that way. About all Spirits is, is just the same old soul in a new body. But the new body has to be just like the old one. Or else the soul wouldn't fit with it. The same body can't last forever, of course. So the soul has to have a new one to take the place of the old wore-out body— just like a plow that is out in the weather, the handles rot out but the point lasts on. A Spirit is not any bigger nor any less than the body it comes from. Spirits don't stay on this earth much of the time. They would be fools if they did. Spirits are not always happy. Dunk's Spirit wasn't in Pairlee. That was Dunk's Spirit Nep Franklin saw in the old mill shed.*

One could hardly call this vigorous discussion a mere set of conventions. Because the speaker's comments are discursive, they indicate strong beliefs. So much talk about ghosts means the world of spirits cannot be far away. In other instances the narrator mixes pagan and Christian attitudes in the normal course of reporting, and soon it becomes obvious that Christianity is a somewhat casual influence in the animistic world of Mary Dorthula White.

This powerful mountain woman establishes her identity in the Prologue of *The Hawk* cycle and towers over much of the action and most of the other characters:

> *I've been Granny-woman to every youngon born in this district for nigh on sixty years. I've tied the navel cords of all the saints and sinners that have seen their first daylight in Hoot Owl District. They all have bellies about alike. There's not much difference.*

Her speech strikes the ear directly from the printed page. The language we hear carries with it the thrust of simplicity and raw strength. The words are coarse, flinty, and occasionally terrifying. Sentence units are short, blunt, split often into staccato fragments. In these unseasoned materials of literature there is no place for circumlocution, none for convoluted rhetoric and tortuous syntax. The meaning lies not in memorable phrases, but, as in the ballads and other oral forms, in the effects achieved with a sparse, direct economy. As a reporter, Miss Haun seems incapable of self-conscious artifices or a single flamboyant vice. Her oral method is simply explosive in its implications.

The diction also serves to characterize the rationale and temper of the narrator. She observes, for example, that antique-hunters would find her house "if they had to cross hell on a rotten log." She reports that Amy had a beau who started "bossing her around like a slut dog." When Old Ad Kanipe was sowing a late crop of wild oats and sparking young girls, the blunt comment from the community is, "An old dog like that ought to be cut." Fearing the worst for her granddaughter, Mary Dorthula says, "All the years that I have been Granny-woman I never have give anybody a thing to knock a youngon. Heaps of women have begged me to. It is just one of the things I always said no to. But with Cordia it was different."

The simple figures of speech are taken directly from like-
nesses in the natural world: "hot as a sunburnt sheep . . . skin
as white as a strawberry blossom . . . face as wrinkled as a
rotten apple . . . ugly as a mud fence dabbed up with tadpoles
. . . as quiet as a snake in wintertime . . . acted like his colt's
tooth hadn't been cast . . . she wilted away like a rose throwed
in hot ashes . . . limp as a hot cabbage leaf . . . he kept his arm
around her as tight as the skin on a poor hog . . . he fell off
till he looked like a birch sapling with britches on . . . spread
over the country like polecat stink."

Bound up with the recurring natural images is the store
of folk superstitions—numerous omens, portents, and taboos—
which provide the tales with conflict and dramatic intensity.
For example, the action in a story frequently pivots on a superstition that is deeply entrenched in the mind of the community.
It may foretell trouble and assure certain doom. Herself affected,
Mary Dorthula White reacts to Chance as if the real world were
governed by a higher order of dark forces which she cannot
ignore and can seldom placate. For her there is no gap between
the natural and supernatural worlds; interaction between them
is constant; the lines of communication are always open. She
hears in the cry of the screechowl a forewarning of death—her
own, the reader comes to know—and she is prompted into a
recollection of ninety-two years. What follows is a kind of
examination of conscience which provides the narrative frame-
work in the cycle of the stories.

When an author selects materials of this kind—when he
mixes realism with the supernatural—he has the task of creating characters so completely attuned to both worlds that the
story which unfolds will achieve its own internal validity.
Without begging her reader's credulity, Miss Haun convinc-
ingly dramatizes the superstitions of her characters and brings
about fictional belief in the caprices of nature as they act upon
and affect a pantheistic universe. For example, certain ruin is
presaged by an act as simple as burning sassafras root in the

cookstove by mistake, by hearing a rooster crow at midnight, killing a toadfrog in front of a woman believed to be a witch, seeing a wren fly through the house, finding a red ear of corn in the crib when feeding the chickens, eating honey on the day a relative is to be buried, getting married when the red haw is in bloom, hearing a screech owl in the rain or seeing a dove on the roof of a house, or, worst violation of all, telling something to a third person which a dying person has asked you to hold secret. In a merely folkloristic context, a catalogue of such beliefs might be summarily forgotten by readers today. Because they are woven into the dramatic fabric of Miss Haun's stories, the superstitions contribute, paradoxically, to the final credulity. We find ourselves accepting the terms and continually looking below the surface for ultimate meaning. At the end we discover a coherent cosmological view. That is to say that we are struck first by the presentation of shocking, concrete details in this dark corner of Creation; then we are legitimately engaged in the untoward events which keep intruding upon the microcosm—informing it, changing it, sometimes creating and sometimes resolving its conflicts. Sooner or later we realize that we remember Homer, Virgil, *Beowulf,* and the supernatural ballads for precisely the same reasons.

For modern readers, however, there is this degree of difference: we must approach Homer and Virgil, sometimes laboriously, in the original tongue or in the formal, literary English of a Bulfinch. But Barshia Kanipe brings the Pegasus experience directly home in the idiom of Cocke County. The same immediate effect on the reader holds true for the other revelations in Miss Haun's world: witches, a talking apple tree, a bleeding ghost, reflections in a spring, an unquiet grave, a Daedalus figure, a witch's effigy, a journey to the moon involving a conversation with its man, the clothes of a dead child's corpse wet with tears, God talking through a bluebird, or the "hant bleach" of doom upon the brow of a boy bewitched. Because of her effective handling of these actions, we conclude that for Mildred Haun of Cocke County these were not book-learned materials from a library shelf. They were, in the course of time and in the nature of things, powerful facts which had been transmitted by ear and tongue, researched in memory, at once felt and imagined.

The crushing fatalism in all but a few of the stories is a result of the whimsical supernatural forces. All the characters know the meaning of "signs"; very few disregard them or dare to profess disbelief in their efficacy. The penalties for disavowal are inevitably severe. Amy in "The Spring is Trusty" attempts to ignore the meaning of the man's face she sees in the water on the first day of May. Enzor does not in fact seem a likely husband, for, as the narrator points out time and time again, he seems motivated by cruelty. But Enzor too is caught in the strict fatalism of the "sign." The night after he has told Amy he is through with her, he arrives with a shotgun to claim her as his bride. The Granny-woman, who has seen more of life than anyone in the community, is painfully aware of her own helplessness. Her will is so subdued that she watches passively at the murder of her granddaughter and the newborn child. At another crucial moment she murmurs, "I've been like a checker on a checker board. I've just moved when pushed. And there I've set till I was pushed again."

Readers insisting upon the Christian doctrine of free will may find that some of the characters are rendered unsympathetic because they fail to respond to the necessity of action. It is quite true that some of them lose their dignity and personality through their resigned, uncomplaining submission. The admirable dignity of the Granny-woman, however, rests in her ability to endure—to remain a person in spite of the dehumanizing world in which she lives.

This loss of dignity is most clearly seen in the way Miss Haun depicts the man-woman relationship, which is analogous to the larger structure of control and submission. The women represent the helpless element in human nature at the

same time that they typify the qualities that could be redemp-
tive in the moral order. Women like Amy, Effena, the Granny-
woman, and Meady stand out in sharp contrast to the men.
Their qualities of love, stability, industry, and kindness are
menaced by the insensitive, wasteful, indolent men under whose
rule they must live. Amy says that women are fit for nothing
but marriage. Nettie, the central character and narrator of
"For Lead," says that women have to be taken care of. Iron-
ically, of course, the men do not take care of the women. Their
lot worsens when they marry. Mary Dorthula White finds that
Ad lives off her labor. She watches him and her stepson Linus
sell her household belongings to an antique-hunter; then they
bring in cheap replacements for her carefully accumulated store
of tradition. These instances suggest that marriage is little more
than a bitter continuance of the social order and that any
happiness shared by men and women is short-lived.

With his conniving and incestuous desires, Linus is the em-
bodiment of male depravity—as are Lom and Hubert in "The
Look." Linus kills the husband of his sister Effena and moves
in with her. Although taunted by the husband's ghost into
confessing his murder, he remains unpunished. (In fact, civil
law is conspicuously absent in these stories.) When Meady
marries a Melungeon to spite Linus, his power over her remains so strong that she drives her husband away. Linus stays
with her through the birth of her twins, one of whom he
throws into the fire because he will not tolerate another man's
children. Even then Meady is passive, without the will to
retaliate.

Other stories reflect the same theme: women are to be con-
trolled by the dark psyche of the male. This recurs in "A Feeling of Pity" when Cora endures inhuman treatment from her
husband Eli and his father Noah. After the father dies, Eli is
openly unfaithful to Cora, but no one can persuade her to leave
him. The narrator explains, simply, that Cora felt pity for
people and things that could not exercise a moral control over

their actions. Thus the relationship comes full circle: the men, who seem to typify the unprincipled forces of nature, are merely the helpless agents of its overriding power. The one gleam of hope comes in the last chapter, in which Amy narrates her mother's final triumph over Ad—and her redemption of him. Thus the female principle becomes part of the higher forces and the possibility of grace is open.

It is obviously worth noting that, aside from the serious themes, there are three of the later stories which show an extraordinary talent for humor. These are "Shin-Bone Rocks," "The Turkey's Feather," and "Dave Cocke's Motion," all of which are comic sketches reminiscent of the popular tradition exploited by the Southwest humorists. As an example of local color, "Shin-Bone Rocks" is a robustious tale in which the rowdy Rocky Point boys challenge the Low Land gang over Shorty Fuller's courtship of Neppie Arwood. There is a masculine toughness at the core that suggests Sut Lovingood, Simon Suggs, and Davy Crockett. In "The Turkey's Feather" and again in "Dave Cocke's Motion," Miss Haun demonstrates through the first-person narrator that a female humorist can be as amusing as the boys who whittle on the steps of the Tumble Bug store. Here again, like the Southwest writers of last century, she turns to advantage the mountain idiom, employs the supernatural for humorous effect, and maintains a brisk country wit without being coy or bawdy.

Having noted some of the rich components, one searches above and beyond the parts for a comprehensive term to describe the body of Miss Haun's work. What do we say, finally, about *The Hawk's Done Gone* and the later stories which are obviously segments of the same family chronicle? As originally published in 1940, *The Hawk* gave some reviewers pause, for generically it is not an easy work to classify. Because the chapters are not organized around a central action, or actions, and new characters come and go in successive installments, it can hardly be called a novel. On the other hand, the stories are held together by a central character and each chapter forms a part of the same family history which she attempts to record. One recalls certain parallels with Hemingway's *In Our Time* and Anderson's *Winesburg, Ohio,* and remembers that a few critics still argue novel status for these collections.

The form Miss Haun chose—or which she let evolve—is more like that of a long traditional tale in which disparate themes occur and technical unities are not always strictly observed. Only a few of the stories—singly and out of context—are complete enough to satisfy the requirements of the well-made story like the best of Hemingway and Anderson. In arriving at a working classification of *Wuthering Heights,* Northrop Frye offers a tentative suggestion:

> *The conventions of* WUTHERING HEIGHTS *are linked rather with the tale and the ballad. They seem to have more affinity with tragedy, and the tragic emotions of passion and fury. . . . The shape of the plot is different: instead of manoeuvering around a central situation, as Jane Austen does, Emily Brontë tells her story with linear accents. . . . Conventions so different justify us in regarding* WUTHERING HEIGHTS *as a different form of prose fiction from the novel, a form which we shall here call the romance.*[2]

But if the romancer, as Frye goes on to say, does not attempt to create "real people" as much as he creates "stylized figures which expand into psychological archetypes," then Mildred Haun effected a daring combination. If Heathcliffe and Catherine are stylized figures and psychological archetypes, Mary Dorthula White and the Cocke County people remain consistently earthy in spite of their dark psychological inclinations.

Consciously or unconsciously, few writers in the twentieth century have set down as complex a rendering of romantic fantasy and realism. Perhaps few have had as informed a "folk"

---

2. Northrop Frye, "The Four Forms of Fiction," in *Discussions of the Novel,* edited by Roger Sale (Boston: D. C. Heath. 1960), p. 4.

background or been as willing to take as many chances with their readers. The thematic premise, bluntly put, insists upon equal parts of witchcraft and herb medicine. The memorable narrator is simultaneously a witch-doctor and mountain mid-wife. Thus the final integrity of these disparate elements makes for strong purgation. Because the stories are always within hear-ing distance of the folk tradition, they provide us with a link between the ancient oral tale and its full-grown modern de-scendants. To read them is to confront again those same powers operative and prevailing in epic and myth; they are the passion-ate, supernatural forces which are at work simultaneously in Miss Haun's corner of the universe and in Homer's.

HERSCHEL GOWER

The Hawk's Done Gone

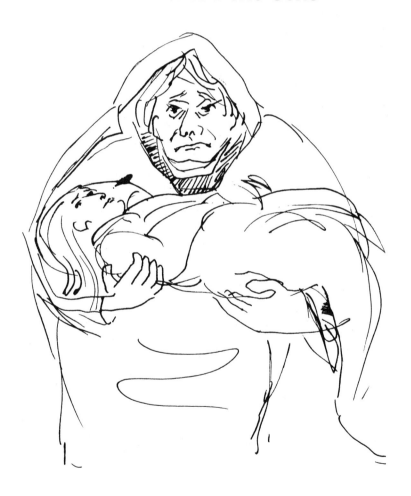

Births

Mary Dorthula White, Jan. 6, 1847

Joe White, bastard son of Mary
    Dorthula White, June 5, 1863

Ad Kanipe, January 1, 1847

Barshia Kanipe, son of Ad and
    Marthy Kanipe, April 30, 1862

Linus Kanipe, son of Ad and
    Marthy Kanipe, Sept. 4, 1865

Amy Kanipe, daughter of Ad and
    M. Dorthula Kanipe, Mar. 4, 1883

Effena Kanipe, daughter of Ad and
    M. Dorthula Kanipe, Aug. 13, 1885

Meady Kanipe, daughter of Ad and
    M. Dorthula Kanipe, Sept. 1, 1887

Wilbur Kanipe, son of Ad and
    M. Dorthula Kanipe, July 30, 1890

Bessie Brock, bastard daughter of
    Joe White and Tiny Brock, Feb. 16, 1893

Cordia Owens, daughter of Murf and
    Effena Owens, June 1, 1902

Rozella Hurst, daughter of Burt
    and Meady Hurst, Aug. 5, 1908

Drusilla Hurst, daughter of Burt
    and Meady Hurst, April 3, 1913

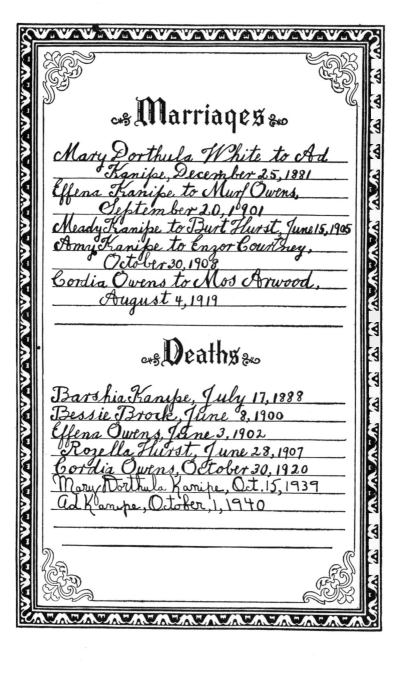

Marriages

Mary Dorthula White to Ad
    Kanipe, December 25, 1881
Effena Kanipe to Murf Owens,
    September 20, 1901
Meady Kanipe to Burt Hurst, June 15, 1905
Amy Kanipe to Enzor Courtney,
    October 30, 1908
Cordia Owens to Mos Arwood,
    August 4, 1919

Deaths

Barshia Kanipe, July 17, 1888
Bessie Brock, June 8, 1900
Effena Owens, June 3, 1902
Rozella Hurst, June 28, 1907
Cordia Owens, October 30, 1920
Mary Dorthula Kanipe, Oct. 15, 1939
Ad Kanipe, October, 1, 1940

CHAPTER 1

PROLOGUE

P UTS me in mind of Letitia Edes Mountain, this page of names in the Family Bible does. It has grown so fast. Maybe it's because I've thought a heap on Letitia. Always in the summertime when I'm out on the porch I can see that mountain. It raises up over in Hancock County, head and shoulders above any hill here in Cocke County. I can see it just back of Lead Hill. Even when I'm in the house this way I can see it through the window.

When I was a youngon folks would tell me tales about that mountain, how Letitia Edes wanted, worse than a hungry dog wants a rabbit, to grow bigger than any mountain she ever saw. She growed so big that when she died they couldn't get her out of the house to bury her. They had to climb up on the hills around the house and shovel the dirt in on top of it. But Letitia, she didn't stop growing. Not even then. Every year the mountain grows a shoulder span higher and spreads out at the bottom like a rotting haystack, till folks that used to live in the hollow all at once find themselves living on the hillside. Sometimes I nigh think I can see it growing—by watching where the shadow

5

of it falls on Sals King Mountain. I take note of it when I am watching the sun set down behind it.

Letitia Edes Mountain climbs up over there in the west, and Reds Run Mountain is in front of the house, jig-jagging up to the top like a stair-step, covered with spruce pine that stay green all winter long. And on the east side of the house there's that little old haystacky-looking hill Ma always called Sals King Mountain. I have a time hunting heart leaves and ginseng on it. It goes straight up into a point and is harder to climb than a greased pole.

There's something restful about being fenced in by the hills up here at the end of the hollow. They make me feel safe from the wind and from everything else in the world—everything save them antique hunters. There's no getting shut of them. They would come if they had to cross hell on a rotten log.

But I was talking about the Family Bible. I'm proud the antiquers didn't get it. The back is frazzled a little on the edge there. It ought to be fixed someway. And that square hole in the front cover. Joe cut it out with a case knife. He liked to cut on things. Some folks—all folks I reckon—talked about me because I had Joe before I married Ad. They don't know all that I know, of course. But it makes me feel peaceable as a full kitten just to set here and look at the Family Record page and think on all the names.

My own. It's always the first one I see. Mary Dorthula White, born January 6, 1847. On Old Christmas. The cows all kneel at midnight on Old Christmas to pray for any youngon born then. They pray that the youngon won't ever die. And it never will. Or so folks say. The breath may go out sometime. But the body goes on doing the same thing it did while it was breathing. Letitia Edes was born on Old Christmas. That's the reason she keeps on growing. And will always.

Mary Dorthula White. The pokeberry ink is faded till it looks like the name is writ with catnip tea. Seems like half of Forever since I heard the name spoke. Folks here in Cocke

County call me Granny. It's not because I've got so many grandyoungons of my own that makes them call me that. It's because I've been Granny-woman to every youngon born in this district for nigh sixty years now. I've tied the navel cords of all the saints and sinners that have seen their first daylight in Hoot Owl District. They all have bellies about alike. There's not much difference. But it's getting so I can't climb the hills like I used to. And I have that feeling nigh all the time—like I've been sent for and couldn't go. Somebody else will have to take my place sometime, I guess. I've been teaching Amy; she learned fast. She is my oldest girl and it is right she should. But then she married Enzor Courtney and moved over in Hamblen County. She'll be needed there. I'll have to go on for a while yet anyhow. Of course, there is that town doctor man that lives in Del Rio. Folks say he don't know much. But them that lives too far away from here have to put up with him sometimes. And have to pay him to boot. I don't want to think about not being any more use. It is my place, seems like, to doctor sick folks and bring babies into the world, and lay out the dead. It was just this morning I heard a screech owl hollering—in the daytime—giving warning that a death is nigh. It might be Dona Fawver. But she seems strong. I can't think who it might be. If it got so I couldn't doctor folks I might not ever see anybody. The end of this hollow is so far from the road. And it is so rough to get into that folks claim the devil's apron string broke loose here. And nobody much comes just to be coming.

But I am naturalized to the place. And never do get lonesome—no more than the old red oak over there by the spring does. In the summertime there's the little chickens to take off and feed. There's always the jay birds trying to take a bath in the water bucket. And the calico bushes all over the Lead Hill with their white, closed-up blossoms that open when they feel a bee light on them. In the fall of the year this way, I can watch the piedy colored leaves drop to the ground. And that old dogwood tree that leans out from Bays Mountain like it is trying to pull away from the hill. It is the one I chopped them chips out of to take the warts off my feet that time. It sheds off its leaves in the fall and puts on little red seeds, round and hard as gravels. Then there's hickory nuts to hunt this time of year on Sals King Mountain, and hickory tree leaves falling to the ground—yellow as the full moon.

But I hain't always been so peaceable and quiet here. Being a Granny-woman is techy business. There was Jake's and Tessie's baby that time. I was uneasy about Tessie from the time I heard she was called to straw. I told Jake I wanted him to have some other woman come too. But he went logger-headed on and didn't do it. It took me nigh all night to get the baby born. And when I did get it to come it was as black in the face as a Melungeon. They are the folks, you know, that live over in Hancock County and have that reddish-black skin, and nobody knows how they got it. No outside folks don't. They are not Indians and they are not Negroes. And they are not a mixture. They are just a queer tribe of folks that live over there on Newman's Ridge and Blackwater Creek. They have lived in Hancock County as long as the hills have, I reckon, and have tended to their own business. Letitia Edes was one of them. Well, the baby looked just like one. Of course it wasn't. But there wasn't any more sign of breath in it than there is in a burnt rock. I splashed it in a tub of warm water first and then in a tub of cold. I blowed breath down its throat and swung it up and down in the air. But there wasn't any way to get it to breathe, no matter what.

Some folks allowed I killed the youngon. They claimed every time they passed Jake's house they saw a fat, crooked form dressed in a dirt-colored lindsey dress with puffed-out sleeves and full-gathered skirt. That was me, they said. Claimed it looked for all the world like me, with my thick white hair strung down to my waist as it is when I am combing it. They saw it walking around in the yard toting a baby on a fork. Red flames spouted up from the handle of the fork and smoke flew around the baby like a swarm of bees around a limb.

Some folks say they have seen me riding through the air in a flour sifter too. And Froney's man laid a broom across the door to see whether I would step over it. A witch won't ever step over a broom, you know. I had half a mind to stoop down and pick it up just to see what he would do or say. But when I didn't, Elzie climbed back into his shell like a snail.

There's more to being a Granny-woman than some folks think there is. A body has to bear blame sometimes where blame is not due. But I just scour them things off my mind. It is not hard to. Not when I can set here by the fire and look out at Letitia Edes Mountain there, then down at this page of names that grew fast too. And think on them. They're all in here, all my own youngons. And Ad's boys by his first old woman, I put their names in too. It makes the page nigh full of names—

CHAPTER 2

THE PIT OF DEATH

Joe White (born June 5, 1863)

JOE was dark, and smooth-skinned like a paw-paw. I reckon it never was hard for folks to tell he wasn't Ad's boy. He was tall, and I don't blame Tiny Brock for setting so much store by him. All girls would have if he had give them any chance.

Some folks thought Joe was queer. He was a black little baby —nigh as black as night. Pleasant as a flower and different from other youngons as a dove is from a buzzard. I am proud he was. Even when he was in his gum and sheepskin days he had a way with him that made me do everything he wanted me to do. I don't know why. Or I guess I do too. He did Tiny the same way.

I recollect the first time Joe and Tiny ever played together. Joe was three months old. Tiny was a week younger. Sadie Brock brought Tiny over here. I put them down on a pallet to play. I give them some spools and two fall pippin apples. I give Tiny the biggest apple. Joe reached over and took it out of her hand and give her hisn. Tiny looked at him like she thought it was right. Then handed him her spool. Joe took it. Soon he handed it back to her. Tiny laughed and showed them dimples in her cheeks. Tiny was suited for Joe, I thought. Her skin was fair as a lily. And them sad-looking blue eyes, always seeming like something sorrowful was going to happen to her. Different from Joe's brown eyes that were smiling all the time like his pa's did.

After Tiny got big enough to come by herself, she come to see Joe nigh every day. Sometimes she got in such a hurry she would come before breakfast and stay till almost dark. I hated to tell her when it come time to go home. But I knowed her ma would be uneasy about her, having to pass that cave between here and their house. I never had been scary of that hole—not till Tiny told that dream she had. She come down here one morning before good sunup wanting Joe to play with her.

"Let's go holler into the cave," Joe said, "and hear it holler back to us."

Tiny looked at him with her sad eyes like she was afeared of something. "I dreampt about that cave one night," she said. Something in the way she said it made me take note.

"What did you dream?"

"Hit was scary. My pa and another man, a stranger man to me, they caught us throwing rocks into the cave. They grabbed Joe and throwed him in. Just like he was a rock too. I heard the echo. When I woke up I thought Pa was whipping me and I was crying."

I didn't ask Tiny if she eat breakfast before she left home. I wondered if Sadie had ever told her not to tell a dream before breakfast if she didn't want it to come true. I started to ask her. But somehow I didn't want to know. I tried to raz it off my mind. I couldn't do it.

Always after that I had an uneasy feeling when Joe and Tiny were playing around the cave. If they stayed too long I would go over that way to pick up wood or look for a hen's nest or something. But Joe promised me he never would go back into that cave. All the time afterward it seemed like I felt better when they played around here close to the house in sight of me or in my hearing. They would make mud houses over

there on the red bank. At least Joe would make them. Tiny
would stand and watch. That was about all she ever did. Joe
would gather up the sticks and make the house. Then he would
dob the chinks with mud and make a top of dried-up grass.
They were right pretty. Or I thought they were. Tiny never
did offer to make the house any different from what Joe said.
And he always named what they would play.

"We'll play hop-scotch," he would say.

When they got tired of that they would play with making
mud cakes. It seemed like they always ended up by making
mud cakes. "Ma, will you give me some red beans out of
that jar? And some white ones too?" Joe would keep begging
till they used up nigh all my seed beans for candy to put on
mud cakes they made. Joe did all the patting out of the cakes.
"You will get dirt under your fingernails," he would say to
Tiny, or, "You will get mud on your dress." Joe never did
like to see womenfolks go dirty.

Sometimes they would play at keeping house. Joe would
throw a stick over his shoulder and start off, calling, "Be sure
and have an early dinner." He would go away and set under
a bush for a while. Tiny would stick the beans on the cakes
and make them look pretty. Joe would come back when he
thought she had them ready. "I got the corn plowed out," he
would say. "Is dinner ready?" Tiny would give him the
cakes with beans on them. Sometimes she would put a flower
in the center. A black-eyed daisy if they were in bloom. That
was the flower Joe most liked. Tiny seemed to know nigh
everything he liked. At times I wished she didn't. I wished I
was the only one that knowed. I ought not to have had them
thoughts. Joe and Tiny would sing while they were playing.
Always they would sing:

> "And that young couple got married,
>   And married let them be.
> And that young couple got married
>   And why not you and me?"

They didn't even know what the song was about. Joe learned it from hearing me sing around here. I liked to watch them play.

But one time—it was in the fall of the year—they were playing over there under that oak tree by the spring, and I went after a bucket of water. Joe was laying down as still as a rock, all covered up with leaves. "Joe is dead," Tiny told me when she seed me come up. "Somebody kilt him dead." She was a-making out like she was crying. Joe, he got up and started walking around real stiff, looking like he didn't know where he was going. Tiny begun running and hollering, "You'd better watch out or the ghostes will get you—the ghostes will get you and take you too." They both went to laughing. I turned my head the other way. I thought Joe did look like a ghost. I couldn't help but think about that dream. I told them I thought they ought not to be playing dead.

Joe made things for Tiny to play with—the same things he made for himself, save littler. They liked to fish and hunt, him and her did. If Tiny got to go along it had to be at a time when the Old Man Brock was not at the house. But Sadie would let Tiny go anywhere with Joe. Joe caught some big fish sometimes and he was proud as a pup when he did.

Tiny was tickled too, when Joe caught a big one. She would show them dimples. "Look what Joe caught this time," she would say. And I could see a little sparkle in them sad eyes. Joe would be plagued but I could tell it did him good for Tiny to brag on him. Even that little. He said he just wanted her to go along to watch. "Girls hain't much good at fishing," he would say. Tiny would look at him and not say anything.

I couldn't stand the smell of old stinking fish. I told him not to bring any home to me. Sometimes, though, boylike, he was so proud of the big ones he caught that he would hang them on a stick and tote them home to show to me. Other folks craned their necks too, of course. But nobody could find out where he caught them. He wouldn't tell, not ever. He would

say he caught them in Slop Creek. But they couldn't find out
whereabouts in Slop Creek. No matter how hard they tried.
And they did try—harder than a preacher for mourners. Joe
used to make rabbit boxes out of hollow logs. He bought steel
traps with the money his rabbits brought him. Folks soon
found out that he sold furs—he sold several every winter—
and they itched like fleay kittens to find out where he trapped.
They never could find the place.

A few folks thought Joe knowed some paths through that
cave between Brocks' house and here. They allowed there were
all sorts of animals in there but nobody had ever been able to
get further back into it than five or six yards. They allowed
Joe might have found a path through it or maybe some other
opening. I don't know. He did sometimes grin mighty big
when he heard folks talk about that cave going straight down
instead of back into Reds Run Mountain like other caves.

Joe kept on trapping after he growed up. He would go to
his traps at two o'clock in the morning. I wasn't bothered by
it any more than the spring is bothered by a little frost. He
told me about his jaunts. He cut canes and made whistles so
as to keep himself company on the way. One icy morning,
after a wet snow had been falling all night, Joe said he had a
good time that morning. He said them big patches of bull weeds
looked like soldiers. Looked like soldier men marching with
swords across their backs. Big strong soldiers with silver swords
—no blood. He had heard about soldiers. I told him all that I
knowed. And when Ad was sparking me he used to be pretty
good to tell Joe stories about soldiers. I wish there had been a
war Joe could have gone to. I used to watch him and Tiny
act out them play songs. Always they liked to play "Soldier
Boy and Fair Lady."

> "The soldier boy come riding by,
> And there he spied a fair lady."

Joe would take Tiny's hand and play like he was running off
with her.

But old bull weeds covered with ice don't look any more like soldiers to me than sweet williams look like men. I guess I don't ever see any further than my own nose. But Joe in a war. He would have looked good dressed up in soldier's clothes. So tall and straight. Tan. Tan would have made his brown eyes show up. Joe would have looked like his pa. For all the world like his pa. And maybe come marching by Tiny's house and kept the soldier men from harming her things. All the other soldiers would have minded what Joe said.

But the way it plagued Joe to tease him about the girls—nigh to death. His face would turn as red as a rooster's comb. And make his eyes look browner. More browner than they were. The little old girls all feisted around him at school. But he never had any use for any of them save Tiny.

He was always mannerable toward Tiny. I couldn't help but take note of it. I don't reckon there was a day that they didn't go on to school together of a morning and come back together of an evening. Joe led the way—mashed down the briars and held back the bushes for her. I never did take time to teach him that. He did it of his own accord. And helped her across the gullies. "Here, give me your hand and I'll pull you across—you might fall in."

It was funny the way he looked on Tiny. He wanted her to do everything he did. But he wanted to be the one that showed her how. And he wanted to act like he was stronger than her. He made her flips and shotguns and things like that. Sawed and hammered and whittled away on things for Tiny. He had her climbing trees and throwing rocks and doing all sorts of things like that.

The time Tiny clumb that old rotten oak. The one over yonder on the other side of Reds Run Mountain. Barren of limbs full halfway up. She thought she seed a 'possum's hole and she climbed up further than Joe told her to. A limb broke with her.

That was one time Joe was scared white as a young buzzard

when he got home. Them big old brown eyes were popping like a screech owl's. I couldnt' help but laugh. And yet it wasn't funny. At least no laughing matter.

Then that fuss Joe and Tiny had with Basil Shipley. Basil was a snotty-nosed little old girl from down in the slates and she made fun of Tiny's apron because Tiny's ma made the cloth. Joe, he took up for Tiny and told Basil the buttonholes in her dress looked like pigs' eyes. I wonder what made Joe ever think of a thing like that. Youngons can think of funny things. Or Joe could. At least I thought he could. I don't guess Old Lady Shipley did.

Tiny was a bashful little critter. As modest as a dove. She never did any harm to anybody. But Basil pinned a sign on the back of her dress tail that evening. It was cut out in the shape of a tag, and had "Lost Dog" printed on it. Joe had took note of everybody looking at Tiny and laughing. But he didn't know what it was all about till Tiny turned off down there where the path separates to go to her house. Then he saw that tag, and he stooped down and pulled it off.

When Tiny got home that night she found dirt and gravel in her dinner bucket. And a note that said, "Tiny Brock's hair looks like it has been fried in hen oil—nobody but a bastard would spark her." She told Joe about it the next morning when she met him at the forks of the path. She cried like a pinched baby and said she wanted to stay home from school that day. But Joe begged her to go on.

That day at dinner recess they all got to playing "Go in and out the windows." Joe was in the ring and when they come to that verse that said:

> "Go forth and face your lover;
> Go forth and face your lover,
> For love has gained the day,"

Joe walked up and faced Tiny just as he always did. When they sung the verse that says, "I'll measure my love to show

you," Tiny stretched her arms out full length and Joe did too.
And their finger tips touched.

Basil Shipley went to laughing and she begun singing:

> "Lost Dog is in love with a bastard,
> Lost Dog is in love with a bastard,
> And he is in love with her."

Joe and Tiny, they stood there for a span. They didnt' know
what to do. Tiny finally spoke up—the first time she ever did
—and she said, "You're just mad because Joe won't spark
you. That's what's wrong with you." Basil pointed her finger
at Tiny and begun hollering:

> "Oh, Tiny's mad and I am glad
> And I know what will please her:
> A bottle of ink to make her stink,
> A bottle of wine to make her shine
> And Joe White to squeeze her."

Then Basil's brother, that sawed-off one that they called
Shorty, took it up. He said, "Oh, look at little Joey, the sparking man—he is mad. Look at his green eyes. Oh, he is mad
and I am glad." Joe looked at Shorty and said, "You shut
your big mouth or I'll knock you into the middle of next
week." Everybody got quiet as a snail. Joe and Shorty stood
there looking at one another. Both of them swelled up like
toad frogs. The girls went to walking off. They huddled together up on the bank where they could see good. The boys
that were for Shorty kept getting up closer to him and the
ones that were for Joe went to easing over to him by the littles.
Somebody said they had better get them off down below the
bank so Miss Omie wouldn't see what was going on.

Joe and his side, they started. But them on Shorty's side
couldn't get Shorty to budge a smidgin. He stood there red
in the face and begun to shake like a trapped rabbit. They tried
to push him, but he slapped at them and wouldn't be moved.
Them on Joe's side begun hollering:

"Coward, coward, that's what's right,
Shorty's a coward, and he won't fight."

They got to hollering pretty loud and Miss Omie come out of
the schoolhouse to see what was wrong. She went to asking
questions and Shorty spoke up that Joe had threatened to slap
him into the middle of next week and was trying to make
him go down there behind the bank to fight. Basil butted in
and told that Tiny started it.

All the youngons begun trying to tell what had took place.
First one and then another told his side. And they all told
different things. They told so many different things that I
reckon Miss Omie didn't know which one to believe. She
ended up by making Joe stay in after school. It was good dusk
when she let him out. Tiny was waiting for him a little ways
from the schoolhouse. She set down in the path and waited
for him to come. It was dark as pitch by the time they got to
the fork in the path. Joe went on with Tiny till they got in
sight of her house.

That made him a good whet after dark getting home. I
didn't fuss at him any when he told me about it. I thought
it would work out somehow. The next day when he went
to eat his dinner he found a dead rat in his basket. Of course
he knowed Shorty Shipley put it in there but he didn't make
any name of it.

But, sometime during the day, Basil Shipley got hold of
Tiny's book and grabbed a note out of it—one Joe wrote
Tiny, of course. Tiny jumped up to take it away from Basil.
Basil hollered out, "Teacher, here's a note." Miss Omie took it
and read it out loud to the whole school. She made Joe and
Tiny go up to the front of the room and stand with their
backs to one another. Made Joe stand on his left foot and Tiny
on her right one. She kept them both in after school that
evening. And give them a good shaming about writing notes.
"Hain't you big ones to be sparking?" she said. Of course Miss
Omie never had sparked anybody.

That was on a Thursday. The next Monday, on the way to school, Tiny and Joe found a nest of little garter snakes. Joe caught them and put them into Tiny's dinner basket and they took them on to school. At the first recess Tiny put them into Basil Shipley's desk—just poured them out into her desk. Books were called and Basil got in her seat. Directly them snakes, all quiled up together, fell out into her lap. Basil jumped up and hollered. She hollered and bawled and took on like a dying calf. Miss Omie got mad as a wet hen.

But nothing kept Joe and Tiny from sticking together. They were fitted for one another. And then not getting to marry. Joe took it as well as anybody could, I reckon. I believe what Tiny's pa said hurt his feelings. Joe said he didn't pay it any heed. He might have said that to kept from making me feel any worse than I always did. I wasn't ashamed. But I didn't see why it should be held against Joe for what I had done.

Joe took Tiny to a cake-walking over at Holiways church house one night. Just a few nights after me and Ad got married, and Ad moved over here with me and Joe. Tiny slipped out after the Old Man Brock went to sleep and Joe waited for her down the path a piece. Ad caught on that Joe was going and he thought he must be aiming to take Tiny. So he followed him. Ad had a grudgment against Joe from the start, seemed like. After he seed Joe and Tiny meet, he went and called the Old Man Brock out of bed. The Old Man and Ad both took themselves to the cake-walking. Just to cause trouble, of course.

The cake-walk was going well. Joe and Tiny were having a big time. They looked pretty together because Joe was big and dark, and Tiny was so fair. The fiddlers were playing "Shoot the Buffalo." Joe and Tiny were dancing around and the caller was giving them a good looking over. They were trying for the best-looking pair. Just about the time the walk was ready to end, Old Man Brock stepped up and pulled Tiny out of the ring. Tiny looked at Joe like she hated to leave him. Joe stepped out of the ring too.

"You hain't a-sparking my girl," Old Man Brock said. Joe answered back. One word led to another. They stood there and growled at one another till Joe took note that everybody was watching them and he told the Old Man they had better get out of the crowd. They went off down into the thicket— just left Tiny standing there by herself looking like a scared deer. Joe and the Old Man went to the thicket, but they didn't go by themselves. Ad was tagging along right by the side of Old Man Brock. And six other men followed them. They were for Joe. They told him to go on—they would see it was fair.

When they got down there in the thicket, the Old Man Brock begun cussing Joe. He called him everything save something decent. Joe doubled up his fists and started at him. The Old Man grabbed in his hip pocket. He was grabbing for his pistol. But the other men took the pistol away from him. "You're going to fight it fair," one of them told him. The Old Man Brock looked around at Ad. Ad was standing there shaking all over and the Old Man wouldn't move an inch to hit Joe. It was his place to hit first because he started the racket. The Old Man and Ad kept easing off by the littles till finally they went on away and didn't show themselves again that night. I recollect how Ad was breathing when he come home. When Joe got back into the crowd he found Tiny still standing there by that old cedar tree. Shorty Shipley was trying to get her to walk with him. But Tiny wouldn't do it.

Old Man Brock give Tiny a whipping when she come in that night. And her eighteen year old. He allowed as how he would kill her and Joe both if she ever slipped off and went with him again. He watched her close for two or three weeks after that. Joe didn't get to see her scarcely any. But the Old Man Brock couldn't stay from town on Saturday nights for long at a time. And Joe watched his chances.

A short while after that Joe told me he had asked Tiny to marry him. Told me all about it. I can nigh see them now—the both of them setting there, either one thinking of tothern. It was dusk-time—after supper when Tiny had come to the spring to fetch a bucket of water. The stars were popping out, one here and one there, then two over there and like that all over the sky till it was beginning to get speckled. There was a whippoorwill hollering. They could hear it away across the field. All the other birds had gone to roost. They could hear the branch a-talking to the sweet-smelling flowers on the bank. And near make out what it was saying. Or play they could.

They set down on the bank of the branch and asked riddles to one another. Tiny asked hern:

> "There was an old woman didn't have but one eye,
> But she had a long tail that she let fly.
> Every time that she went through a gap,
> She left a piece of her tail in a trap."

"I never could rede that," Joe owned up. "What is the answer to it?"

"Hit ain't anything but a needle—that's all."

"Do you like to sew?"

"I like to try. Ma says I have a right smart sleight at it. I've pieced eight quilts. One of them is puckered some—the first one I made."

"Your hands are teeny and you can make little things, I bet."

"I can tat right good."

They got to singing. They sung them old love songs over again. The same ones they used to sing—save this time Joe would look at Tiny and Tiny would look at Joe and each one of them knowed the other one meant the words in the songs. Till Tiny took note that it was getting late. "Ma will think I have fell into the spring."

"But let's sing one more."

Tiny laughed. "Maybe we'd better sing 'Till We Meet Again,' " she told him.

But Joe wasn't to be outdone. He said they would sing "That Young Couple." Tiny did like she always did—she give in.

> "And that young couple got married,
>   And married let them be.
> And that young couple got married
>   And why not you and me?"

Joe set there for a right smart while. He crumbled up a clod and let the dirt run through his fingers. He would look at Tiny, and then he would try to say it. Finally, he got it out, "I don't reckon you've got any idea of ever marrying me, have you, Tiny?"

"You hain't never asked me yet, have you?"

"But I don't reckon you would."

"Are you going to ask me to?"

Then Tiny laid her head on Joe's shoulder and he put his arm around her, real clumsy and bashful-like, and she told him she would marry him. That was all.

But Tiny had to ask her pa first. That was where the rub come in. The next Saturday night they met at the spring to see what her pa said. He had a knack for saying the wrong thing. Always. The Old Man Brock did. He said he was a Christian man, a member of the Holiways church house, and he couldn't afford to have the name of his girl marrying a bastard, and he wouldn't have. Joe vowed he would marry Tiny anyhow. I looked at him. And thought about Tiny's dream.

I didn't know it then. But I learnt about it afterward, that Ad had something to do with Old Man Brock not being willing. I never did cheep it to Joe. I thought it best not to. I've always had a hankering Joe thought the thread come from a ball somewhere. He knew Ad and Old Man Brock were thick as two in a bed.

I tried to make Joe promise he wouldn't ask Tiny to go against her pa's will. I didn't want him to do anything to make the dream come true. He wouldn't promise me. He had a dream too, he said, about a snake trying to wrap around Tiny's neck. Joe tried to kill the snake. That made me more uneasy. But I didn't tell him dreaming of a snake meant he would be killed. I didn't think I ought.

Folks thought Joe never did see Tiny any more after the Old Man Brock told them they couldn't mary. But I had a sort of hankering. I didn't think it humanly possible for Joe to stay away from Tiny nigh twelve year. But still I don't see how they managed to get together. Joe, he went on trapping. Got so he would stay away two weeks at a time. Sometimes longer. And him and Ad didn't have anything to say to one another when he did come in. Then it got out that Tiny was called to straw. Old Man Brock didn't take note of Tiny's shape till nigh four months before the time. He allowed as how he was going to kill Joe if he ever set foot on his place again. It spread around over the country like polecat stink that he said he was.

It was talked around that the Old Man Brock tried to beat the youngon out of Tiny. I don't know. Sadie Brock just told me afterward that she tried to get Tiny to take pennyroyal tea to knock the youngon. But Tiny wouldn't do it. Said she and Joe were going to get married and she wanted to have the baby. Said she was old enough to have a mind of her own. I don't know what all took place. I just had to go by hear-tell.

The word got around that Old Man Brock wasn't ever going to let Tiny out of the house again. And there was talk that the Old Man and Ad were getting even thicker. It seemed like everybody in the country was waiting for something to happen. Just waiting for it to. But hoping maybe it wouldn't.

I could tell Joe felt it. The last several times he come in home he was nigh pale as a ghost. And that smile—his pa's smile—got to seeming like it wasn't meant for anybody to see. But just a smile without a meaning. A smile like ghosts have, almost. I didn't like it.

Joe come in one day and told me what he aimed on doing.
I argued with him. I asked him if he recollected Tiny's dream.
"Yeah," he said, "and she told it before breakfast." But Joe
said he wasn't afraid. He was going after Tiny. It was about
her time and he was going to bring her down here so I could
take care of her. He didn't care what Old Man Brock said
and he didn't care what Ad said. He had already told Ad.
I couldn't reason with him. He went walking off, humming
like a ghost:

> "It's 'possum when I'm hungry, I'm hungry,
>   It's whisky when I'm dry.
> It's heaven, heaven, sweet heaven,
>   It's heaven when I die."

I stood there too stiff to move. Stood there and watched him
go. And knowed he feared more than he let on.

I thought of the blacksnake Joe dreamed about. I thought
of Old Man Brock. And I thought of Ad. Ad was out somewhere with his gun. Joe didn't take hisn. I put a stick of
wood into the stove. And seed it was sassafras. The worst of
bad luck. I knowed then. Old Man Brock would have an
excuse. I set there like a bump on a log. Set there and didn't
think nor bat an eye.

Ad come in about midnight and I was still setting there. I
don't know what he thought. He looked sneaking—more
sneaking than a sheep-killing dog. He sort of glanced at me
and turned his head the other way.

Nine days after that—exactly nine—Tiny had the baby. It
was after dark when I come back from helping. I feared to
pass that cave. When I got close to it, I felt like woolly bugs
were crawling all over me. It was so quiet I could have heard
a feather drop. I tried to run past. My legs wouldn't work.
Something made me stop—right in front of the cave. Chains
rattling in it. Animals hollering. And a man's voice—Joe's
voice. I knowed it was his voice. And I was sure.

CHAPTER 3

DARKNESS COMING DEEP

Bessie Brock (born February 16, 1893)

I TOLD the bees about Bessie three times. Thought maybe that would take it off my mind. I don't know. Somehow, I have thought on her ever since—not ever knowing her real pa and ma. But I reckon it was best that she be took. Reckon it was meant that way.

Bessie was a pretty little booger though. I have missed her worse than a bonnet. Old Man Brock didn't want her, and him her own grandpa. And Ad, he raised Cain with me. I knowed it was best. Joe never did get to see Bessie while he was alive. But afterward, well, I reckon he did.

It was just three weeks after Bessie was born that Sadie Brock come running down here on evening late and said Tiny was bad sick. Nigh unto death, she thought. I put on a clean apron and went.

When I got there Tiny was already as cold as a cornstalk. Laying on the floor in that little old lean-to with no cover on her. And it snowing outside. I went on and laid her out. Old Man Brock said he wished the damned bastard baby would die too. "One damned bastard begets anothern," he said. I didn't pay him any heed, or tried to act like I didn't.

Sadie bawled a little and said she was shedding tears over

Tiny's going to Torment. "That awful place where whores and bastards go," she said. "And liars and hypocrites and killers," I could have added. But that wasn't any time for adding.

The Brocks didn't offer to have Tiny laid out on the bed in the big house. But I lugged her on in there anyhow. And there was the baby—Bessie, laying there in all that filth. I couldn't keep my hands off her. Not to have saved my hair and hide, I couldn't.

But I do feel halfway ashamed for the way I treated Tiny. I pert nigh throwed her body down and picked Bessie up. It was the first time I had seed her since the day she was born. And Tiny wouldn't have cared if she had knowed. She hadn't been used to any treatment anyhow.

Old Man Brock and Sadie stood there like locust posts, not turning over a hand to do e'er a thing. I held Bessie in my arms as long as I could without my conscience hurting me too bad. About not laying out Tiny. I took note of Bessie's eyes. Joe's eyes and them pretty dimples. But she stunk worse than a cow stable, she was so wet and dirty. If it had been summer the flies would have been blowing her.

"She ought to be changed," I said.

Sadie looked sullen and answered shortly, "Well, if you want it changed, you can change it yourself."

The Brocks didn't have a sheet on the place. Old Man Brock is about like Ad in some ways. He never sees the use of women-folks having anything decent for the house. But I washed Tiny and laid her out on them old dirty quilts. All wet with where the baby had been. I could tell how things had been going. Tiny had tended to the baby till she couldn't set one foot before the other, and then just laid down and died like a wore-out horse. Might nigh dropped dead in her tracks wait-ing on the baby. It hadn't been waited on since. I wonder how Tiny managed to let it nurse.

As soon as I got Tiny laid out I went down to Sue Ella

Whetsel's and told her about it. Sue Ella got out some clean sheets and towels. Me and her sewed two of the bed sheets together to make Tiny's winding sheet. The news soon got norrated around. Dona Fawver fetched two sheets and that Lone Star quilt of hern. We fixed Tiny up like a decent corpse ought to be fixed.

Tiny was pretty as a calla lily laying there in them white sheets. Dona had them done up so good and clean. And that Lone Star quilt—pieced out of red and green and yellow, with more red than any other color. When that was laid over Tiny the red shined up against her cheeks and made her look colorful. Like she was laying there a-sleeping.

Dona hollered out once during the night. She said she seed Tiny open her eyes and turn her head over sideways just like she was looking to see if the baby was all right. I was back in the kitchen at the time and I don't know whether Dona was just scared or not. She vows and declares it to be so. And I never have heard tell of Dona and the truth being very far at outs.

All I know is that during the night when Dona and all the rest were setting there snoring like hogs a-grunting, that— well, I didn't know what to think at the time. I knowed it was midnight because I could hear Whetsel's rooster crowing. The sound come across the hill. I had a feeling—some kind of queer feeling that I never had had before. I thought, "I wish to my Lord Sue Ella would wake up."

About that time I thought about the door. We hadn't left it ajar. It was still cold and Sue Ella said we had best shut it till nigh midnight. I thought to myself real quick—I had better jump up and crack that door so Tiny's spirit could get out. Well, I tiptoed over there and opened it part way open. I started tiptoeing back to the corner. I didn't even look toward the bed. But I heard the lowest voice. It had been so long since I had heard Tiny say anything that I didn't quite memorize how her voice sounded. But that voice said, "Bessie's pa will care for her."

It dumfounded me for a right smart whet of time. I don't recollect whether I stood there like a scared chinch or whether I went back to where I was setting. I just don't recollect.

But the first thing I memorize taking place after that was Dona saying, "Granny, you're nigh tired to death, hain't you?" And I did feel all at once like I was about to fall to staves. But I didn't give my answer. I just set there. I guess I must have looked like a scared lamb. I didn't want to set Dona off to talking about it. I didn't feel in the mood for talking.

We had the burying the next morning. It was a pitiful sight. Dona fetched Bessie some things to wear. We talked it over about taking her to the burying. We didn't make any name of it to Old Man Brock nor Sadie. We put the clothes on Bessie and toted her. It wasn't such a fur piece to the Holiways church house.

When Henry Buckner—he was the man that sort of took the burying in hand—when he said that folks could come around and look at the corpse, you would have thought Tiny didn't have any folks at all.

Other folks, of course, waited for Old Man Brock and Sadie to make the move. But the Old Man, he set right there without moving a smidgin. Sadie begun twisting and turning like there was a cockle-burr in her seat. It was right plain she was wanting to go but was waiting for the Old Man to make the start.

It got so quiet there in the church house that it seemed like folks had quit breathing. I thought it was time for somebody to make a start. I got up from my seat and took Bessie up there in my arms. Old Man Brock and Sadie followed.

After Bessie got bigger I talked to her about her pa and ma. I told her all about Joe, how he looked and how much he set a store by her, and learned her to call him Daddy. She talked about things Daddy used to do, just like she recollected.

"Daddy is so tall," she would say. "Are there any little girls up in Heaven for Daddy to love? Is Mamma there too? Why did they go? Will I ever die? Will I go to Heaven? Will my kitten go? Are you too old to go to Heaven, Granny? When will I go?"

I lugged Bessie back over to Brocks' after the burying. The Old Man allowed as how I could just keep her if I wanted to. Said he wasn't used to raising bastards. I brought her on home with me. Ad soon got over it. And Amy did pert nigh all the taking care of her.

It seemed like Bessie never did get started off right. She was pale and sickly from the first. I kept having hopes that she would get all right. I thought maybe it was because Tiny had to do like she did, that maybe she hadn't give enough milk for Bessie. I give her bone-set tea and iron-root tea. But it seemed like there was a little something wrong with her all the time. She wasn't exactly sick, but she didn't have the life in her that other youngons have. She growed up skinny and gangling like a sunflower. Seemed like her legs weren't strong enough to hold her body up.

Ad even took notice of it. I thought it would be good for her to stay out in the air as much as she could. I was forever telling Amy to take her out in the yard. Sometimes the other youngons would try to teach her to play hop-scotch or "Love Has Gained the Day," or "Babes in the Wood." She wanted to play as bad as a crippled pup. But she couldn't stand it long. Her breath would give out on her. Then she would have to set and watch the others. Set and look on with pitiful eyes at Effena and Meady playing.

Bessie was a queer youngon—like Joe. And yet not like Joe in everything. She acted like a grown-up woman from the time she started talking. She liked to mock Amy's ways. She thought the sun riz and set in Amy. And she liked to stay around in the kitchen and talk to me when I was cooking. She was a heap of help.

All my youngons thought as much of Bessie as a cow does of its first calf. They treated her like she was a fairy. Seemed like they felt she wasn't as stout as the rest of them. I never named it to them. They always made her set in the shade while they picked the strawberries. When they went to the spring they would give her that little old pint cup that Barshia made a bailing wire handle to. That was all they ever let her try to tote up the hill. But Bessie was as sharp as a bright new pin. She took note of it. She said she was a big girl, she could tote a bucketful.

After a while, though, she got so she didn't offer to go to the spring with them. "I'm going to stay and help Granny," she would say. When I was over at the meal box and needed a knife or something out of the three-cornered cupboard I would tell her to bring it to me and them little old brown eyes would glitter. Or sometimes I would tell her to put a stick of wood into the stove. And it made her as proud as a bird pup with his first quail. "Granny, do I help much?"

"I couldn't get along without you."

"Am I good help?"

"You're handy as a pocket on a shirt," I told her.

Seems like everything happened so sudden-like that I never did get my senses together enough to know just what took place. I've been like a checker on a checker board. I've just moved when pushed. And there I've set till I was pushed again.

Amy called Bessie to get up that morning. It was on a Wednesday, and she said all right. Amy come on back into the kitchen without thinking anything uncommon. I thought it a little queer. Because Bessie was generally up by the time I got the stove fire going good. "I got up early because the early bird catches the worm," she would say. Then she would look up at me, "Let me make up biscuit bread for you, will you, Granny? I done already washed my hands—see? They're clean as a pin."

I kept wondering why she didn't come on. It wasn't like

common for her to go back to sleep after she was waked. Amy called her again and asked her if she was sick. She said she wasn't.

The rest of us all set down to eat. Somehow I didn't feel hungry. I went on into the big house. I called Bessie. I could tell from the way she made answer that something was wrong. I took hold of her hand and it felt to me like it was hot as an iron. She put her hand up to her head. "I hurt all over, Granny," she said.

I told her to lay still. I went on and did up the work. I didn't say anything to Ad about it. I didn't know how he might take it. Him and the boys went off to the store that morning soon as they got their breakfast down. To loaf all day and tell yarns.

By the middle of that evening Bessie had little tiny red spots on her legs. I put my finger on them and they turned white. Right then I knowed what was wrong. "Hit is mountain fever," I said.

Me and Amy made her plenty of cherry-bark tea. That is the first time I have ever seen it fail to cure the fever. We poured it down her by the cupfuls. But it didn't have any effect on her at all. For twenty whole days she laid there without any change one way or the other. I couldn't hardly sleep or do anything else waiting for the twenty-first day to come. I knowed the night of the twenty-first would bring a change one way. Even Ad hoped and thought the change would be for the better. They all did. I didn't think, nor say I thought—nor even hope nor say I hoped. Amy didn't either.

The twenty-first morning she seemed pyeart as a pup. She riz up in bed and said she wanted to see her kitten. Amy went and fetched Old Boots into the room. Bessie took it up on the bed and rubbed it and asked it if it had been lonesome. It played with her easy-like. Just as if it knowed. She wanted Old Shep, she said. Amy called him too. He put his front paws up on the bed and licked her face and whined. Bessie laughed and said

Old Shep thought her face needed washing. But it didn't. Me
and Amy kept her clean.

It was the first time she had took note of the youngons
in a week. Effena was standing there eating a walnut and
Bessie said, "I want the boy's britches out of that walnut."
Effena handed it to her. I didn't say anything against it. I'm
proud now I didn't. She looked around at them, plumb bright.
"We could play eleven hand here on the bed." Amy motioned
to the youngons. They all went over there and set around on
the edge of the bed. But Bessie's arm was so weak she couldn't
lift it. Old Shep hung his head and moseyed out of the room.
When I took note of him it seemed like all the hope went out
of me. The youngons stayed in there with Bessie. After a
while she went to sleep and they come out. Effena looked up
at me. "Is Bessie going to be better?" she asked. I didn't
answer.

I set by the bed as much as I could that day. And while
I was setting there that evening I sort of went off into a
trance, I reckon. Anyhow I thought I was talking to Tiny
again. I heard her say, in the same voice that sounded like it
did that night, "Take her to Joe . . . the cave." Then Bessie
must have stirred, for I woke up. She was laying there looking
at me. Seems like I was more uneasy about her than I had
ever been about any of my own youngons. I set as much a
store by her as I did her pa. Joe would have been proud to
have seed me with her. She just laid there and kept looking
at me.

"Tell me a story, Granny, will you?—the one about the
man in the moon. Did he burn brush, Granny?"

"Yeah, he burnt brush. You recollect it well."

"I hurt, Granny—all over. I hurt worse than a shot bird."

"I'll get you a fresh drink of water. Hit'll make you feel
better."

"Kiss me, Granny. I feel as hot as a sunburnt sheep."

I give her a cold drink and put a wet rag to her head. But she didn't seem to give any heed to what I was doing.

"I dreampt I saw Daddy up in Heaven last night, Granny. He wanted me to come up there too. Hold my head up, Granny. I'm tired. I'm tired as a dog ater a fox hunt."

I propped her head up on the pillow and it seemed like she looked more stronger than she had for over a week. Amy brought her some snake-root tea. But she was fretful and pushed it away. "I don't want it, Amy. Hit tastes worse than gall."

Amy said she was going out and bury something of Bessie's. I told her I feared there wasn't any use. But she went on. Bessie didn't give any more heed to her going than if she had been a fly.

"Tell me the story about the Christ Child, will you, Granny? And the one about the man in the moon, will you? And the man's ghost that stalked around without his head?"

It was hard for me to get through them stories. But I went on. "Well, one time there was a man. He knowed hit wasn't right to work on Sunday. But he went on and did it just the same. So one day, when there wasn't any call for it, he was out a-burning brush on Sunday evening. The brush didn't get quite burnt up. He didn't want the fire to spread so he stayed with it till after dark. Directly the moon come up. And when it seed him down there burning brush it come right down and got him."

"Is that the same man that's still in there?"

"That's the one you see in the moon every time you look at it."

"Can he see me?"

"He can see you too."

"Tell me about the man that didn't have a head. Could he see without a head?"

Somehow or nother, I didn't care to talk about ghosts. I don't know why. Or at least I didn't exactly at the time.

And yet I felt like I ought to humor Bessie. Just felt that way. So I went on. Amy come in about the time I got it told and said supper was ready. I told her to let the rest go on and eat. To keep the youngons quiet and keep them out of the big house.

"And the one about the Christ Child, Granny, will you —now—?"

"One time—it was on a cold Christmas Eve—there was a little boy child a-wandering around through a big place somewhere, I don't know how come him—"

But I didn't go any further, for I looked down at Bessie and saw she was sleeping like a full kitten. I set there till it was a right smart whet after dark and I heard Ad snoring out on the back porch. I thought it was time I took myself to see Joe. I put on a clean apron. Joe never did like to see me dirty. I felt pert nigh afeared and yet I wasn't afeared. It was a pretty night. The pines looked white when the moon shined on them. The red buds were a purplish color. And that dogwood tree was in full blossom. The blossoms looked like they were a pale blue. The moon changed everything—the sweet williams smelt sweeter and it seemed like the air smelt more fresh-like. It was more cooler than general too.

It just made me wish I could live outdoors all the time. Everything was still—just one frog hollering somewheres, and two birds a-singing real low. I looked up at the moon. I couldn't help talking out loud to myself, or I guess to the man in the moon. I sort of grinned at him. I felt like he was looking at me and listening. "I bet you don't know little Bessie likes to hear stories about you," I said, and I thought I could see him smile back at me. I wish I could have told Bessie more stories. But after I got married I never did feel like singing or asking riddles or telling tales or anything like I used to do for Joe. I forgot all pretty things.

It seemed like it was a right far piece to the cave. But shortly I heard the frogs hollering over at Brocks' pond and I could tell I was near the cave. I was getting closer and more closer with every step I took. Then I thought I saw something. I did. Like a man with no head. "But that's not Joe." I felt like the ground was shaking under me—felt like the earth had fell down and left me standing there on nothing. Once I thought I would go back. But that was what I had come for. I hollered to him. He didn't answer. Then I thought, "Well, no wonder, without a head."

I felt like I was facing the Judgment Day. I kept on easing up, a real short step at a time—and every step kept getting me closer and closer. I could see it was Joe's form, his britches, his shoes—everything. I batted my eyes. They flopped to and open—like a frog in a hail storm, I guess. It seemed like I could see a head on his shoulders. I started to turn around. Something made me take another step. Something pushed me up—the air, it seemed, back of me. Then I was sure. He did have a head. It was Joe. Just like he always was. He come toward me.

"Don't be afeared of me, Ma. I won't harm you."

"I'm not, Joe. Joe, I come to tell you Bessie is sick—your youngon—she is sick. Can't you come and see her?"

"I can't move from here, Ma. Bring her to me tomorrow night. I have to go back now. My time . . . is up."

I hollered at him—I guess loud enough to deafen a preacher man. But he was gone like a blowed-out candle. I think I must have gone blind there for a minute, for I never did see which way he went, or whether he went any way.

Things were razed from my mind after that. I somehow didn't feel all bothered up inside. So I went back to the house. The moon was shining in at the door and showing there on Bessie's hair. It looked like a brown diamond, Bessie's hair did, it was so shiny and soft. I couldn't help going over and feeling of it. Bessie didn't stir a limb nor leaf. I could tell she was breathing—easy and content—like a purring cat. I had the best feeling—felt just like a body does when he's been looking for somebody he wants to see real bad, and then all at once they come into sight—just tip the hill. That's the way I felt. I went right off to sleep and didn't wake up till Ad yelled for me the next morning and said it was high time I was getting out of bed.

Bessie was already awake and pyeart as a jaybird. "I woke up before Granny did. I want my kitten to come and play with me. Where's Effena?"

Seemed like the youngons felt eased about Bessie too. They talked and laughed with her and didn't act like they had pity for her. I didn't scold them for running through the room, or jumping on the bed or anything like that. I thought they might as well. Effena fixed Bessie's pillow. Bessie set up and looked pretty and right strong even. She sent Effena to get her some strawberry preserves between a biscuit. Amy had to go down to Fawvers' and ask for some preserves and biscuits too. Ad had been spending my eggs and butter money for liquor and I hadn't had time to keep up and try to scrounge in a little flour.

"Hit tastes good," Bessie said. And she wanted more. That evening Dona Fawver brought a jam cake up here and some cucumber pickles. "I want more cake and pickles," Bessie would say. Again and then again. Her and Effena eat till that whole cake was gone. I never did tell Ad. He would have laid it all on that. Amy understood. She knowed, it appeared.

All day Bessie played and talked with the youngons. I didn't ask her how she was feeling—if she hurt anywheres. Amy didn't either. We just felt. The both of us just felt. We laughed and talked too. Me and Amy. It looks like we wouldn't have. Everything was razed off our minds. All day that day.

It was a Saturday night. Ad didn't come in that night. Out with that woman in town, I guess. The moon was up. It was big and full again. I put all the youngons to bed. Amy helped me to. Amy knowed, it seemed. And I don't know how she knowed. I hadn't named it to her e'er a time. But she did. Amy seed things quick. I reckon it was because she was my oldest girl and always had to help me with the other youngons.

Bessie was asleep. I thought I would pick her up real easy and take her. Then she wouldn't wake and know. She opened her eyes. I felt like a chicken-eating cat. But I pulled myself together.

"Don't you want to go see your daddy, Bessie?"

"I dreampt I seed him up in Heaven last night, Granny."

"I could take you to him."

"To Daddy? Now? I'm not much heavy, am I?"

I took her up. There wasn't a sound, not a motion. Bessie was light—so light it seemed I was carrying a pillow. She put her hand up against my neck, and talked.

"The moon's big tonight, hain't it, Granny? Do you see the little Christ Child up there in it? Granny, do you reckon there is room for me in the moon? It's big."

"There might be."

"I'm powerful tired, Granny. And I hurt. I hurt right here. Granny, can you make it quit hurting?"

I couldn't make her any answer. The question scared me, even if I did know. Somehow, I didn't let my mind think on it till I had to. Bessie never had been out of her head before. That was a sign of more fever. I couldn't tell as she was any hotter. But I could see that I was nearing the pit. An easy feeling come over me.

"If the moon does come down and get me, I'll live with the little Christ Child, won't I? Hold my head plumb tight, Granny. I hurt. Would I be sick any more if the moon come down and got me? . . . Granny, you know when you woke me up a while ago? Well, I thought I was a-going some-wheres with the Christ Child."

I hadn't noticed that I was at the cave till I heard Joe say-ing, "I'll take her now." I put Bessie into his arms. I felt dog weary and tired. So tired that I shut my eyes and set down there on the ground. "I'm tired too," I said out loud. But I was sure I had done my part. Tiny said take her to Joe—to the cave.

"You can take her now," I heard Joe say. And his voice sounded happy. Again he said, "My time . . . is up."

I reckon I must have set there like a knot on a log. I don't recollect saying anything. I felt Bessie in my lap. Then I thought. Or I think I thought. I wasn't sure I had seen Joe. I thought I had heard him. I was sure Bessie was in my lap, looking up into my face.

"Where are you, Granny?"

"Here I am."

"I've been somewheres, Granny. I've been to the moon. Everything was pretty and the moon was full of little girls and little boys. They were happy as humming birds. Everybody was just a-singing. They sung better than Barshia did when he played the fiddle. Daddy was up there too. . . . Don't you cry, Granny, and I'll tell you about the man in the moon. He said for me to come to him. He said I could live up there always. . . . And he said I never would hurt any more. . . . He said I would be happy . . . and could sing like all the other little girls, Granny. . . ."

Then her breath give out. All the time she was talking I could feel her breaths coming slower and slower. I heard Brocks' rooster crow for midnight. The words of that song run through my mind:

> "At the silent hours of midnight,
>   In the darkness coming deep,
> Pressed against her mother's bosom,
>   Little Bessie fell asleep,"

and I couldn't help but hum them. I heard other roosters' crows coming up the hollow and across the hills from every side. And Old Shep howling.

CHAPTER 4

BARSHIA'S HORSE HE MADE,
IT FLEW

Barshia Kanipe (born April 30, 1862)

"SO TIRED. So tired," he said. Always Barshia said that. And I guess it did tire him to keep his foot going up and down. All the time. But that's all he ever did save just piddle with fancy things. Pretty fancy things. And when he stretched out in bed at night, that foot kept a-going. Even in his sleep, it went. I told Amy if ever that foot stopped going I would know Barshia was dead. His heart would stop before his foot did.

Sometimes I lost patience with him. If he would have moved the rest of his body some. I ought to have had more pity on him. But I didn't understand at first—not till Dona Fawver told me that about Teelie—I didn't. You see, Barshia was Ad's oldest boy by his first old woman. I thought he was just lazy or crazy one. I didn't know which. Or maybe both.

Barshia could take up more room than anybody I ever seed too. He would set there by the window with his legs all sprawled out. And that foot a-going. When I was sweeping I would try my best to get him to move. But, mind you, he wouldn't even move a smidgin. Not to save my soul, he wouldn't. And he wouldn't say anything about why he wouldn't. He would just look at me. Like he could run through me. Or squall out at me to bring him everwhat he had need for.

He didn't talk much—just set there. Sometimes he would tell me or Amy one that he wanted a drink of water. Amy was a youngon then and seemed like Barshia kept her trotting all the time, bringing something to him. We always went out and got him water when he asked for it. Sometimes I went and got him a drink on my own accord. He always took it—just swallowed it down. Sometimes after he took a drink, he would say that he was tired. Always he was tired. No matter what. He looked like he was stuck to that chair. But we could get him to come to the table nearly every meal. We learned we had to call him a long time beforehands. If we waited till dinner was on the table he wouldn't come at all. Ad would make me or Amy one fetch his victuals to him. Ad never named anything to me about it—ne'er a word. I don't know whether he thought what Dona did or not. I just don't know. If I recollected to call Barshia before the sun got on the porch at all, he would get there by the time it got three planks in on the floor. He was pretty dauncy about his eating too. If we didn't have everything to suit him, he swelt up like a sycamore ball in wet weather. And he would throw a plate at me every time he got mad when he was at the table. Ad would take it up and side with Barshia.

It was at the table he done most of his talking. He would set there after he got through eating and tell about the big things he had done and the big things he was going to keep on doing. Always making his words keep time with his foot patting. He was a-going to get him a fine big brood sow. That he was. And he was a-going to have the finest hogs of anybody in the whole country. He would raise him some turkeys too. Big bunches of turkeys like he had heard about. Like other folkses had. He could make money, he said—a heap of money off a big bunch of fat red turkeys. Red turkeys with white wings. He could hear them gobbling. He liked to hear them gobble. He was going to take that money and make him a fine big house to live in. It was all in his mind's eye. He was going to make a heap of good furniture to put in it too. Pretty furniture like Grandpa used to make.

But the house never did get built. Barshia would set there without moving anything save his right foot. From daylight till dark it went up and down. It made just enough noise to get on my nerves and aggravate the life out of me. Even after Dona told me that—even if I did have pity on him—it still wore on me.

He wouldn't allow me nor Amy neither one to sing around the house. Every time we started to sing he would tell us to shut up. Said we sounded like a buzzard trying to sing. Then he would show us how. When Amy was three year old she could sing right well. But Barshia fussed so much she soon got so she didn't even try. And Barshia could play the fiddle. He was good at playing and singing anything. Them things he made up hisself and sung, I thought were good.

I couldn't hardly spin or weave or do anything around where he was. But I had to. I would put a dip of snuff in my mouth and go on and thole it the best I could. Sometimes I wished he would lose the use of that right leg. That was before I knowed. Having him forever patting the floor was enough to run a hog wild. And just seeing him setting there with his legs all sprawled out. All sprawled out and one foot a-going up and down, pickety peck—no matter what a body was trying to do.

Womenfolks didn't like to come here much because he set there no matter what nor who. None ever come save Teelie Edes. Teelie come to cut his hair for him and to get him to help her make some things. I didn't think it strange for her to come—not till Dona told me what she was.

In the summertime he set right there by the window. All summer long he just set there. That is the most coolest spot a body can find in the summertime. I never have seen a day when there wasn't a breeze blowing through there. Of course

Barshia set right in the window and knocked the breeze off everybody else. Sprawled out in the only chair on the place that set good. That big one he made one day. The one I had such a time getting the willows for. The one he said he dreampt the pattern of.

When cold weather come on he would tell me to move his chair up in front of the fireplace. He would sprawl out there in the same way all winter long. There wasn't room for anybody else to get around save just at the sides. Every time anybody set down he would rare about them killing time. "Setting here hain't buying the baby a new dress nor paying for the one it's got," he would say. And he would keep on patting his foot. Whether he was piddling with anything or not.

Sometimes though he wanted us to pop popcorn for him, and we did. We never could pop it to suit him much. He said he just liked to see the white balls go up and down. It did seem like they went up and down just like his foot—fell right into the time. He made us crack walnuts and pick out the kernels for him. One time he got so mad at Amy because she didn't get the boy's britches out whole that he grabbed the hammer and hit her on the head with it. He knocked the breath plumb out of her. That was before she was yet four year old. I thought he had kilt her and it near scared the daylights out of me. Barshia didn't do a thing but set there and grin like a 'possum all the time I was working with her. Amy has still got the scar on her face. None of us ever told the truth about the scar. We always just said she bumped into the crib door over there.

Barshia said he liked to watch the blaze and see the sparks fly up. Sparks like the color of his hair. It was right pretty. And Barshia thought it was pretty—he was stuck on himself. Sometimes the smoke would puff out in the room and he would say, "Look at it. It comes right toward me. Smoke always follows beauty." I guess he was right pretty. But just setting there all day. Even when he was making anything. Then stretching out in bed at night. He laid so still you never could have told whether he was dead or alive if it hadn't been for that foot. It kept going.

Ad said Barshia was the thinkin'est boy in the world. And he could think. I know that too. He took it by spells. He could think of more pretty chairs and tables to be made out of willows and green hickories. But he never would budge out of his chair to get the things to make what he wanted. He always sent me out to get the kind of wood he needed. Of course, I did all the hard work in making them too—always looking to be hit over the head any minute. And Amy toted pegs and things that Barshia would call for. It's a wonder me and her are still alive. We made some mighty pretty tables and they come in right handy too. He fixed them hearts and horseshoes and things between the table legs.

When anybody come in, me and Amy always quit working on the things. Of course no womenfolks hardly ever come save Teelie. And sometimes Dona. Barshia would tell Teelie he was making them chairs and things while it was bad weather and there wasn't much he could do outside. Teelie always bragged about him making them so pretty. And she would get him to show her how. Said she liked to do things like that too.

I couldn't help but notice some things Teelie did. Even before Dona told me about her. Of course, I didn't think anything at the time. But I just noted. She watch his foot like a hawk. Her head would go up and down to keep time with it. And her eyes would sparkle like a toad's eyes. She looked like it done her good. I took note of it. I never did name it to anybody else. How her eyes looked, you know, that witchy stare.

Barshia could make nearly anything we needed that way. But we had to let him do it when the notion struck him. Nigh every time we asked him he would say he was too tired. "So tired," he would say. Or he would say he was busy right then.

"As busy as a tick in a tar bucket," he would say. He made that washstand there. Hewed it out with his hands. And cut out that place there in the shape of a rooster. Then filled the place in with red cedar. It is a handy old washstand. And that red rooster setting up there on the drawer. Any kind or bird or varmint he could carve out of wood. Made walking sticks and carved all kinds of heads on the handle ends of them.

And them monkeys. He made them for all the girls that asked him to. He would make things like that for girls. And chains made out of little fine twigs, all lapped around and fancied up. He would do that, but he wouldn't talk to a girl hardly at all. Of course, none of them wanted him to. Teelie was the only woman I ever saw him talk to much. He would talk to her. And sing for her. She said she liked to hear him sing. He would sing the songs he made up hisself. Teelie would keep time and watch his foot.

I wish Dona had told me sooner. For a long while after I married Ad I thought Barshia mighty queer. Right from the first I took note of it. For a long time I wanted to ask somebody about it. But I never could bring myself to name it to Teelie. For Teelie was counted queer too. But one day Dona Fawver come and spent the day with us. She helped me get dinner. And I named something about Teelie a-coming to see Barshia and cutting his hair for him. Dona asked me if I ever feared Teelie. Some folks talked, she said, about what Teelie did—things a witch would do.

Then she lit in on Barshia. I didn't see any link between them. But she switched from one to tother. I was glad to hear anything I could. I wish she had talked before. She told me about how Barshia's ma had raised him up to think he was something on a stick, and how she had learnt him to think he was too pretty to work. That was the reason he had got so he didn't want to move. He had got used to setting there and having other folks wait on him like he was a king.

That was the reason he was so everlasting hateful and always

poking fun at other folks. His ma had learnt him to think
he was better than anybody else. I guess that is the reason
he always made fun of me and Amy when we tried to sing.
He was always throwing it up to Amy about being so ugly
she had to whip her face before she could go to sleep. Every
little thing she did he would call her as awkward as a blind
buzzard. From the time she was big enough to know what he
meant he fussed at her that way.

And Barshia was always talking about his red hair. Everybody said they thought he was right pretty. Pretty as a speckled
pup, some said. He did look all right. But I never could think
about that. Not with that foot a-going. Up and down.

He was fat as a mud ball, you know. Never did anything to
sweat the fat off. Just setting there. His skin, it was white as
a strawberry blossom. Some folks said he looked like he had
the hant bleach. He was afeared a little dirt would get on him.
Always hollering for me or Amy to bring some water and
wash his face for him. It seemed like a blue million times a
day we washed him. He wanted us to keep him clean as a pin
—shirts and everything. And he was foreverlasting fussing
about us not keeping the house clean.

The house got to leaking like a sifter. There wasn't a place
in it where it didn't leak. Not a spot big enough to keep a
bed in. Every time I said anything about splitting the boards
to patch it with, Barshia would argue there wasn't any use
because it wouldn't be but a short while till he would have
us a new house put up. He said he had it in mind to build a
fine one. Ad, he acted like he thought it was so. He would
talk about it. Barshia said he had it all planned out in his
mind and he was going to cut the logs as soon as he got rested.
He said he was tired, so tired, he said, from working all the
summer long, and he needed a little rest before he started in on
something like that. That is what he said in the fall. Every
time me or Amy either one spoke a word he would tell us to

shut up because we were bothering his thinking about the new house. And that foot.

Dona kept on telling me things by the littles. Every time I would see her. She knowed Ad's first old woman well, and had seen all the youngons grow up. Said Barshia hadn't always been like he was now. But said he was wild as a buck when he was younger. Said when he was born he didn't weigh but two pound. And said Marthy—Marthy was the name of Ad's first old woman—said Marthy like to have died when Barshia come. He was the first youngon, and she wasn't quite fourteen year old yet. Said Ad had kicked and cussed her about so much it wasn't any wonder she had a hard time. He wouldn't go after Marthy's ma to help get Barshia born, Ad wouldn't. Just went after Teelie Edes. That is all he would do. Said he wasn't going to have Marthy's ma around him. Claimed it was easier for Teelie to come anyhow—all her youngons being dead, and her living over there in that old place by herself. That was before I started being Granny-woman so much.

It was on the last night of April Barshia was born. A rainy, sloppy night, Dona said. She heard somebody pass by her house on horseback a little before midnight and she just allowed it was Ad. Said she had a feeling everything wasn't going off all right, and something told her she ought to go. So she got up out of bed and went right over there.

Said it was a good thing she did too. For it was a long span of time before Ad got back. He come by himself and walking. Ad said Teelie thought there wouldn't be any use in coming till nigh daylight, because a woman never was ready when she thought she was. Teelie sent word for Marthy to lay still and she would be there in plenty of time. So Ad left Old Maud for her to ride when she got ready to come and he footed it on back. Dona said, sure enough, along a short span after chicken crow, Teelie come riding up to the porch on Old Maud. They got Barshia born about the crack of day. Dona said she was scared to death. Marthy laid there for twenty-one days just as black in the face as a Melungeon. Folks thought she would die, sure as the Lord. But Teelie waited on her, and she got all right.

Barshia growed off all right too, Dona said. Teelie brought her cow over there and left it so Ad and Marthy could have milk to feed him on. You see, they had to raise Barshia on a bottle because Marthy didn't give any milk. She laid there them twenty-one days without knowing she had a baby. Ad went and got one of them old blowzy Goolen girls to do the work while Marthy was in bed. And then he slept with her all the time. Right there in the room where Marthy was. Dona said he took Marthy's chickens to the store and sold them to get that old huzzy clothes.

Dona said Teelie was mighty good to Marthy. She helped out a lot. She just about stood on the edge of Marthy's grave and kept Marthy pushed out. She went every day. She set and stared at that Goolen girl till the girl got scared and upped and went home. The old Goolen girl caught up Old Maud and went riding her off. Left word that she would turn the horse loose when she got home and let her come on back by herself. But before she got out of sight of the house Old Maud got scared at something and throwed her off. Teelie said right then she always liked Old Maud and that made her like her better.

When Barshia was a youngon, folks told Marthy he couldn't live. Everybody save Teelie. And Teelie always said he would live longer than Marthy. Teelie tried to get Marthy not to give in to him so much. Told her it was going to be the ruination of him. Of course Marthy never paid any attention to Teelie. Nobody did.

Marthy never did make Barshia mind anything she said. He just run the whole place. Dona said he was so tiny when he was a baby that Marthy had to nurse him on a pillow to know she had anything in her lap. She worried all the time about how she was going to live without him when he died.

Even after he got to be a great big hulk of a boy she worried about him. But Dona said she believed Teelie got mad at Barshia the day she told him not to kill that toad frog and he went on and did it anyhow. He was three year old then. And Teelie was still letting her cow stay over there. Out there in the yard, right in front of Teelie, Barshia killed a toad frog. The cow started giving bloody milk, of course, and got so bad they had to kill her. Marthy's ma give them another cow.

Dona said Barshia was worst when he was about fifteen year old. That was when he went to running after whores. The same ones Ad run after—only he was worse than Ad. He spent everything he could get his hands on. Of course he couldn't get his hands on much. He borrowed every cent he could from everybody that would loan him anything. Sometimes he would come in drunk and beat Marthy like whipping a cow. Ad would take up for him. Always, Dona said. Ad would say he was the best youngon he had.

Barshia and Ad got together and sold off Marthy's last chicken, and the last cow. There wasn't anything a body could say to Barshia that would do him any good. When a body tried to tell him anything he would get mad and cuss a blue streak. Nigh everybody was afeared of him. Nigh everybody save Teelie. She would talk right straight to him sometimes.

Dona said folks give him the name of being one that would fight a circle saw. Everybody looked on him as having sense enough too, if he would just use it. He could tell other folks how to do anything. But even back then he never would do anything himself. He never walked anywhere either. Always rode Old Maud. Everybody talked about it being a shame the way he run that horse. Teelie would stand and stare at him every time she seed him running her that way. He made Maud come and stick her head out the door for him to put the bridle on her. He would beat her and try to make her get down

on her knees for him to get on. Teelie always said he tried to
make Old Maud have more sense than he had.

Every time he got on Old Maud he would just lay the lash
to her. The more she run the more he whipped her. He wore
a spur on his right heel, and kept that foot going up and down
all the time to spur Old Maud. His foot went up and down,
rolling that spur wheel into Old Maud's side. He would take
boys on behind him. Sometimes as many as four would ride her.
Along nigh Christmas time he got some firecrackers and would
light them and lay them between Old Maud's ears. She was
always afeared of loud noises.

But finally, one day, he run her all the way from home to
Del Rio, and she dropped over dead—right in front of the store
porch. Barshia burnt dried grass under her after she was dead,
trying to make her get up. Teelie was there that day with a
basket of eggs and she told him not to burn that grass under
Maud. But he went right on, and set his foot up on her to stick
that spur in her. Dona said she had heard several folks name it
about how Teelie watched Barshia's foot as it went up and
down sticking the spur into Old Maud's side.

Dona said she never had named it to another living soul,
but she seed Teelie pull off her dress one time and there was
a brown spot on her left breast in the shape of a frog. That is
always a sure witch sign. I don't know. But if Teelie ever dies
I am going to help lay her out. I want to know for sure. But
Marthy got Bob Gollahon to take his team of mules and drag
Old Maud in home. She skinned her and kept the hide for a
keepsake. She kept it propped up in the stable. And when Ad
moved over here he brought it along with him.

After that, Barshia managed somehow to get another horse.
Bought it on credit. He run it all the time, till Delley Sample
had to take the horse back because Barshia never did pay for it.
Then Barshia tried to make Marthy borrow enough money to
buy him another horse. And he tried to borrow other folks'
horses to ride places. But, of course, nobody would let him have

one. He throwed it up to Marthy that she didn't try to get things for him. But said someday he would have a horse finer than anybody in the country and they would all want to borrow hisn.

Dona said that was the way he did up till he was seventeen year old. Carried on that way for nigh three year, you see. Then when he didn't have anything to spend it got so nobody would have anything to do with him. There wasn't much left for him to do save to stay at home. Marthy never would so much as let him turn over his hands to do a solitary thing. She never would let him set his feet on the ground in wet weather for fear it would hurt him.

All Marthy could talk about was how pretty Barshia was. She wanted him right there in the room to do the talking no matter who come. She would brag about him saying such funny things. Dona said everybody did think he was plumb pretty back then before he sprung out and got so fat. Red hair with a big wave in it, blue eyes. That fair skin, white as a lily. And his teeth too. I guess I would have thought him pretty if I could have ever looked at anything save that pattety foot. Me and Amy catered to him like Marthy had done, and washed his face every time he told us to. He always had us wash his hair in egg. That made it curly and shiny, he said. I reckon it did. Something did. He said hair needed working just like plants did, so he made us scratch his head for him every day. Me or Amy one.

But Dona said it was caused from the way Marthy let him do—his pride and laziness was. That foot—it didn't go up and down till Teelie saw him kill Old Maud. She said Teelie liked Old Maud. And, more than that, Barshia killed that toad frog. I don't know. I never have named it to anybody else. Me and Dona talks. Maybe too much.

For the most part I let Barshia alone and didn't pay any more attention to his fussing than to a little dust in the sunshine. But right there toward the last—for them last two weeks.

It all come about so fast and yet so slow. He was setting there one day, stone-still, you know, save for his right foot. It hadn't been going up and down any faster—just the same. All the morning he set there like his mind was galavanting away off somewhere. A little while before dinner he told Amy to fetch him the Bible book. That's how it all started. He said he could understand the Bible better than a preacher could. He could too. But when he told what he had been reading about, he always fixed it up and told it to suit his own mind. He didn't ever tell a thing like it was in the Bible. Never.

Soon that evening Teelie come. Before we got dinner over. I was glad to have her come. Her and Barshia made things together, and me and Amy got to rest from being bossed about and dogging for him. For a short span, we did. That evening —it was a pretty evening—the sun and robins and everything. Everything just budding out. Teelie was cutting Barshia's hair for him again. She said she liked to cut that hair. I took note, mind you, that she put some in her apron pocket.

Barshia started telling her them stories he had been reading in the Bible. Told her some of them were good stories—the one about Jesus Christ himself. How he was buried by some trashy folks, you know. And how, after they stuck him down into the grave, he riz up and up and up—plumb up to Heaven. Teelie, she said she didn't believe them tales much. She believed they were something somebody made up on the Lord. So she told some that she liked better. Teelie had a good memory and she knowed lots of things. She clipped the hair and he patted his foot and she nodded her head and talked. Clip-clip, pat-pat, you know. I set and took it all in—all I could.

Teelie told the tale about the man that made the flying horse—the same old tale. The one Ma used to tell to me. How he flew right past his slow-pokey brothers, into the rich girl's window—and won the pretty fair lady. And a pot of gold too, of course. Always they won money with the girl. The same old story. But Teelie, she put more to it. She knowed a man—Old Bogus Snyder was his name. A man that might nigh made a flying horse. But died before he got it done. She said she never did see the horse but she had seen Bogus.

Barshia, he just set there. He blinked and blinked like a toad frog in a hail storm. Teelie watched his foot, and kept her head going up and down with it. Up and down. That owlish grin on her face. Barshia seemed not to want to speak e'er a word. She didn't try to get him to.

She stayed till late that evening. Said there was something she wanted Barshia to help her make. They worked on it. But I could see Barshia's mind wasn't so much on what he was doing. She wanted him to cut her the shape of a horse out of cedar. Said she wanted something pretty to set on her center table. He helped her all that evening, making it. It was right pretty too, I thought. Before she started she asked me to loan her some beeswax. Said she needed some. Amy went and got it for her—a right smart dab. She asked Barshia if it was soft enough to work into anything. He took it in his hands and squez it. She nodded her head up and down with his foot. That was to get him to touch the wax, I guess. I guess it was.

But that night we couldn't get Barshia to go to bed at all. He said he was going to set up and think. Think and plan, you know. Ad said about the new house, he guessed. But I didn't think it was any house. Barshia set all the next morning. Set and moved that foot up and down. Every time I looked at him I thought I could see the picture of a horse in his eyes. I guess I just thought that because I had a hankering. A while before dinner he hollered for Amy to come there. Right then I knowed what was up. Or thought I did. And that was what it was.

Me and Amy went up on Sals King Mountain and I cut the things that evening. The kind of little saplings and things he told us to. We toted them up to the woodpile. He said he was going to bow out some little limbs like ribs and make a sort of frame of a horse, and then stretch Old Maud's hide over it.

That is what he did. He clumb up on top of the fruit-drying kiln. Said he could have a good start from up there.

Me and Amy worked on that horse. Amy toted things and run after things till I feared she would stop growing. We took Barshia's cussings and beatings. He would hit us with everwhat he had in his hands when he got mad because we didn't do things to suit him. We had two 'possum hides there that Barshia took to make the wings out of. Fixed them, you know, sort of like a kite. So the air could suck up under them. I sort of thought it a crazy stunt. But then I had seen so much. I never was quite sure what to think. A body never knows, you know, with folks like that, just what might happen. It did, of course.

Ad, he didn't say a word while Barshia was working on it. Didn't give it much heed. Nobody didn't pass through here during them two weeks. So just Barshia and me and Amy knowed much about it. We worked and worked. Me or Amy one had to be right there on the ground to take things up the ladder to him. Always we had to be there—one of us. To take him things. To help him saw and hammer and nail and cut and measure and measure. We never did know when he was going into one of them mad fits and knock us off. He never stopped that foot. He set up there in that chair and kept his foot going up and down. When I was nailing I would fall into the time he kept with that right foot—pit-pat, bang-bang, crack-crack. And sawing with the handsaw, pit-pat, push-pull, see-saw. Teelie she come and helped sometimes. She nodded her head with his foot and grinned—like an owl. That grin. I wondered at Teelie.

Till finally he got it made. It looked queer. Bent willow limbs for ribs. Hickory legs with knots for knees. But it did look like a horse's bones. And a pedal on its right side. A pedal so that when it worked up and down the wings would flop-flop, you know, up and down. And that would make the horse fly through the air.

Ad, he still didn't pay it any heed. Just me and Amy. We

seed it all. Rainy days we worked right on. Then he sent us to
the barn to bring Old Maud's skin. We unripped it down the
belly where it was sewed. We clawed the straw stuffing out.
I hated to. I thought of Marthy—how she would feel—and
somehow of Teelie too. All the while.

Teelie, she come that very evening—just as we got the hide
stretched over the frame. That stiff dry hide. But it fit all
right. Barshia could measure things—just with his eyes. He
was good. At that, he was, and it looked right well. We sewed
the hide back together down the throat and down the belly.
Twine strings through them gashes in Old Maude. Teelie, she
grinned when we split a place in the hide for that pedal to
stick out. And them kite-like wings. Horsehide and 'possum
hide. 'Possum-hide wings. It looked all right. Barshia made
me pull out the top riddle in the kiln. It slanted down. And
lift the horse out on it. I did. I feared it might slide off if
the wind should blow or if anything jarred it.

Barshia set there and looked at it. Teelie watched his foot
and her head went up and down with it. She took hold of
the pedal—moved it just a smidgin and the wings begun to
move too.

The next day—it was Sunday—Ad and the boys went galavanting off somewhere. I don't know where. Me and the girls
were by ourselves with Barshia. And even Amy wasn't big
enough to help much. She was company though, and generally
I was pacified when she was with me. But that day I felt different—somehow, I did. A little wren flew through the house
that morning. I looked at Amy and she looked back at me.

All that morning Barshia kept us busy. His foot kept on—
up and down. He talked to the time of it. He was going to
Heaven, he said. Going to fly to Heaven. God was calling him
home, and he sung "To See the Shining Angels, and Don't
You Want to Go?"

The primping he did. We nearly wore our legs off waiting
on him. Made us wash and scrub him up good, head and all.

In that soap that we made and scented up with horse-mint leaves. Said he wanted to be clean when first the angels seed him. Said he would marry one of them. One with yellow curls. He liked yellow hair, he said. Next to red it was the prettiest. His own hair did look pretty that morning. Plumb pretty—like a star, or like the sun almost. It shined and was so fluffy.

He cleaned his teeth and had Amy clean his teeth and had me clean his teeth. Till he wore out all the beggar-louse-root toothbrushes Amy had. He told her to go get some more. But it was so early in the spring. They weren't big enough yet. I told him so. "Borrow some," he said. "Go, borrow some for me. From Teelie. She keeps them all the time. Enough for the whole country." Amy went. It was a right fur piece for a youngon to go.

It was after midday when she got back. I had done took Barshia's dinner to him. She give him the toothbrushes and he started cleaning his teeth again. Rubbed them up and down as his foot went up and down.

Me and Amy set down to eat. She looked at me. I looked at her. And then she talked. Like youngons will, you know. About what Teelie had in them shelves where she kept her toothbrushes. Thorns and leaves and everything. Said that little wooden horse Barshia whittled out was laying on the floor. A little beeswax man was fastened on to it. A man made out of old, dirty-looking beeswax. His head was broke off and laying there, made out of clean-looking, new beeswax, the head, with hair stuck on it—Barshia's hair. A thorn was stuck through the man's right foot, Amy said. Said she took note of it. I looked at her. I don't reckon she was old enough to know. But she did look like she was thinking about something strange.

After dinner, Barshia set there in his chair for a short while. Me and Amy set there in the chair looking at one another and at his foot. It went up and down till I thought I couldn't thole it any longer—e'er a bit longer. I felt pity for him too. I got to thinking. And sure enough fearful things of Teelie, as never before, even with Dona's talk and all.

Barshia got up and went to the door. He turned around. In the door, he turned around. Said for us to tell Ad and them where he had gone. He was tired of this old world, he said. And he was tired of living and working. Said he wanted to go some place where he wouldn't have to even think.

All along I had halfway thought that it wouldn't happen. That maybe he was just talking to hear his head roar. That was what Ad had said. When I seed him in the door I knowed he wasn't just talking. Standing there in the door, bearing his whole weight on his left foot, I knowed he wasn't. That right foot still going up and down. I had pity for him. In a way. And yet. Then he went out.

I watched out the little window door. I could see from there. I told Amy not to look. He clumb up the ladder. I had made it out of poles so I could get to the top riddle easy. He clumb up the ladder slow. Like a caterpillar climbing. Every time he set his right foot on the poles of that ladder, his toes went up and down. I set there and looked. He got to the top.

I saw it all. He got on Old Maud. That is what me and Amy had been calling it. He got on and tied his left foot to Old Maud's side. Pulled the string through the holes he had made in her. He fastened on his spur—the same old spur. That thing. Them sharp points in the wheel. He started working the pedal up and down.

Them 'possum-hide wings, they begun to flop. Sure enough they could flop. Up and down. Old Maud, she begun to move. Just sliding a little, I thought. But she got her front feet to the edge. I held my breath. He kept working the pedal, you know. It looked like Old Maud went straight up. Up into the air. And them wings a-flopping. "Amy, it is going up. It is," I yelled. I shut my eyes.

When I opened them again, I saw it going down. The wings still flopping. But going down. Head foremost down. Down to the ground on its head. His head too, I guess. I didn't look at him. I didn't want to see it all. "Amy, he's kilt," I said. "Ad ought to have knowed."

Amy went twirling around like a leaf in a whirlwind. I did too. We got to him. He was laying there with his head all bent down under his chest. Old Maud's was too. The sticks in her neck were broke. I didn't look at Barshia's head so much. I looked at his foot. "He hain't kilt," I said. We untied him from Old Maud. Him and Old Maud.

Barshia was heavy. You know how fat he was. I couldn't tote him in. He didn't say a word. Not e'er a word, he didn't. Amy helped all she could and we managed to drag him to the house and get him in. I didn't listen to see if he was breathing. I watched that foot. Up and down. Just like Old Maud, I thought. We stretched him out on the bed. I saw his neck was limber. Limber as a dish clout. "I'll splinter it up," I said. But something told me there wasn't any use. Not in that.

I took a-hold of his neck and watched his foot. Always that. His head rolled over a little. He looked at me. "I won't be so tired. So tired," he said. Keeping time.

I stood and watched him—like one dog watching another die. He laid there like common—stone-still save for that foot. Then it stopped.

CHAPTER 5

THE SPRING IS TRUSTY

Amy Kanipe (born March 4, 1883)

AMY jumped out of bed that morning sooner than she ever had before. At first, I couldn't make out the reason for it. But she went toward the spring, and I saw what she was up to. It was May morning and she was going to see her future husband's face.

I don't reckon the spring had much trouble picking out a face for Amy to see. Enzor Courtney and Eloyd Fawver were the only two boys left around here anywhere that were as old as she was. Amy was twenty-five year old, a-going on twenty-six. And when a girl gets up that close to the line she quits dreaming about princes that will come riding by someday.

I thought all the time it would be Eloyd or Enzor one. I didn't know which, and didn't bother over it. I just reckoned it out that there was about six of one and half-dozen of the other. Enzor was ever as queer as a white eagle, I thought. And I didn't figure Amy would ever be able to make him understand. I allowed Amy wouldn't be what he wanted her to be, and then he would fuss. He fussed at her as it was—when they were sparking. Enzor was pure and seely. But it seemed like Amy was just drawed to him. On account of that, I reckon. He never touched her when they were courting and he didn't want Eloyd to touch her either.

Eloyd was good to Amy when they were together. I took note of that. As good to her as a cat is to its sick kitten. Amy couldn't help but notice it too. Eloyd understood, of course. He was as deep in the mud as Amy was in the mire.

Amy vowed she didn't want to marry anybody at all. She said she didn't see the use in beating the devil around the stump or talking about it—she just didn't want to. She would hold her head up in the air and go around singing:

"Single life is the happy life,
  Single life is jolly.
I am single and no man's wife;
  No man shall control me."

But Ad had already cut several throughs about her not being married. Everybody in the country was talking about it. Somehow, I sort of found myself making excuses for her when folks named it to me about Amy getting to be an old maid. I would say that I had always told her, "Time enough yet," because she was my oldest girl and I wanted her to stay at home and help with the other youngons. Of course in a way I did want her to stay with me as long as she could. But it was getting plaguing to Amy to have it throwed up to her, and she said she aimed to get married so folks would quit tormenting her. Even Preacher Jarven teased her about it. He said the Bible spoke of widows being in Heaven but there wasn't e'er a word about old maids. That was what led Amy to act like a frying chicken on May morning.

She told me about it when she come back to the house. The spring didn't look very clean and healthy that morning. But it was a right smart of fun to play like she was as young as Effena and Meady. She didn't see any face in the spring though. She didn't see anything save old faded redbud blossoms that had dropped in. She started to come on back.

But then she thought she seed something rising up from the bottom. It was Enzor's face. Boiling up. Coming toward her.

Looking at her like he wanted her. But changing to a frown, looking grim at her like he was fussing. Then she couldn't see him any more. She could just see herself in the water. She saw herself go through a change. At the last she looked old and broke down, and her face was wrinkled as a rotten apple.

Then she thought she heard something. A horse. Enzor's horse. She thought it was a token, maybe. Enzor always rode horseback to see her. Eloyd walked. She saw something forming in the spring again. A coffin. Somebody in the coffin. A man. Eloyd in the coffin. But Amy said she knowed well enough that there wasn't anything to what the spring said. It might have been her own shadow anyhow, that she saw. She didn't believe in any such.

So she went on as general, trying to spark them both. All summer she went on that way. She got so she didn't tell me much. I couldn't make out whether she aimed on marrying either one of them or not.

Everybody around here tried to get her to give up Enzor and let Eloyd have a fair chance. But she shut her ears to things folks would say. Even when they teased her about the queer way Enzor treated her—bossing her about like a slut dog and forever threatening to quit her. She would get aggravated with him sometimes and say she was going to marry Eloyd— no matter what. But when Enzor come back she would be proud to see him.

One time Eloyd asked to take her to the poke supper up there at the Cedar Grove schoolhouse and she wouldn't go. I thought and everybody else thought too it was because she was afraid of Enzor. Afraid of that look he would give her when he was fussing at her about throwing herself away on Eloyd Fawver.

The more Enzor fussed the more Amy got so she could stand it. She let him treat her like a dog. Right before everybody too. I hated for folks to name it to me. But I thought she was old enough to know what she was doing.

Enzor would go to church with her and not go in. One time

he bolted in the church house and made her get up and go out because the preacher man spoke to her. It looked like Enzor didn't care much for her himself. But he didn't want her to have anything to do with anybody else. I took note that she never did act herself around Enzor. Always, she feared she she would do something he wouldn't like. The way she looked at him before she would open her mouth to say a word.

Well, Amy turned down Eloyd and went to that very same poke supper with Enzor. He come by for her without even letting her know he was coming. Then he wouldn't even bid on her poke when it was put up for sale. Eloyd was there by hisself and he bid on it. When Enzor saw him bidding on it he got up and left and dared Amy to eat with Eloyd. Amy didn't. That was where I thought she played the fool, giving in to Enzor. But she went up and set with Sue Ella Whetsel. Told Eloyd she wasn't hungry. Then she had to come on home, walking along with the old women. Of course, Eloyd asked her, but she wouldn't let him come.

Just before they got to Whetsels' house they saw Enzor standing there by the side of the road. Amy stopped to talk with him. I reckon he must have fussed something awful that night. Amy was bawling like a stung baby when she come to bed. She said Enzor wouldn't believe her when she told him she hadn't eat with Eloyd.

One Sunday evening after that Amy told Eloyd he could come and set with her. While he was here Enzor come sneaking up. Amy saw him in the distance and she made Eloyd slip out the kitchen door.

I believe Eloyd would have had a fight and settled it all with Enzor if Amy would have let him. She always begged him not to. Eloyd had just had too good a raising to act like it might have been best to act. But Enzor did beat a buck at slipping around and seeing when Eloyd was here. Many was the time he come when I know good and well that Amy wasn't looking for him. He would even come sometimes when she was over the wash tub, or when the other youngons were sick, and make Amy stop her work and go off somewhere with him. Just go off some place where he could set and look at her and fuss.

There was one time when Amy had to do some tall begging for Enzor though. That was the time I let her go with the Whetsels to the ice-cream supper at Low Land. They got up a wagonload of folks that wanted to go. I didn't think about Eloyd nor Enzor neither one a-being there. Amy didn't either. It was so far.

The first person she seed when she got out of the wagon was Eloyd. He asked her to cake-walk with him. Before they much more than got started Enzor stepped up and pulled her out of the ring. Eloyd went after him that time like a cat after a mouse. I reckon they might nigh had a fray. Everybody come crowding around like ants. Amy pulled Eloyd back and told him to go on away from her, she didn't want any fighting. Then Enzor didn't even cake-walk with her. He was too stingy to blow his nose.

I could hear Enzor say hurtful things to Amy too. Sometimes I could. He told her she was ugly as a mud fence dabbed with tadpoles—throwed that up to her one time when he was mad. That hurt because Amy wanted to be pretty and she never was. Big and rough. But that wasn't her fault. That comes from too hard work. And she is looking old now. Too much thinking, I guess. If she thinks. And I reckon all folks do—all that can. But no matter how spiteful Enzor was, it looked like he just sort of charmed Amy like some folks charm bees and flies.

I had a queer feeling all that day. Amy had been going around mighty content-looking, and that morning she dropped her dish rag. She picked it up and give it a good shaking like it was something she liked pretty well, and she said, "Uh, oh, Mr. Dish Rag, I fooled you this time. I'm looking for him tonight." I didn't say anything. Somehow, I had that queer feeling like a body has before somebody gets killed or a storm comes.

I didn't think so much about it till I went to milk that night. I got my bucket and called Old Heif. "Soolk, Heif, soolk, soolk." But there wasn't any use. I soon saw that. Old Heif was always one to play deaf if she didn't want to come up. I started out across the field after her. All that bunch of starved chickens and turkeys started after me. I seed I might as well go back and feed them. I clumb in the crib and shucked the corn. I was shucking away and calling the chickens at the same time, "Chickey, chickey—pee, turks, pee, pee, pee, pee," when all at once I took note that I had a red ear. I stiffened up all over and set there with it in my hand.

I reckon it was because it set me to thinking about Amy again. Amy and Enzor went over to Arwoods' to that corn-husking. Amy never will outlive that. Enzor found a red ear that night and then he wouldn't even kiss her.

Carlous Hull said he was going to kiss Amy in Enzor's place, and Enzor raised Cain with Amy about it. She said she had a good time that night in spite of everything. Eloyd was there and he shucked right into the jug of liquor. That is just the way Eloyd has always been. I told Amy I bet he come early and helped hide it. Eloyd will drink. But I don't blame a body for that. Folks that drink have better natures. I don't guess Enzor ever drunk a drop in his life or used a cuss word either.

I fed the chickens and went on to milk. I took the bucket with me. I noticed that it was a smotherly evening. And that the grass was all dead. I couldn't see how Old Heif lived. She was hid in the furderest corner that evening. Poor old critter—that was the only fun she ever got—hiding from me. It was right aggravating that evening. It was drizzling rain and somehow it made me feel all out of sorts.

I went on up to her. She was standing under that old cedar tree. Trying to keep herself dry. Just as I got up to her I thought I heard somebody playing the dulcimer. I stopped. It stopped. I started again and it commenced again. I kept on looking and directly I found out what it was. It was my milk bucket. It was carrying the tune good—just as clear—

> "My daughter got married,
> She married the wrong man."

I told Old Heif to saugh and I would milk her where she was. I felt that the ground under my feet was soft. I looked down and saw that I was standing right on an ant hole. That meant bad luck—the worst of bad luck. But Amy had been arguing me that signs didn't mean anything. She said there wasn't a thing to that May morning sign. Said it tried to make her think she would marry Enzor, and shortly after that Enzor got mad at her, so mad he wouldn't speak. Eloyd kept on coming.

It was on the last Saturday night of the meeting at Holiways church house that Amy and Enzor had their row. Enzor made her to understand that he was through with her. Amy went to the protracted meeting that night. Enzor was there and he didn't say anything to her. She spoke to him and he didn't give her any more answer than a deaf man's ghost. After meeting she started walking on home with the crowd of old women, and the first thing she knowed she heard somebody say, "Well, Topper needs some company tonight." Eloyd always called her Topper. I don't like it. But Amy, she seemed to. At least back when he first started calling her that, she did. Amy didn't give him any answer. Didn't even say howdy. It sort of addled her brain, I reckon, him slipping up behind her that way. He started walking along by the side of her. The old women picked up a little. There wasn't anything left for Amy to do save to walk on with him.

They hadn't gone over two dozen steps till they heard a horse come a-loping it up the road. Amy said it sounded to her like it was flying off the face of the earth. She knowed right then it was Enzor and she begun shaking all over like a cold dog. Eloyd kept on talking. Acted like he didn't hear a thing. The horse kept coming up behind them at fox-chasing speed. Amy screampt and pulled Eloyd out of the road. Enzor would have run over them both. He passed on by them, then stopped his horse as quick as he could and turned square dab across the road in front of them.

Of course Amy and Eloyd stopped. That was the only thing they could do. Nobody didn't say a thing till Enzor said, "Get yourself on here behind me." Amy, like she was charmed, went to going toward him. Eloyd stepped up and grabbed Enzor by the leg. "Come on down, Enzor, I've had enough of your damned stubbornness." But Amy pushed Eloyd away like he was a pup and yelled for him to stay out of it. She leapt up on that horse like a cat. The horse lit out. She thought she would fall off, but she grabbed Enzor around the waist. And then she was glad he took her away from Eloyd. They heard Eloyd holler that he would settle it yet. Enzor almost run over the crowd of old women when he passed them. He didn't slow down any till he got to the house.

He stopped and Amy just set there with her arms around his waist. He said, "Hain't you never going to get down?" Amy slid down and stood there like a bayed cow without saying a word. But Enzor, he looked at her and said, in that hateful way he had, "I'm through with you for good this time. I never aim to speak to you again." And he rode off.

He didn't come to meeting another time after that. Meeting broke the next Wednesday night and he wasn't there then. Eloyd was there though and he went in and set with Amy, and walked on back home with her that night.

Eloyd said he waited that night down where the Slop Creek road turned off—waited for Enzor to come on back. He was going to have it out with him. But he said Enzor must have got a hankering some way, because when his horse come along Enzor wasn't on it. He thought Enzor turned the horse loose to go on in by itself and he cut through the fields a-walking.

All the way from church that night Eloyd pled with Amy to marry him, but she didn't give him any answer. Enzor used to say he would kill Eloyd if Amy ever married him.

Eloyd said he wanted to come to see Amy the next Saturday night and she told him he could come. Eloyd always fixed it to come on Saturday nights. Because he knowed Ad and the boys always traipsed off over to Collins' to the dance on a Saturday night. It never failed. When I got in from milking that night I saw Ad and the boys were back from the store and ready to go again. I knowed they wouldn't be back till chicken crow. Somehow I wished they wouldn't go. The first time I ever wished it. Amy watched them out of sight, proud that they were going. "Ma, I've done eat a snack," she said. "Eloyd Fawver is coming to set with me tonight."

That made me think. I don't know why I thought. But I had noted it three different times. "Well, that accounts for it," I told her. "I've seen two hens a-fighting out here in front of the steps three times today. But that means two folks, Amy."

She didn't pay my words much heed. "Huh uh, just Eloyd is all I know about. Me and Eloyd are thinking about getting hitched up together. I'm going to make answer tonight."

I looked at her. "Have you let on to Enzor?" I asked.

"Huh uh," she said. "But me and him ain't fitted. I wouldn't have minded living with him a short span though."

"Amy, you recollect what the spring said, don't you?"

"A ground hog can see his own shadow and get afeared of it. What can a spring tell a body?"

I tried to eat my supper. Somehow I wasn't hungry. Everything was quiet as a ghost. I kept listening for some noise. No birds. I told myself it was because it was a cold night. I thought Amy and Eloyd would need a little fire. I built it for them. I took note of how everything around the house stunk. Worse than a dead rat, it seemed it stunk. Old wet filth, I reckon. No frogs. I noticed that it was getting dark. The night was black as a crow. Everything quiet save for the rain. Sizzly sizzly soz.

Pittity pittity pat—splash. It got harder. Kept a-getting more harder. I felt pity for Eloyd. I reckoned a boy had to think a heap of a girl to come out in a rain like that to see her. And Amy, Amy seemed happy too. She sung away to the top of her voice:

> "Oh, boys, why don't you marry?
> There's no place like home."

In the big house there combing her hair, she was. Combing her hair after dark. I had warned her more times than one. But Amy never was one that feared bad luck. She was by them signs like she was by the face in the spring. Said they didn't amount to a drop of water. How could combing her hair after dark bring bad luck, she would ask. I wouldn't know. And I didn't blame her for wanting her hair combed. She looked like a fright when it wasn't.

I heard something else. I thought I did. It was Eloyd. A right fur piece off yet. But singing. Like an echo, it appeared:

> "Oh, boys, why don't you marry?
> There's no place like home."

Both of them with the same thing on their minds. I thought it was right nice. Eloyd got to the house before I could much more than turn around.

"Hello," I heard him holler. He sounded happy—like a body in love.

Amy, she went to the door. Amy knowed how to act. Amy had always had manners. "Come on in the house," she said. "Get you that chair there. . . . I heard you singing, Eloyd."

Eloyd seemed beat for a while. But just a short while— it was hard to ever get ahead of Eloyd. He come back at her with, "That was to warn you the devil was out. Did you hear what I was singing?"

Amy saw she didn't have anything on Eloyd and she stumbled around for what to say. "I didn't pay any atten— yeah, Eloyd, I heard."

"You might as well make up your mind to marry me," Eloyd said, blunt straight out. "I'm going to keep on tormenting you till you do."

He went over there to her. She was scared, I reckon. She hadn't looked for it to come about so quick. She allowed they would talk a while first. A short while anyhow. But Eloyd didn't. Then the way the night was. It seemed so cold. All of it did. To me it seemed cold. Eloyd put his arms around her. She leaned her head back a little. "Monday?" he asked. "As soon as I can get the license?" Amy didn't know what to say to that. She hadn't thought about a license. She thought they would just go get Square Newberry to marry them. But she pulled herself together.

"Hit suits me," she said. They weren't the words she had been practicing on before the looking glass. A woman never does, I reckon, say the words she aims to say.

I held my breath. Amy and Eloyd got quiet. I heard a horse running. Coming right up to the door. I stayed in the lean-to. It was all I could do. But Amy told me afterward. Told me what part I didn't hear. She heard the horse run up to the front steps. She looked up. There was Enzor in the doorway. With a gun in his hand. That grim look. He pointed the gun at Eloyd, and started toward him. Amy, she went to squalling out, "Eloyd, don't you! Enzor. Enzor, you said—"

But she caught herself. She saw there wasn't any use in talking. Enzor wasn't listening. He was eyeing Eloyd. With his gun pointed right at him. Amy stood there. Stood there wondering why Eloyd didn't run. Why he didn't get away from that gun.

Enzor took his pistol down. He stared at Amy. Right straight at her. With that look. "Which one are you going to marry?" he blurted out at her. In that way he had of blurting, like he was scolding a slut dog.

Amy could tell he meant for her to answer. "You. Enzor, do you want me? You said you didn't want me."

Eloyd started at Enzor. Like a biting sow he started at him. Right into the face of that gun. Amy went to hollering again. "Eloyd. Eloyd, don't you do anything. I don't want you." Just as she had always done. Shielding Enzor. She was afraid Eloyd would grab that gun out of Enzor's hand.

"But, Topper—" Eloyd tried to reason with Amy. She wasn't to be reasoned with.

"You know I didn't mean it. Never—" Eloyd was out of the door before she finished what she started to say.

Amy said she felt numb as a clod after Eloyd went. She didn't move. She was afraid to look at Enzor. But she had to look at him. He drew her eye to him, like general. Standing there stiff as a dog iron. Pale. Grim—like he was in the spring.

Enzor's lips quivered like a snake's eye. "I seed his hands on you. . . . I'll let daylight through him. . . . Don't I suit you?"

Amy stood there and shook like a frog's leg frying. She never had seen Enzor quite like that before. Not quite like that. She didn't think words would do any good. But she got some out. "Enzor, you know you suit me." She started to say more. But Enzor butted in.

"I'll come after you Monday," he told her, and he went stalking out the door. "Be ready," he yelled back at her.

Ready to wear herself out for him. Ready to see Eloyd in a coffin. That was what Enzor might as well said. And I reckon Amy saw it at last, saw the spring was trusty.

CHAPTER 6

APPLE TREE

Amy Kanipe

Part 2

A MY went over to Buck Golden's every once in a while. She went to play dolls with Pairlee. Then after Pairlee died I didn't see any harm in letting Amy go to see the old man. She was the only person that ever had much to do with him. But she knowed Buck about as well as the bark knows the tree, I reckon. He was always just as mannerable as a dog to her when she went to play with Pairlee. He was foreverlasting picking up rocks and bringing them in for them to put in their playhouse. Fancy rocks that sparkled like diamonds, and flint and such.

You know, Buck never did have but one youngon of his own. That was Pairlee's mammy. They called her Dunk. Buck's woman died on the very day that Dunk was thirteen year old. Dunk told me that while I was laying out her ma. I know I thought about bad luck at the time she told me. Dunk eat honey on the day her ma was buried too. I don't reckon the youngon had ever been told any better. It might not have made any difference anyhow, though, one sorrow never does come but what there are two more to follow it. That has always been.

Bad luck did come. There wasn't anything a body could do to keep it away, I reckon. About three years after Dunk's ma was buried, I begun to hear it rumored that Dunk was called to straw. Folks are always ready to talk, if it is something bad they can say about a body. But let them hear something good and they keep as quiet as a snake in the wintertime.

I don't reckon Buck ever noticed Dunk's shape. He never was around the house any much. He stayed out in the field or over at the mill one, pert nigh from daylight till dark. He thought more of his goats than he did of anybody. They were his only friends. I guess goats are pretty safe things to have for friends. They don't speak our language.

Then Dunk had Pairlee. Dunk never has been seen since. Some folks think that Buck doubled her up and burned her right there in the fireplace. I can't think that. Some folks think he killed her with the ax and buried her under the floor of that old mill house. Nep Franklin is the one that started that. There may be something in it. I don't know. But I do know Buck never did run the mill any after Dunk was missing. I don't see any loose stave in the tale. Nep tells it. He says he got caught in a storm one night coming from the Holiways meeting house. He had to stop in at the old mill to keep from getting sousing wet. He hadn't been there long till he heard a baby squalling. Then a rifle go off. He says it sounded for all the world like that old muzzle-loading thirty-eight of Buck's. He says he set there and shook all over.

Nep thought Buck was shooting at him for being there in the mill house. He says he started to get himself out. The minute he started, there was a flash of lightning and he saw Dunk Golden standing in front of the doorway. He says he stopped stone-still—he didn't want her to touch him. For if a body is touched by a dead person that comes back to earth he will die and go where that person is—especially if a body is kissed. And Dunk might kiss him, he thought. But I don't guess she was so anxious.

Nep says Dunk was all dressed up in some sort of dress that was as green-colored as blue grass. Said her skin was green too—a sort of glow-worm green. He lit in to telling her that he wasn't going to harm anything any more than a dove would, that he had just stopped in there out of the storm. I bet Nep looked like a scared deer that didn't know which way to run. He says he kept on trying to explain to her. Dunk smiled at him and said, "God, He knows more than other folkses do." Nep claims he wasn't scared after he found out it wasn't anybody but Dunk. He says he noticed for sure that she didn't have a gun. But I bet he was scared so bad he couldn't have told a gun from a cornstalk. He said as soon as he saw she didn't have a gun, he went back to the corner and set down on a log—one that was laying there.

He says he looked up several times and seed her still standing in the doorway. Then he felt the planks under him being raised. Another flash of lightning come. His eye caught sight of her going under the planks. The planks dropped back. And Dunk was gone.

Nep says he took his chance. He run out of the door as quick as a mouse. Lightning nor thunder nor a good sousing nor anything else didn't keep him from going. He swears he run more faster than a deer. But I don't know. Nep is pretty apt to measure things by a 'coon's skin with the tail thrown in.

Buck never did say a word about Dunk. Never cheeped a thing to a soul. He never had any reason to. There might not have been anything to cheep. Nobody will know. And nobody will be the worse off for not knowing.

Buck raised the baby on goat's milk. There is something about goats. I have heard tell as how souls of dead folks live on in them. I don't know. Folks have missed Buck's mill.

Preacher Jarven says Buck will be held to account for killing Dunk. He says Buck owes it to God to tell all his sins to the preacher man. But Buck never did move an inch toward the meeting-house door. Buck's woman, you know, had always had a good name. And then Dunk doing the way she did so soon after her ma died. It was enough to addle his brain a mite.

Buck and his woman moved here from Virginia—let's see —the winter that Dona Fawver's old piedy cow died. He bought that little place from Old Man Brock and run that little mill. It was a lot more easier to take a turn of corn to him than it was to grind it between two rocks for yourself. His mill has been missed ever since—as much as a huckleberry patch would be.

Buck never did any harm to anybody. I went and stayed all day with his woman once. She was plain as an old shoe and just as common as anybody. Preacher Jarven said she never did come to meeting and tell any experience. But I sort of believe folks can be saved without giving Preacher Jarven the last poke of meal they've got.

And Buck set enough store by Pairlee to make up for anything else. Pairlee set a heap a store by him too, of course. She always looked like a little fairy. Some folks think she was Dunk's Spirit. They think the soul went out from Dunk and lived on in Pairlee. But common sense would tell a body that is not so. Spirits don't do that way. About all Spirits is, is just the same old soul in a new body. But the new body has to be just like the old one. Or else the soul wouldn't fit with it. The same body can't last forever, of course. So the soul has to have a new one to take the place of the old wore-out body—just like a plow that is out in the weather, the handles rot out but the point lasts on. A Spirit is not any bigger nor any less than the body it comes from. Spirits don't stay on this earth much of the time. They would be fools if they did. Spirits are not always happy. Dunk's Spirit wasn't in Pairlee. That was Dunk's Spirit Nep Franklin saw in the old mill shed.

More than that, Pairlee didn't even favor Dunk any more than a humming bird favors a buzzard. Pairlee was the spitten image of Nep Franklin. Everybody already thought Nep was Pairlee's daddy even before he told about seeing Dunk's ghost.

He was the only one that ever had a chance to be. He was the only one that ever sparked Dunk any. He courted her for nigh three year. Then all of a sudden he dropped her like a hot poker. Buck, he acted like his colt's tooth hadn't been cast.

They say he just let Dunk lay out there on the branch banks with Nep many a Saturday night till after dark. But I reckon Buck didn't know any better. He was good himself and he thought everybody else was good.

I know it is so—that saying that a cowbird's egg don't hatch an eagle. But Pairlee couldn't help it because Nep was her pa. I let Amy go over there and play with Pairlee on Sundays. Pairlee never did go off the place. She never did know any better than to stay there with Buck all the time. I reckon the youngon thought him and her and Amy were the only folks in the world. She never even saw a team of oxen. I wonder how big she thought the world was. But she was better off than folks that know too much.

When Pairlee was a baby Buck let her crawl around in the house naked as a needle. I made her some clothes and sent them to her.

Amy said that Buck was forever and eternally out piddling around at something. Said the house always looked like a perfect hurrah's nest—pet goats and everything. Pairlee learned to do the cooking when she was five year old. She did every speck of it up till the time she died. Amy said Pairlee was quick, she could move around like the wind.

Amy kept on going over there even after Pairlee died. Some folks thought I ought not to let her go. I never did see why. Her and Pairlee had played together ever since they had been knee-high to a tadpole. I didn't see any harm in letting her go to see Buck. I cooked him some sallet and sent him. Several times I did that. I would have sent him more things if I had had them. That time he was down in his back I sent him some dried fishing worms to rub with. Amy made him some ash cakes every time she went. She makes right good ash cakes.

Buck kept right on finding and making play-pretties. Even if Pairlee was dead. He wanted Amy to play with them. I don't reckon he ever did see that she was growing up. But all he made the last several times she was over there was wooden dolls. Wooden dolls and coffins to put them in.

Amy, she went on and played with them just to pacify him. Him and her would play like the little dolls were dead. They made the coffins out of the bark from that apple tree, and they lined the coffins with apple-tree leaves—green leaves that were soft as kittens' fur.

You know, he buried Pairlee under that apple tree. He told Amy it had stayed green every winter since then, all winter long. They would have the buryings out there and Buck would pray and sing. Of course, Amy and Pairlee had played that way. It was all right for youngons. But it is different with grown-up folks—it looks queer, or others think it does. Amy said Buck got more fun out of playing that way than her and Pairlee did when they were little. She said that he always prayed the little dolls would go to Heaven so they could play with Pairlee. He said he was sure Pairlee's Spirit flew as straight to Heaven as a bee martin to its gourd. He always sung the lines of that song about

> "Death, grim death, did not stop here,
> For I had a babe to me most dear.
> Death, like a volgul, came in a whirl
> And took from me my little girl.
> I have a hope that cheers my breast
> To think that she has gone to rest."

I reckon he kept that song on his mind all the time, from daylight till dark, from dark till daylight.

Amy said Buck always raised enough corn to have plenty of meal. But nobody ever saw him tending it. I don't know how he got the ground broke. He didn't have any oxen. Preacher Jarven said Buck never got out in daytime because he was ashamed of his sins. Buck did keep himself hid like a crippled deer. That's no test, of course. Others go for show.

Amy said he wasn't ever the same after Pairlee died. She said he just set out there under the shade of that apple tree and whittled. Pairlee, that was all he would talk about. He told Amy that little things Pairlee had done and said would come back to him like baby songs his ma used to sing. And it's a funny thing—his byword, it was "God, He knows."

He told Amy that God knowed him and Pairlee would spend all of their time together. He always had said that. He kept on saying it after Pairlee was under the ground. He sung some more of that song. I reckon he made it up. Something about

> "My life is all so lonely
>   My heart is troubled sore.
> Her dearest presence only
>   Could make me weep no more.

> "Sad was the hour of parting
>   She said in words so sweet,
> Come, Grandpa, I am dying,
>   We must in Heaven meet.

> "Oh yes, I'll meet you, Pairlee,
>   On that eternal shore
> And there we will live together
>   For parting will be no more."

Buck said Pairlee had been coming to him ever since she died. But not enough. He said he didn't want to keep on bothering her by weeping so much. Said she come back to let him see that her clothes were dank with his tears. That is about the most he ever told Amy that amounted to anything.

Amy said he set there and whittled and his mumbling went on and on like his old corn mill. Him being so sure of going to Pairlee was one thing that made me think Buck wasn't at outs with the Lord. He prayed enough. Every time Amy went, he was setting there with his head bent down.

Preacher Jarven said Buck couldn't get forgiveness unless he should come to the mourners' bench. But the bench under that apple tree. God would be closer. Or it seems to me he would. God talked to Dona Fawver through a bluebird. And he could talk to Buck through an apple tree. Different folks have to have different sorts of signs. I would rather do my own praying. Then I'd know it was done.

But Preacher Jarven stood right up in the pulpit and preached a sermon on Buck. He said there was a killer living right in our district, a killer that didn't even ask the prayers of the Christian people. He said he could close his eyes and see fire spouting out from that killer's ears and mouth, like smoke from a 'possum's hole. He could see his wicked flesh torn and slashed to threads. He could see him sinking deeper and deeper still into the boiling lead that never hardened. He said he could see him driven by the master he had served—driven not with a raw-hide whip as oxen are—but with a whip made of a burning blaze of fire. He said he thanked and praised his God that Buck was getting what he earned. But it is just like I told the youngons when I come home—if I had my druthers, I would druther the Lord knowed about my sins than for Preacher Jarvin to. The Lord wouldn't tell everybody in the whole country.

The weather was so bad during all the wintertime that Amy didn't get a chance to go see Buck e'er a time. Ad and the boys never went around him after he quit running the mill. Me and Amy thought about him several times. We allowed he was setting over there by the fire a-whittling. Amy said she didn't reckon he would set out under the tree during wintertime. He made Pairlee's coffin out of the limbs of that apple tree. And buried her under it. It was in full bloom then.

All Amy found him doing for the last several times she was over there was setting out under the apple tree whittling —whitting and humming and mumbling. It didn't plague him any for her to catch him setting there talking to himself. He allowed as how he was talking to that old tree. Said it talked back to him. It was the only friend he had now that the wild dogs had killed his goats. It was the only thing he had to talk to him. He set out there pert nigh from sun to sun. Said the shade was cool-like. Said he just hoped and prayed that when he died the God that made the tree would let his bones rest amongst its roots. He said he wanted, worse than a hungry bird wants a worm, them roots to loop and twine around his body tight. So he would know the tree was still close to him like it was to Pairlee. Their Spirits would be together, he said, and he didn't see why their bodies shouldn't be. He said that tree had been the meeting place of him and Pairlee ever since her Spirit had been wafted away to Heaven. The good old apple tree— a home for the little birds that sung her burying song, a place for her pet squirrel to use, a place for the fairies to dance—it had done enough if it never did any more. It is funny why he said that. And now it won't. More funny things happen in this world. I sometimes wonder.

One time Buck told Amy that this world wasn't going to be around him long. I guess his mind was a little too worried. His grief had stung him worse than a hornet. He said this world was dying. He could see things wilting around him like pizened dogs. He said him and Pairlee had set out in the shade of the tree that day. She died that night. He didn't see any earthly reason why Pairlee was took from him. He never mentioned a word about Dunk, ne'er a word. He said Pairlee hadn't been sick. Death, it just slipped upon her like a cat upon a mouse. He stood by her dying bed. She wilted away like a rose throwed in hot ashes. He had always been good to her, the Lord would vouch for that.

There were some pretty big storms that spring. One cloudy night, after the thunder and lightning had quit and the rain had slacked to a mere sizzle-sozzle, I went out on the porch. All around me the things looked light—just like the moon was shining. I went back into the house. I told the youngons I felt like something strange had happened that night. They laughed at me—like youngons do.

Next morning before breakfast Amy told me about a dream she had had that night. She dreampt about Buck. And she aimed to go over there as soon as we got the work done up. But it had rained harder than she thought and the branch was up so big she couldn't go. The next day, somehow, she didn't get started. One thing and another happened to keep her from going. It is easy to find excuses for not doing the things a body ought to do. But dreams didn't bother Amy any more than a lie bothers a preacher man.

It was a month before she went. When she got in sight she saw the chimney standing by itself. She had dreampt the lightning struck Buck's house and burnt it down. She stopped stone-still and looked at the chimney. She saw the apple tree was blown up by the roots. She went on up. She said she smelt something that smelt worse than any dead thing she had ever smelt. It was Buck she smelt—piled up there in that place the tree had gouted out. The bank above the hole was ready to cave in. It was ready to cover him. Things are not always planned by men. I don't know that they are.

CHAPTER 7

THE NEW JERUSALEM

Effena Kanipe (born August 13, 1885)

IT WAS scary, of course, all of it was. But Linus's face was the scariest. The way he looked—like a blowed-up bladder going down and down till it was nothing but flabby skin again. And Effena laying there talking to the ghost. Like it was something alive. Just like it was Murf come back alive.

I had a feeling all along that something would happen. Linus was against Effena marrying Murf Owens from the start. Said Murf would make Effena join the New Jerusalem church over in Hancock County where all the Melungeons went and tore down stove pipes a-shouting. Effena had no business getting into anything like that, he said. He didn't believe in such mixing up. I thought he was just watching out for Effena's good.

Linus was Ad's youngest boy by his first old woman, and Effena, mine and Ad's second girl, was twenty years younger than he was. I didn't think it was any of Linus's business, though, what his half-sister done. Murf was a Melungeon, but I didn't see why that should make any difference. Linus claimed there was a man come over in Hancock County from somewhere down the country and tried to let on like Melungeon folks had Negro blood in them. But of course that man didn't know anything about it—no more than a frog does. Melungeon folks can tell about themselves—how they are an old race of folks, and how they were started somewhere on a ship. They had some kind of trouble on the ship and ended up here. The old folks know about it. Murf was a good worker and he thought a heap of Effena. Done had a crop rented over there on Heaths' place and the house all ready to move into.

The day they married I had a gloomy feeling hanging over me. I took note of it that morning when I went to milk. The red haw bushes were in bloom. I never have seen bad luck fail to come to folks that got married when the red haw was in bloom. I didn't name anything about it to Effena. Me and Dona Fawver talked about it the next day. Dona said if Effena didn't know they were in bloom, maybe it wouldn't make any difference. But, of course, Dona didn't know all. I didn't either. Not then.

I didn't rest easy till I heard from Effena. Ad went over there on Sunday and he said she seemed happy as a jay bird. Everything seemed to be going all right. I didn't hear any more till one day Effena come over and spent the day with me. Murf was working in the old locust field right above Heaths' house. He was going to eat dinner with them, she said.

Everything was peaceful with her and Murf and she was going to have a baby—a boy baby, she said, one that looked just like Murf. Smooth black skin, and had his ways. I didn't ask her any questions. I thought it best not to. I didn't know. She went on home that evening. Late.

The next day, along up in the shank of the evening, Ad come in. I saw there was something wrong. He set down in the door and couldn't set still. Kept going back and forth to the water bucket. Took a sip, and put the gourd back into the bucket. Dipped up a gourdful and poured it back. Directly he upped and spoke his mind—what was on it. All.

Murf wasn't at home when Effena got back that evening.

She went down in the locust patch to look for him. He wasn't there. Heaths hadn't seen him since dinnertime. Nor heard him chopping. Effena rung the dinner bell. He didn't come in that night. All night that night she set and watched. Over there by herself. She looked in all the stables. She looked every place where he might have fell or got fastened under something.

The next morning come. She blew the fox horn and folks from all around come in. Ad and Linus were up at the Silver City store house and they heard it there. They looked everywhere they could think to look. Everywhere there was to look. Every place where he might have got hemmed up by a horse or cow or where he might have got caught between something.

Linus was going to stay with her that night, Ad said, and on till she found out. I couldn't help but think. Ad said he didn't know what to make of it. I don't know how much Ad knowed. I didn't speak my mind to him.

I went over there the next day. Effena was all upset, I could tell that. She wouldn't come home with me. Said she was going to stay there—stay there and wait till Murf come home. Said for me to go on back and let Linus stay there—it didn't matter now. She looked like she wanted Linus to stay there with her by herself. I didn't know how to make it all out. So many folks kept coming I couldn't talk to her much. I come on home.

Some of us went over there every day and things were just the same. She still said Murf would come back. Most folks allowed he had took a notion to go out west. Thought he had slipped around and caught onto a train somehow and just gone off. Said he used to talk about going out west.

Linus stayed over there three nights and then he come home. He said Effena was plumb hog-wild, didn't know what she was doing, didn't sleep in the house at night. That made me think some more but I didn't say anything. He said she laid out in the fields and slept. It was getting fall.

I sent Amy over there to stay that night. The next day I

went again and Effena talked to me. Linus had a reason for wanting to stay with her. That was the reason she slept out in the fields at night. But it was just one night. She said she had a hankering, but she didn't know for sure—she would have to wait. She didn't know how long. But she would know for sure even if she had to keep on trying till the Judgment Day.

She had had a dream, she said. She went off into a trance that night—that night she slipped off to keep Linus from bothering her. She told me all about it. It was the night before that, though, that set her thinking.

She went to bed back there in the little lean-to and told Linus to sleep in the big house. Well, Linus did. But sometime during the night he got up and got in the bed with Effena. She moved over against the wall, she said. And Linus didn't say e'er a word.

About that time she heard a noise under her bed—a dinging like somebody pounding on something under the bed. Linus drew himself up into a knot and just laid there. Effena struck a match and looked all over the room but she didn't see anything. Her match went out and she heard the noise again. It sounded like somebody down under the floor trying to tear out of a box.

"Did you hear anything, Linus?" she asked him. He told her hell no, and he wished she would cut out that crazy stuff. But Effena took note that he was mighty quick to get out of the bed and go back into the big house. She twisted and turned for a while and finally went off to sleep. She had been awake so much she couldn't help but sleep.

Directly she was waked up again by that same noise. She thought she was just upset from losing so much sleep and everything. But something kept on dinging. She got a match off the table. She struck it and looked under the bed. She didn't see anything under there. But the knocking kept on. It sounded like the planks were about to bust. She tried to run to the door but she couldn't move. She tried to holler to Linus

but her lips wouldn't work. She fell down on the bed and
rammed her head under the pillow. And kept it there till
Linus called her the next morning. Time to get up. She went
on and cooked his breakfast for him.

Linus went off to the store that morning. Told Effena he
wouldn't be back till late in the evening. Effena said she felt
so trifling she thought she needed to be away from everybody
—especially Linus. So she did up the evening work and started
off before Linus got in.

She walked along the cow path till she got to the watering
place up there. She laid down in the grass, above the place
where the water fell off that little rock cliff in the branch. It
smelt so good there. She could tell from the way the sky looked
around the sun that it wasn't a-going to rain that night.

She set down. Thought she would watch the few scattering
clouds. But the sun hadn't quite got down behind the hills
yet. She could barely see the top of it. She said it looked like
the sky was on fire with streaks of red-gold clouds around the
sun. The clouds were all moving—like they were trying to get
down behind the hills and hide themselves. The sky was full
of birds—about as full of birds as strawberry is of seeds. They
were going somewhere to roost. To some tree on Sals King
Mountain. They looked like little black specks swirling around
in the air. She kept her eyes on the clouds. One of them made
a big white dog. He had a basket in his mouth. Then it turned
into a cow—a white cow with a calf by the side of her. They
were running as fast as a scared deer. Then it turned into a bear
running after a man. The man fell down. And broke himself
all to pieces.

The wind fawned her cheeks. She felt happy. She shut her
eyes. There was a jay bird over her head fussing about something. A mocking bird was singing too. She didn't know a
mocking bird could sing so sweet. She thought it must be trying
to sing her to sleep. She never had heard of one trying to act
pretty before. She took note of the brown threshes up there in

the catawba bush. She reckoned they would take care of her
for the night. The waterfall was playing for her. She couldn't
quite make out what it was playing. She tried to sing, "Oh,
sweetheart, I have grown lonely living thus alone," to its tune.
That wasn't it. She tried another. Then she caught on. It was:

"And oh, what a weeping and wailing
  When the lost ones were told of their fate."

And she commenced humming to the music:

"They cried for the rocks and the mountains,
  They prayed but their prayers were too late."

She lay there and counted the stars as they popped into the
sky. Counted them till they got too many to count. The night
jar flies and the crickets begun to sing. She recollected what
Murf had told her. Murf said God made all them pretty things.
She never had believed there was a God. But now she was
sure there was. She felt Him—she almost seed Him. He was up
yander in the sky.

She raised up on her elbow and looked at the water in the
branch. The moon made it light as day. She raised up a little
higher. She could see the watering hole. The water stood still
in it. And there was the moon. She looked up. The moon in
the water was exactly like the moon in the sky. She told herself there had to be a God. She thought about things Murf had
said. Murf said she ought to go to the New Jerusalem. She
never had prayed. But she said she somehow or nother felt
like she had to then. She shut her eyes and said it out loud:
"Oh God, you are a good God, and you love Melungeons and
widows and orphans as well as anybody else. And God, Murf
loved You. He said You did everything right. I'll be much
obliged to You, God, if you'll send him back to me by—by—"
then she thought—she would have to give God time—"by the
time little Murf is born. Amen. And, Lord, I forgot to tell You,
I am a-going to the New Jerusalem as soon as little Murf is
big enough." She said she didn't know whether she ought to

be talking to God about little Murf or not. But she reckoned
He already knowed.

Effena took note that it was getting late. The air felt like
it was blowing over dank leaves. She thought getting a little
damp wouldn't hurt her. An owl—a screech owl, she reckoned—screamed down below her. Another one up the hollow
answered it. They kept on answering one another. Owls—bad
luck—death. All that went through her mind. But she tried
to think the owls didn't mean any harm.

She heard a noise. She tried to not think of panthers. She
tried to think there wouldn't be any danger in Linus finding
her. She tried to crouch closer to the ground. She caught on to
what it was. It was a dog barking, away off somewhere. Still
she kept thinking. She listened—afraid to move. The bass and
alto of the frogs sung her to sleep.

Something made her wake up. She wondered where she had
been. She remembered going somewhere. She could tell it was
near the crack of day. The roosters were crowing. One rooster
crowed and another answered, and then one from further off
answered him. They kept on answering one another.

It was a dewey morning and she made up her mind she
would stay there in her dry place till the sun come up—so she
could see the spider webs in it. When she thought of spider
webs shining in the dew she thought of Murf's eyes shining,
then of Murf's ma—how her eyes shined that night. Then she
recollected where it was she had been. She got up and went to
the house to get Linus's breakfast for him.

When she got near the house she saw a dove setting on top
of it hollering. That meant death inside of a year. She wondered
if little Murf would die. Then she made herself not think of it.

Linus was already up. "Where in the hell have you been?"
was the first thing he said to her.

"To Heaven," she told him.

"Get on in the bed and get you some sleep."

"I'm not sleepy," she told him, "I'm not sleepy at all. I'm

sort of tired out—that's all. I reckon you want a snack to eat, don't you?"

"I cooked my own breakfast," Linus yelled out at her, "and you can do the same, or do without."

She could tell he was uneasy and she thought she had better keep on. She said, offhand-like, "It was a right fur piece to go."

"Who did you see up in Heaven?" Linus asked her, like he was talking to a crazy person.

"God Almighty and Murf's ma. Murf's ma said Murf hadn't come to Heaven yet. Said he wouldn't be there for ninety-one days. Said he got in a racket and got killed. She kept saying to me, 'Go to the New Jerusalem, Effena, go to the New Jerusalem.' She told me that three times. Said Murf would have to stay in the middle place because—"

But Linus wouldn't let her go any further. He looked at her real hard and said, "Aw, God damn it, shut your mouth and dry up this crazy stuff around here." And he started to hit her.

Effena told me all that. And said for me not to say anything to Linus about what she had told me. And for me not to pay any attention to the things she said to Linus. But it was true she went off into a trance that night while she was asleep up there in the field and she did talk to Murf's ma and Murf's ma said Murf was killed and wouldn't be to Heaven for ninety-one days. Effena asked her who killed him but she wouldn't tell that. She didn't give any answer. She just said, "Go to the New Jerusalem, Effena, go to the New Jerusalem," and Effena didn't see any more of her.

I couldn't make Effena come home with me that night so I left Amy over there to stay with her. For three whole months Amy stayed with her. I went over there every chance I got. Sometimes Effena appeared all right. But the last two or three times, I thought I could tell a difference. The last

time I went she talked and talked till I know her tongue ached
from talking.

She talked about the New Jerusalem. Said Murf had aimed
to take her there as soon as the protracted meeting started, and
now it was going on. She had been slipping and reading the
Bible every day since Murf left. Linus took it away from her
when he caught her reading it. And Amy looked at her like
she didn't know what to make of it. Effena said all she thought
about was that old new-fangled song and she hated it. She
hated it, she said. But she set there on the step and sung it:

> "My husband left me just a week ago today
> And he never said a word before he went away."

She talked about Linus. She hated him. Even if he was her
half-brother. She said he let on like he didn't want her to
marry Murf because Murf was a Melungeon. But Linus just
wanted to keep her for himself. That was it. And that was
the reason he was so willing to come and stay with her. Murf
was black and she was proud he was black. He promised to
tell her all about where his tribe come from. Like his grandma
used to tell it to him. Little Murf would be black too whenever he come into the world. And his skin would be smooth
and have that reddish tinge. She looked up at me as pitiful as
a shot dog and said she hoped she could keep herself together
till little Murf got born into this world.

She said she could tell she was about to get out of her head.
It wasn't all just let-on to scare Linus up. Hadn't been alto-
gether—even from the first. Then she recollected something I
had told her—about me going up there to the Rocky Pint
graveyard to graze Old Heif one day before she was born.
While I was up there that old crazy Malinda Adds come across
the hill with a butcher knife in her hand telling me not to
step on her grave or she would cut my throat for me. I got
scared and was afraid Effena would me marked by Malinda.
She brought all that in. Said she was marked. Said it was her

birthmark. She was birthmarked to go crazy. I tried to talk her out of the notion but she wasn't in a way to listen to me.

She said she was going to be careful while her baby was making. She wasn't going to grab herself anywhere when she was scared. She wasn't going to birthmark little Murf like I had birthmarked her. From little Murf she jumped to Murf—how much she thought of him—and then to Linus again—how she hated him. Then she upped and told it all. What I had hoped wasn't so but feared was so. The thing she had always wanted to tell me but feared. Afeared of what Linus might do to her. She upped and told it all—how she had feared her first night with Murf and how he took it good, she thought:

The young folks around give her and Murf a big serenading. All the folks from miles around come in. It lasted till midnight. All of a sudden the menfolks quit beating the circle saw outside. And the womenfolks started fixing Effena for her first night with Murf. That was the first time she had let herself think of it. And it scared her nigh to death.

The womenfolks pulled off her last piece of clothes. She stood there limp as a hot cabbage leaf and let them put the gown on her. It was the first gown Effena had ever had. She made it herself. With a pink and white tatted yoke in it. Pink ribbon run through the tatting. I recollect how much time Effena spent on it and how she took pains to hide it when Linus would come around. Dona Fawver raised Effena's arms up, and somebody else slipped the gown over her head. All together they lifted her up and laid her over on the far side of the bed—on the side next to the wall. The cow bell rung. The women all giggled.

"Remember the old saying," Dona told her, "about keeping your back turned to a man, and—" "It's funny how they are all plagued to death," somebody else broke in. They all went to gabbing about how they themselves acted the first night. Effena wadded herself up into a knot and shook with sobs.

She crouched as close to the wall as she could get. She said she wished she could crawl through the wall.

She heard joking voices. She could tell the men were breaking up the serenade. She could hear them teasing Murf: "We're having a getting of stove wood for you tomorrow, Murf. I bet I can work you down for once in your life." And, "Hey, Murf, I'll finish that wrestle with you tomorrow." She heard everybody laughing like a bunch of silly geese. She liked to hear folks laugh. She heard somebody holler back from the top of the hill. "Hey, Murf, I can't take your cow because the calf's too lousy." Murf was already trading and planning. He aimed to make her a good living, Effena could see that. She had laid off and laid off to tell Murf the truth after he said he wanted to marry her. Now she wished she had gone on and got it over with. She heard heavy shoes fall on the porch just outside the door. She held her breath. Murf was whistling:

> "She is pretty, and as pure as a lily,
>   And as charming as the tiny flower of May.
> Oh, there never was a maiden half so lovely
>   As my pretty little darling was today."

"You hain't asleep, are you, Effie?" She could tell from the way he said it he was happy as a turkey gobbler with thirteen hens.

"Huh uh, not yet," she told him, and she guessed her voice sounded happy too. She was happy, she said, just as happy as a violet on a creek bank. She couldn't help being. She loved Murf. She had always set a heap a store by him. She wanted to tell him everything—tell him it was Linus and tell him Linus made her. But somehow or nother she feared. She begun easy-like to see how mad Murf might get.

"Murf," and she said she could hear her voice trembling like a scared rooster's, "hain't there a lamp over there on the table?"

Murf jumped around like a blown-up bladder in the wind.

He said there was a brand fired new one bought just for Effena. "Will you light it?" she asked him.

He already had it lighted before she got it out. She propped up against her pillow, and let her hair fall all about her face— all over her pillow, and down nearly into her eyes, so Murf would take note of her eyes. She could tell from the way he looked at her, he thought she was pretty as a humming bird. She wanted him to think it. She said she didn't want to go through the wall after all.

"Murf," she asked him, "you know there's nobody else in the whole world I love save you, don't you?"

"I allowed maybe I might be one of the persons you liked pretty well."

He put out the lamp and jumped out of his clothes. She could tell he wanted to get her in his arms. She knowed she had looked pretty, pretty as a framed picture. Murf's arms were around her then. Somehow, she felt as happy and carefree as a bird. She recollected every little word both of them said.

"Murf?"

"Uh huh."

"You never have called me Effena."

"Well you just wait. After today, it will be Effena this and Effena that, and, Effena, go kill the old yellow cat."

"I'm a-going to tell you something, Murf."

"I reckon you'll be telling me a sight of things before you've lived with me long, don't you?"

"I'm not like you said I had to be."

"I think the same thing about you that a sheep does about a clover blossom—I think you're might sweet, Effena—aw, the devil, I like Effie better."

"Murf, I'm not pyore." She just upped and told him the truth.

"Huh?" And she saw he was choking so bad he couldn't talk. But then he clinched his arms about her tight as a barrel hoop and they lay peaceful. She was hisn. That was all she wanted.

Then I was sure of what I had thought all along. I felt pity for Effena. And for Murf too, of course, and pretty well reckoned what had happened to him. Effena looked up at me as pitiful as a maimed sparrow. "But Murf said he understood— said he didn't hold it against me any, and now—" but she was talked out. She couldn't do anything save cry.

I saw I had better stay with her so I told Amy to go on home and get dinner. Effena sent word for Linus to come. Said for Amy to tell him it was best he should come. I didn't know what to think. I feared the worst. I didn't know what the worst might be.

Anyhow, Linus wasn't long in getting over there. Effena said she wanted to get dinner by herself. When we went to the table she passed the sallet. I took some out in my plate and looked at it. "What kind of sallet is this?" I asked.

"The kind that grows on lilac trees," she said. "The kind that grows around King Solomon's swimming hole." Then she lit in again—like she had been doing all day, as hard and fast as she could talk:

She had been on a trip, she said—to King Solomon's swimming hole. It was a queer-looking place, but it was pretty as Heaven. It was about like being in Eve's garden. She went on horseback, she said. She got up and got a soon start. King Solomon, he met her at the pearly gate and handed her the key —a big gold key. She said she went on the inside. Then she stopped and looked at Linus, "Guess who I met inside?"

"King Solomon again?" Linus asked.

Effena went right on, "Naw, I met him, and I said—"

"Who?" Linus asked her again.

"*Him*," she said, and she went right on talking.

Linus stopped her again and asked her who it was she saw.

"It was Murf," she told him. And she went on to telling what the swimming hole looked like. It was a big round thing

made out of pearl bowls set on top of one another. There was
a gold man standing on top of the last one. He had a bucket
of water in his hand. He kept pouring the water out into that
little top pool. It would run over into the next pool. All the
pools did that way save the last one, and it held all the water
the little gold man poured out.

There was a pretty little branch that snake-bent around
there every which away close to the swimming hole. It had a
great high bank. There was an oak tree there on one side of
the branch with two roots that reached across to the other
bank and grew into the ground. The roots made a sort of foot-
log so her and Murf rested there and watched the fish and
things. She said it was a sight to see.

There were red fish and black and gold and green and blue
and spotted and striped and everything else. There were gold
and silver mud turtles. And the woods there on one side weren't
made out of anything in the world but wild cherries and red-
buds. They were all a-blooming.

She said a body couldn't step without stepping on the
flowers. They felt so soft to her feet that her and Murf took
to walking again. Then she happened to think about the key.
She remembered she hadn't put it on the inside of the gate.

Effena stopped talking for a little while to draw a long
breath. She looked right straight at Linus and said, "And Murf
said you had followed me like a pup and was on the inside.
And as quick as a gun can go off, that moss-like feeling went
out from under my feet."

Then she said all at once Murf was gone and there were all
sorts of colored scorpions and snakes crawling over her feet.
She couldn't run, she couldn't stand still or fall down. She
screamed like a dying panther. Then she felt somebody lifting
her up on a critter of some sort. She saw it was a big white
horse. She rode the horse on out to the gate and crawled off.
She got on Old Doll and come back home.

I watched her and Linus too. She looked hard at Linus. He

looked like somebody just come out of a trance. Set there and
his eyes looked like two cups in a saucer. He didn't say a word.
He got up and left the table. Effena grinned at me. "Don't you
pay any heed to what I tell him," she said. "Maybe he'll make
something out of it."

I helped Effena with the dishes. We set out on the porch
for a short span and then she said it was time for us to go to
bed. Linus said he wasn't sleepy and he was going to stay up
for a while longer. But Effena went on and turned down the
cover for him. He got in. Looked like there was something that
pushed him about—something that made him do everything
Effena told him to do.

Me and her slept back there in the lean-to. She got to talking about herself. Said it didn't matter a frog's hair what
happened to her now—she hadn't felt little Murf kicking for
three or four days. And it had been hard for her to breathe.
Somehow she didn't believe little Murf would ever come into
the world. She guessed she had done something she ought not
to have done. But she aimed to go to the New Jerusalem before
she died—even if she had to walk.

She said she hadn't really aimed to cook lilac leaves for supper.
But she had done it. She didn't feel sleepy. She felt like she
was about ready to fall to staves. She kept twisting and turning
and finally she dropped off to sleep. I did too.

Directly, both of us woke up. There was a noise under the
bed. Effena reached over and took hold of my hand. "It's not
anything," I told her. But the knocking kept on. Sounded like
the planks under the bed were busting. "Is that you, Ma?"
Effena asked me. Then, "No," she said. She screamed loud as
a panther.

Linus come into the room. "What's the matter?" he stormed
out.

"There's somebody in here. Somebody," Effena told him.
I got up and lit the lamp. "You are just having a little night-

mare," I told her. "You've worked yourself up into a franzy."
But I could tell that wasn't it.

"Aw, she's just on a high horse about something and wants
to act a damned fool," Linus said. He looked like an egg-sucking
dog. "We'll get up soon in the morning and take you to that
damblasted New Jerusalem if that's what you are taking such
a spasm for," he hollered and then flounced out of the room.

I begged Effena to take her head out from under the pillow
lest she should smother. She moved the pillow to one side and
squinched her eyes. "Blow out the light, Ma," she said, "I can
feel his breath against my face. I'm all right. The New Jerusalem."

I got back into the bed with her. I took note that she quieted
down and breathed mighty easy. But I didn't know why till the
next day. We got up soon that morning and Linus hitched up
the wagon. Said we would get to the New Jerusalem by time
for meeting that night.

Effena said as soon as I blew out the lamp she felt Murf's
arm slip around her. She didn't want to holler out. Even if
it did scare her. She reached over to see if she could feel the
man beside her. She could—the scar on his forehead—his
broken nose—his thin lips—his broad shoulders. She was
sure it was him and she wasn't afeared. He didn't have any
shirt on. She put her hand on his chest. Water, she thought
it was. Hot water. But it was too thick for water. She knew
what it was. And her hand felt a big torn place.

She said he kept his arm about her as tight as the skin on
a poor hog. She felt better than she had felt in a 'coon's age.
She wished she could talk to Murf, but he was sleeping sound
as a new kitten. Wheezing away like he always did before that
place was made in him. She felt peaceful as a young tumble
bug. She turned her face over toward Murf and went to sleep.

She told me all that on the way over there. Me and her set
in the back of the wagon and talked. She talked about all kinds
of things at once—so many things. And had that peaceful

look on her face. Just twice we stopped to let the horses blow for a short while. And once to eat the little snack of cold dinner me and her fixed up that morning.

The preacher man, he preached loud and long. He prayed and prayed again, and everybody else prayed. Effena, she prayed too. She knelt down by the side of Linus and prayed. And the preacher called for mourners. "What is your sin?" he said. "What is your sin?" I looked hard at Linus. He turned and spoke uneasy-like to Effena. "Murf is pushing me around," he said. She looked at him. "I done it," he owned. "He picked a fuss with me."

CHAPTER 8

MELUNGEON - COLORED

Cordia Owens (born June 1, 1902)

I DIDN'T know what to make of it when I saw Ad come stomping into the house in the middle of the morning. He was white as a lily.

"Cordia runned off and got married last night," he said. "To Mos Arwood."

"Hit's a tale-idle," I said. "It hain't so."

But he said Square Newberry told him. Then he let in to fussing at me because I let her go over there to spend two weeks with Amy. Said after Amy got married and went to Hamblen County to live she had forgot how to take care of anything. Said it looked like I wanted Cordia to run off and get married. I didn't know what to do. Me and Ad had both been tight on Cordia. Tighter than we were on our own youngons. We never had allowed her to go to any poke suppers or singings or anything like that. Many was the time I had stayed away from things myself just to keep Cordia at home.

Of course, Cordia didn't know but what me and Ad were her real pa and ma. I give Effena a death-bed oath that I never would tell. You know, if you tell something a dying person asks you not to tell you will be haunted by that person the rest of your life. Everybody you tell will be haunted too. It never would have done to have told Cordia—just never would.

97

I didn't see how I was going to do without Cordia. And having to worry about her. That made it worse. I had missed her them two weeks she had been staying with Amy—missed her worse than a cow misses a baby calf. I told Amy to be careful with her. But I could tell about what had happened. And I was right. Amy let her go to one of them Dunkards' suppers. Of course, a Dunkards' supper is the beatinest place in the world for a boy and girl to start sparking. Cordia couldn't see but what she had as much right to get married as anybody else when she was already seventeen year old. Me and Ad had brought her up with our own youngons and she never did know she was just a grandyoungon.

Effena, she died just two days after she bore Cordia. She had had much to go through on account of her man getting killed and everything. Then taking that long trip to the New Jerusalem church house in the wagon just as it was time for the baby to come. And the baby being a girl instead of the boy she already had named "Little Murf." It was all too much for her. She was always the sickliest one of my youngons anyhow.

So when Effena saw she was going to die she asked me not to ever let Cordia know that her pa had been a Melungeon. Said some folks were getting so they held it against a body for being a Melungeon. I reckon it was because of what that ignorant man from down the country said about them having Negro blood in them. Of course I don't know—I never have seed a Negro. But I've heard tell of them. Ad sees them sometimes when he goes to Newport. But other folks claimed that Melungeons were a Lost Colony or a Lost Tribe or something. I don't know. I just know Effena said for me to raise Cordia up to think she didn't ever have any other pa or ma. And she said for me not to ever let Cordia get married. I could see how Effena thought. I knowed if Cordia ever had any boy youngons they would be Melungeon-colored and her man might not understand. I knew, and I promised Effena just as the breath went out of her.

I set out to keep the promise. Many was the time it was hard to keep from bawling when Cordia would beg like a pup to go somewhere and would think hard of me because I wouldn't let her. But I made up my mind not to worry till I had something to worry about. I told myself there might not be any youngons, or if there were, they might all be girls.

Everything I looked at made me think of Cordia. The blue flowers out in the yard. Cordia had gone out in the woods and dug them up along back in the spring. Cordia liked flowers. I can remember how she liked them even when she wasn't any more than knee-high to a duck—how she would slip off and pluck wild flowers of all sorts and come toting them in. She went all over the side of Reds Run Mountain picking sweet williams in the spring. She would make little round rings out of larkspur blossoms. And press them in the catalogue.

Cordia was handy around the house. She took to cooking like a duck to water. And she was pretty. I wish it had been so I could have let her go to big to-dos and have a good time. If it just hadn't been for that blood in her. I would have let her have a big time. Then when she got married she could have had an infare and everything. But there's no use crying over a burnt-up candle.

Cordia come home that evening and brought Mos with her. I tried not to let her see I was worried. But I did talk to her about all the signs there are that a woman is going to have a baby. I made her promise to come right to me and let me know at the first sign she had. I hate to own up to what I was aiming on doing. All the years that I have been a Granny-woman I never have give anybody a thing to knock a youngon. Heaps of women have begged me to. It is just one of the things I always said no to. But with Cordia it was different. What I aimed on doing was to give her a quart of hot pennyroyal tea.

Ma told me about it back when she was teaching me to be a Granny-woman.

I tried to hint around and tell Cordia how to keep from getting big. But Cordia didn't want to keep from it—she said she wanted youngons. So I knew I would have to work easy to keep her from catching on to what it was for. And, on top of it all, right while I was talking to her I heard a dove on top of the house hollering—hollering out its bad luck sound.

Of course I couldn't tell Ad nor the youngons anything about it. And Cordia would know when she had her miscarriage. But I allowed Mos never would know but what Cordia got too hot or jumped down off the fence or something. Then I made up my mind that I wasn't going to worry over a swinging foot-log till I was sure I would have to cross one. I didn't see Cordia e'er a time during that whole winter long. Ad went over there once or twice and he said she was getting on all right. Said she was just broke into harness like an old horse.

It come spring. Spring made me feel so good I didn't stop to worry much over Cordia. I was sure she would let me know. It come a real pretty day. I got up soon that morning because I had a feeling Cordia might take a notion to come home and spend the day. The first thing I seed was Old Puss setting there in front of the door washing her face. I was sure then that somebody was coming. I hurried on and started to milk. I hoped it would be Cordia. I wanted to see her. She hadn't been back any more since her and Mos come the next evening after they were married. Of course, the weather hadn't been fitten for her to come.

I hung the milk bucket across my arm and started out the door. It seemed like I couldn't get my work turned off very well. I just poked around like the dead lice were dropping off me. It seemed like the chickens and turkeys and everything else were hungry. They all started to yelping and running after me. They got on my nerves. I stopped to feed them. Everything

I saw made me think of a baby being born, of a ma trying to save a youngon. I could see the egg hanging in the old gray goose's belly. One of the old turkey hens acted sneaking, like she was going to slip off and hunt herself a nest. I seed a little robin skipping about up there in the cow field. Singing because it was fixing to build itself a nest. Happy even before its babies were hatched out. I had to go plumb to the furderest corner of the field. Old Heif always used around the oak trees over there soon of a morning.

I felt all shook up inside. I kept turning around and looking back. I could see somebody coming down the side of Sals King Mountain. I knowed they couldn't be going anywhere else save here. I couldn't think of it being anybody save Cordia. I went on to milk. I couldn't tell for sure who it was. But I knew in reason it was Cordia. Nobody else would be coming this way. I kept on looking back. It looked to me like everwho it was had on a green hat, a yellow waist, and a blue skirt, and big red shoes. She was leading a cow that had a green head and a yellow neck, a blue body and red legs. Then I caught myself.

I thought if it was Cordia she would go on in the house and make up the beds. I thought nothing had got wrong with her. She never had sent word by Ad that she wanted to see me about anything.

Old Heif was away over in the edge of the pine thicket. I thought I would milk her over there where she stood. It would take less time than driving her up. I seed a snake skin right in front of me. Another bad luck sign. But I had already made up my mind not to let things bother me.

Old Heif had been dry in one tit for over a week. I never had thought much about it before. But I thought about it then. That was the worst of bad luck. Then the sun hid behind a cloud and things looked dark and gloomy. I felt tired and dilitary for some reason. I felt like I was just about ready to fall to staves. The old wet filth in the gullies stunk worse than carrion. I nigh stepped on a tumblebug. It let lose of its ball quick as a frog could jump into the water. That set me to thinking again. Tumblebugs knew how to take care of their youngons. Spiders made a ball to tote their youngons around in too. And dirt dobbers.

And birds—if they thought somebody was going to pester their nests—would grab up the little birds in their mouths and hide them in the bushes somewhere. Then they would perch themselves on a limb and holler. They wanted a body to kill them instead of the little birds. Snakes—even snakes took care of the little snakes. They would swallow them. Then I told myself to stop thinking about such. And then I told myself again that any ma that loved her youngon wouldn't let harm come to it. Cordia was more than my youngon.

I moseyed on back to the house. Seemed like I couldn't hurry no matter how hard I tried. I heard somebody making a racket in the house. I couldn't help but notice that old hen standing in the door. Just as I hollered shoo at her she stuck out her head and crowed. I went over that old saying:

> "A whistling girl and a crowing hen
> Is sure to come to some bad end."

I took note of which one it was so I could ring her old neck for her.

Cordia heard me holler and she come to the door with the broom in her hand.

"Well, howdy doo," I said. "What crooked wind blowed you here?"

"I don't know. How are you all getting along?"

"We are perusing about. How are you and Mos?"

"As well as common, I reckon," she said. She went to talking about needing to be at home. "By rights I ought to be at home working now. But this is the first day it has been fitten to come."

I looked at her. She looked like an old woman—tired and

without color. "How many chickens have you'ns got?" I asked her.

"We've not had very good luck. We had about thirty-seven hatched off. We don't have but nineteen now."

"I'll get this milk strained so we can set down and talk," I told her.

She said for me to go on with my work. Then she said, "I guess I might as well tell you now. I'm that way, Ma."

I jumped. "You don't know for sure yet? You might not be."

"Yeah, it couldn't be anything else. I've been that way for three months now."

"Three months?" I knew I mustn't let on. I didn't know what to do. Pennyroyal tea won't do any good after a woman is that far gone. I tried to think it would be a girl baby. I begun saying to myself that I wished Cordia would die before it was born. Of course I didn't wish anything of the sort. I tried to make out like I was proud. "Who are you going to have with you, Cordia?"

"You and Mos's ma," she said.

For the next six months that was all I could think of. I tried to tell myself it was good enough for Cordia because she didn't come and tell me sooner. I tried to think it would be sure to be a girl baby, and not be black. But soon I got to the place where I couldn't believe anything save that it would be a boy. Then when I recollected that Ad had told me Mos had a Melungeon boy from Newman's Ridge in Hancock County staying over there with him during the winter to help saw wood, I seed that would make things worse.

I had a feeling it would have to happen that night, that night it did happen. It was an awful night. A stormy night in the fall of the year. It was the worst storm I ever saw. I didn't see how Ad could lay there and sleep like a knot on a log. I had to stay up and look out the window. I couldn't have slept if I had all the jimpson weed seeds in the world in my shoes.

The water was slushing against the house. There wasn't any air—not enough for a body to breathe. I thought I was going to smother. I opened the window door and kept it open, even if the lightning did scare me. The hard splashes of water. I had to shut it once or twice—for a short while. It was a regular cloudbust.

I felt certain something terrible was bound to happen that very night. I had been feeling it all day. I dreamed of snakes the night before—green snakes. I hadn't slept any the rest of the night. The wind. I buttoned the door and the window too. And propped the door good. But every puff that come I thought it was going to blow open. I feared to breathe. If the door should blow open the wind would suck through and blow the top off the house. I felt like the wind coming through the window was about to blow me away.

"Ad," I yelled.

"Shet your mouth," he said. Then real quick, "What the hell?"

"The door. Quick," I told him.

I bit my tongue as I watched him fight against the wind. He got it pushed to. I knew he couldn't hold it there. "Hand me the hammer and nails here," I heard him yell. I went to turning around and around. To save my life I couldn't think where the hammer was. A big flash of lightning come. It run all over the house. I thought the world was coming to an end. It looked like the whole world was on fire. "God damn it, hurry up," I heard Ad yelling. "On the fireboard."

I handed him the hammer. I couldn't hold the door to. I tried to drive the nails while he held it. Mashed my finger. More bad luck. And I stopped to think of that right there. I wondered how Cordia was taking the storm. I hoped she wouldn't have the baby that night. It come a keen crash. I hollered out that lightning struck the house. Ad said for me to come on to bed and stop that damned foolishness.

I couldn't go to bed. For the last nine days I had been feeling all turned upside down. The feeling I always had when something was going to happen. Something was bound to take place that night. I recollected about hearing death bells in my ears before midday that day. That meant somebody was going to die before midnight. I thought it meant the whole world. It looked to me like everybody was going to burn up.

I caught myself hoping the world would come to an end. So Cordia wouldn't have any trouble. I tried not to think on Cordia. I went to telling Ad the world was coming to an end and singing, "Will you be ready for that day to come?" I kept thinking about that Melungeon boy that had helped Mos all winter. Ad said he was mighty talky around Cordia. That made it worse. It all hopped around through my mind. I got in the bed behind Ad. I didn't even fool to turn my shoes upside down. Corns didn't matter any more. Not then.

I pulled the quilt up over my head. I had rather not see the lightning. I thought there wasn't any use in trying to stop God's plans. I had almost been warned but I hadn't done anything about it. I thought the Lord would understand.

I heard a noise that wasn't just thunder. It was a tree falling. Sounded like the whole earth was being tore up by the roots. I made up my mind to go. I never had done any harm to anybody that I could think of.

I thought I heard somebody calling, "Granny." I was scared so bad I thought it was the Lord. I heard it again. I was making up my mind to do what Preacher Jarven said and answer, "Yes, Lord," when I heard knocking at the window. I called Ad again.

"Aw, God damn it," he said. Then I heard him hollering louder, "Yeah—yeah, all right, Mos." I felt Ad getting out of bed. It was Mos instead of the Lord. I listened. "Cordia wants Granny to come over there," I heard Mos say. All I could think of then was getting over there and helping Cordia. I remembered that the door was nailed. I was afeared to open the win-

dow on account of the wind. The only thing I could think of
was to lift up a plank and crawl out under the house.

I heard Ad scolding me. "What are you doing?" he yelled.
"Go on out the window like somebody with some sense." I
minded him. It looked like the whole ground was a branch.
I thought I would be drowned. I heard a screech owl hollering.
"A screech owl hollering in the rain, Mos," I told him. Then I
said to myself that it needn't be telling me. I already knew
death was nigh.

Mos said, "Slop Creek is rising like smoke from a brush pile.
I guess the foot-log is gone by now."

That meant we would have to go way up the creek and cross
that swinging foot-log. I didn't think I could ever get across it.
It was kind of rickety anyhow. I made up my mind I didn't
care if I did fall in. The wind was something awful. Things
kept roaring in my head till I thought it was going to bust.
"Mos, what was that?" I asked.

"A tree. It just blowed up by the roots," he said.

I kept talking to Mos. "Mos, we'll be kilt dead before we
get there. I know we will. I dreampt about snakes last night.
That lightning."

He answered me real calm-like, "The ground is soggy. These
here sod soakers make pine trees and cedars easy to blow up by
the roots."

I heard a loud noise—sounded like a gun going off in my
ear. The woods were roaring in my ears. I felt like the whole
woods were blowing up. It looked like there was a tree falling
right on me. I wanted to yell. But I didn't have enough breath
to yell. "That was just a limb broke off in front of us," Mos
said. He said we had better go straight up the edge of the creek
from then on. Then he said, "You will be the only one there.
The Shin-Bone branch is up so big I can't go after Ma."

I was almost glad he couldn't. The water was roaring so I
was afraid to go near the bank. I was afraid it might come
down in a big gush and wash us away before we got to Cordia.

Then I pert nigh wished it would. I never would have known
how it all ended up. I heard something squealing—some kind
of animal squealing. "Look," Mos said. "There goes Dona
Fawver's hogs down the creek. And good God, cow too."

I was so tore up I didn't care what washed away. I made
up my mind to pull myself together. I never had been into
such a shape before. Then was the time I needed to keep my
head. We got to the foot-log. When it lightened I could see
the foot-log swing in the wind. I wished it wouldn't lighten so
keen. I didn't want to see it swinging in the wind. I felt like
if I set my foot on the foot-log I would fall right off. Then
I would go down the creek with Dona's hogs and cow. Hogs
and cows and me, I thought. There were worse things to be
with.

Mos took hold of my hand. Both of us would go together,
I thought. I wondered why the wind had to blow like that,
why the branch had to roar. I got to thinking maybe the world
had already come to an end. I thought maybe that was hell.
Preacher Jarven said it would be raining lightning bolts all the
time in hell. Every drop would be an arrow of blazing lightning
and it would go through your body.

I went to thinking about that song:

> "Will the waters be chilly,
> Will the waters be chilly
> When I am called to die?"

The water would roar and the sinner would fall into it. It
would freeze around his neck. His head would be left up on
top for the burning arrows to stick into. And the thunder.
But I had enough sense left to know that wasn't hell. I told
myself I had better keep my head. Something picked me up.
I thought it was the water. I could feel myself floating against
a cow.

"I'll carry you across," Mos said.

"Don't drop me," I kept on telling him.

He set me down. I couldn't bear to look back. The foot-log would be gone in another second. Mos walked so fast it was hard for me to keep up with him. We got in sight. It looked like the house was on fire. The tree in the yard was blowed up by the roots. I seed that the next thing. I wondered if Cordia had heard all that racket. We had to surround the tree to get up on the porch. Cordia didn't open the door. The first thing I thought about was that she was dead. "Push it open— I can't come," I heard her say from inside. Mos pushed the button off with one big lunge. I followed him in.

"It is done over. Hurry up," Cordia said.

I threw back the quilt. "Heat me some water. Bring me the scissors, Mos," I said.

Mos come running with the scissors. "Its skin!" I said. "A Melungeon! I knowed it." I don't know what made me say it. Mos give the baby one look. "That's why that devil wanted to stay here," he yelled.

I seed him pick up a stick of stove wood. I didn't know what had made me blurt it out. I just didn't know anything. I reckon Cordia was too weak to pay any attention to what we were saying. She was shaking. I seed she was having convulsions. That was what it was. And I took note of the stuff by the side of her bed. She had took too much gunpowder.

"Mos!" I yelled. "Don't!"

But it was too late to yell. I stood there like a post, trying to think. I felt Mos take a hold of me. I thought he was going to kill me too.

"Listen to reason," he said to me. "Are you in your right senses?"

I jumped. I don't think I knowed for sure whether I was or not. I saw I would have to quiet myself down. The baby was alive. With Cordia dead. Mos's eyes—they were as green as a glow worm.

"Me and you can bury her up yander on the hill in the morning," he said.

I stood there. But I recollected the hill. Mos's grandpa and grandma were buried up there. It would be for Cordia's good. It would save her name. All that went through my head. Nobody would blame Mos. Nobody would know about the burying. Nobody would come to the burying anyhow. Both creeks were up too high. I seed it was best. We could tell folks that we had to bury her. I thought of the baby.

I've thought about the things that happened that night. All night me and Mos hammered on the coffin. Old rough planks that he tore out of the house loft. Right there in the room where Cordia was. And her more than my girl. And the little funny-colored baby that I prayed the Lord would let die before we got the coffin made. But it didn't. It kept on whimpering and gasping. I never could have stood it if I had been in my right mind. I was scared out of my right senses. Scared Mos would hit me in the head with that hammer. Somehow, I wasn't willing to die, even if I did think I wanted to.

When we got the coffin done we didn't even stuff it and put a lining in it. We piled some quilts down in it and laid Cordia on them. I did wash Cordia and wrap her up in a new quilt. But we had to break her knees to get her legs to go down into the coffin.

And the baby, it kept on living. Mos, he just picked it up and put it on in. I stood and watched him. Stood stone-still and watched him. We nailed the lid down. It was about chicken crow then. I had to stay there in the room while Mos went to dig a grave. And the baby alive.

It poured down rain while Mos was gone. It was dark as pitch outside. And that cat. That cat kept on clawing at the window. It meowed and screamed and went on. Then I heard that panther scream right out there in the yard. It sounded like a woman's screaming.

A big puff of wind come and blew the door open. And that cat kept on. I was afraid the panther would get in the house if I didn't go shut the door. But I couldn't move toward the door. I couldn't move any which way.

The grave, it was full of water by the time me and Mos got Cordia carried up there. About halfway there we had to set the coffin down in the mud so we could rest a spell. And that cat. When we set the coffin down, it jumped upon it. Mos couldn't knock it off. It fit him right back. It followed us every jump of the way. I could hear the baby smothering and that cat meowing.

I'm not even sure we buried Cordia with her head to the west. We might not have. Cordia may have her back turned to the Lord when she raises up to meet him.

It was seven months after we buried her that the funeral was. I had a good notion not to go to the funeral. But I wanted to hear what was said about Cordia. Mos tried all winter to get a preacher man. The roads were gouted out so bad he had to wait till spring. Then Preacher Jarven come. It was a pretty day. A spring day when the bees and birds and spiders and hens and everything thought about their babies. It would have been a pretty day for Cordia to get married.

It was a big funeral. Everybody in Hoot Owl District was there. I wished there hadn't so many folks come. They all said they pitied me and Mos because the branches were up so big we had to do the burying by ourselves.

There were already several folks at the church house when me and Ad got there. I thought we would be the first ones. We started soon. Looked as if the folks were all staring at me like a cat trying to charm a bird. I thought I saw Cordia setting up there on the front seat by Mos. I told myself to keep my senses. But there was a woman setting by the side of Mos.

"Me and you are supposed to set up hyear with Mos and his woman, ain't we?" I heard Ad asking. Then it come to me who that woman was. It was Mos's new woman. He hadn't waited till the dirt settled on Cordia's grave. That woman looked like Cordia. Cordia pale as a sheet. Mos was pale too.

I wanted to tell Mos how it was. But I knowed that would disturb Effena's peace, because I had promised her. Effena would come back and haunt Mos. Mos would be haunted and I would be haunted.

I tried to listen to what the preacher man was saying. Something about Cordia. Something about he wished everybody was as ready to go as Cordia was when the Lord saw fit to call her home. Something about them that weren't ready would cook in biling molasses the rest of their lives, and smell burning sulphur. Something about Cordia making a bee-line for Heaven.

It begun to get dark. I thought a cloud must be coming up. It was time of year for such. "April showers make May flowers," I went to saying, and thinking about how everything was planned out. Then I heard the leaves. Sounded like there was a whirlwind outside. I thought I could smell something burning. I thought about sulphur, about the church being on fire, about the woods—but the woods were green.

I took note that everybody was standing. Ad pulled me up. It seemed like everybody was hollering about something. Then I seed. They were just singing loud. I went to singing too:

> "In vain to Heaven she lifts her eyes
> 　But guilt, a heavy chain,
> Still drags her downward from the skies
> 　To darkness, fire and pain."

Darkness, fire and pain. They were what I had been through. But God said he understood.

Me and Ad went on out behind Mos. We stopped down there in the hollow and I picked my dress tail full of poke sallet for supper. The sun was going down and the air felt good and cool-like. A honey bee flew around my head, and some pretty pied butterflies. I felt peaceful as a kittten.

CHAPTER 9

WILD SALLET

Meady Kanipe (born September 1, 1887)

I WASN'T surprised when Meady slipped off and got married. Not much surprised at what took place after that. Ad took sides with Linus. They kept her mewed up all the time and never allowed her to see anybody. Linus being Ad's youngon by his first old woman and Meady mine and Ad's youngest girl, it made Linus twenty-two years older than Meady —nigh old enough to be her pa.

I knew how Linus had treated Effena and I told Ad I didn't like for him to be so bossy over Meady like he was. Ad said for me to keep my mouth shut. Said he was running his own folks. I didn't say any more. Meady said she wasn't going to put up with it any longer. Sometime she would slip off and show them. That's what she did, of course. They might have reasoned it would be.

It started that day I sent her up yonder to Arwoods' branch to pick a mess of wild sallet. I wanted some for dinner the next day. It was late in the evening before I thought of it. So I sent her while I did up the work.

She was squatted down in the branch picking when she heard a voice. "Howdy, Meady," she heard somebody say. She looked up, of course. It was Burt Hurst. "What are you doing here?" he asked her.

"I'm picking water cress," she said. "What are you?"

"I'm aiming on picking water cresses too, I reckon." And he looked down at her and smiled that smile.

"Don't you'ns have any up on Slop Creek?"

"Naw," he told her, "we don't have any wild sallet of any sort on our place." Meady said he sounded pitiful as a sick youngon. She talks about it over and over now—she sets so much a store by it. She keeps on talking about it, how she acted and all.

She wrapped her dress tail closer around her legs, as close as she could get it. She pushed the bucket down into the water. The soft mud felt good gushing between her toes, she said. And the cold water trickling around her ankles. She turned her head from Burt and watched the fish play around the rocks. She looked back at him. He was setting there on the edge of the bank. Setting there and reaching out. Trying to pick the water cress. "You can't get the good ones that way," she told him. "You've got to pull off your shoes and wade in."

He laughed. "The stream is pyore as it is," he said. Meady didn't see what he meant. "Well, I might ruin it if I waded in," he told her. She laughed too. She couldn't keep from it. She didn't know whether he meant for her to or not.

But soon she set to thinking. She had heard tell as how Burt Hurst had told around that he fancied her. He had said if he was aiming to marry he would rather have her than anybody in the whole country. She wished he would ask her right then. She would marry him just to spite Linus. Him and Linus hated one another worse than dogs and snakes. She knowed that. Linus hated him because he used to try to spark Meady when Meady was just fourteen year old. Burt hated Linus because Linus always butted in. Ad hated Burt too. He hated him for that. And because he was a Melungeon. Ad hated nigh all Melungeons. He hated them because they claimed they were in this country before our kind of folks come. And Ad thought some of his own kin ought to have the credit of finding the whole new country. Meady didn't set much a store by Burt herself—not then. Because he seemed so old to her. But she aimed to spite Ad and Linus somehow. She might as well do it that way as any other.

She said she didn't mind him setting there on the bank of the branch watching her pick sallet. She was quick at it and she wanted him to see she was. She asked him if he could keep from getting stems in it like she could. She was sure he would say no. She said she looked at him and she could tell what he was thinking. She wanted him to think it. He was thinking if he was married and had a house of his own he wouldn't have to be a-picking sallet for his ma all the time. Everything he did would be for his own self and his own home. He had told somebody she was the workingest girl in the country. She wasn't bad-looking neither, he had said.

Meady frowned at him. "You ought to get up from there," she said. "You are squshing all them pretty violets."

She thought maybe if she named violets he would think about her eyes. Somebody told her he used to sing a song about her being pleasant as a flower, with eyes like the violets that in the meadow bloomed. She asked him if he knowed that song. He went to singing it to her. She liked that. She hoped he did set a heap a store by her. He had told around that he liked her even if she was Linus Kanipe's half-sister. He had bragged about how someday he believed he would up and ask her to marry him. There wouldn't be any harm in it, he laughed and told around.

"Well, I reckon I'll have to pull off my shoes and wade in too," she heard him say halfway to himself.

"Pitch your bucket down here, and I'll pick them for you," she told him.

"You are sweet as molasses," he told her. He said he wasn't trifling, but he wanted to see her do it. Said he liked to watch her. And then his ma wouldn't grumble about the stems and trash he put in them.

Meady peeped out from under her bonnet. She wanted to make sure he was watching her when she moved. She went to a place where the cress was more thicker. She was careful to always wrap her dress close around her legs so it wouldn't drop down into the water.

She kept her mind on Burt. He was getting old and settled and he needed a woman. He had liked Meady ever since he used to see her wading when he come over there to pick sallet out of Arwoods' branch. She knew that. She recollected how he took on about the way she tended to that little old doll she had. The one Barshia made out of corn stalks for her. Said he was going to get her a brought-on doll sometime. He kept on being nice to her after Linus ordered him not to speak to her ever again. He was nice when he had a chance to be. Always he was nice.

"Meady, I wish you would always be around to pick water cress for me. Why don't you marry me?" He asked her, right out of the clear sky.

"Because you never have asked me, I reckon."

"I've laid off and laid off to. What would you say if I did?"

"I don't know. I might nod my head up and down."

"I can get Square Newberry to marry us any time."

"I can slip out Saturday night while Pa and Linus are gone to the singing," she told him.

They planned it all. Burt was to come as soon as he thought it would be all right to come. Meady was to slip out there to that old broke-down elm tree at the corner of the garden. The one that got there first was to wait for the other.

"It might be raining," Burt told her.

"I won't melt," Meady said. "I'm not sugar nor salt, nor anybody's honey—not yet."

"But you are a quare little critter," Burt said.

Meady laughed. She picked up the two buckets full of sallet and waded across the branch. She handed Burt his bucket. She heard a jay bird setting up there in a tree laughing fit to kill.

She didn't blame him for laughing. She thought it funny herself. But she would spite Linus and Ad. She said she made up her mind that if Linus killed Burt she wouldn't worry any more over it than she would over a pizened rat. Or if Burt killed Linus she wouldn't either. She thought she didn't like either one of them well enough to care if they killed one another. But I reckon it didn't take long to know what she thought of either one of them.

"It's getting nigh milk time. I'll have to be moseying on," she told Burt.

"Well, after Saturday night you won't have to milk cows for Linus Kanipe. But you don't mind that, do you?" Burt asked her.

"Naw," she told him, "I've been his dog long enough." And she started on home toting the bucket of sallet.

Ad and Linus took a duck fit when they found out Meady had slipped off and got married. They cussed everything and everybody for a while. Soon it all died down and they never made mention of Meady nor Burt neither. At least not to me, they didn't. I don't know what they talked between themselves. I don't need to know.

I thought everything was all right. Meady thought everything was all right too. She thought it till that day Burt come in with blood all over his clothes and skin. She said he looked like a spring just spouting up blood—like a bucket with a big leak in it—blood streaming out of the leak. She went to yelling, "Burt, who's killed you that away?"

She soon found out. Burt wasn't hurt so powerful bad. At least not so bad but what he could tell her how it was done. While he talked she watched the blood gush out of his upper lip. She got some devil's snuff and some spider web to doctor it. And listened too, of course.

Burt and Linus had met up together. Up there in the pine thicket above Burt's house. Linus threatened to come and take Meady back home. They fit and fit. Burt didn't get hurt bad.

Just his lip cut. And a little gash on his neck where Linus was trying to cut his throat for him. But Burt cut Linus's guts out. Cut them out and left Linus laying up there on the ground trying to put them back in. Laying up there by himself.

Meady, she flew up. Always before, she thought she hated Linus. But she had been his dog so long she still wanted to do for him. She told Burt she wasn't going to let him lay up there in the thicket and die like a ground hog. She went running to him.

Burt followed her. Helped her carry Linus to the house and tie his guts back in and wait on him. Meady thought Linus was killed and she took the spite out on Burt, of course. She was two months called to straw and easy to upset. She told Burt she couldn't tolerate him any longer—she hated him. She didn't want to have his youngons. All sorts of things she told him. I don't know what all else.

Burt got enough of it. So he upped and left her. He went back home. Said Meady and Linus could live over there together if they wanted to. If she didn't want him he didn't care —not a whit.

Meady and Linus lived on together there. Ad said Linus wasn't able to come home—not for a long while he wouldn't be. And he give me orders to stay away from there. I didn't know then just how far gone Meady was—when she might have need of me. Ad said Linus would let me know.

But then he didn't. It was in the wintertime and dead cold too. Linus had took things in his hands and burnt up all the furniture save the bed. Then let Meady get out and get in the wood they had to have. I don't know why Meady put up with it. She never has give me any reason. Just because she had been used to Linus's treatment, I reckon. I don't know.

Meady nigh worked her arms off the day before the babies were born. Out in the cold getting wood to keep Linus warm, out in the sleet nigh all day. And Linus was able to do anything he wanted to then.

He let her lay off there in the kitchen, on the floor, and have the twins. Let her do her own doctoring and everything. He slept in the bed. Didn't even get up to see about her till morning.

Meady said it just seemed to fly all over him when he seed the babies. He said one of Burt Hurst's youngons was enough for him to keep up. He allowed as how he would fix one of them—nobody would ever know. Nobody had reason to know that there were two of them. They were both girl babies. It didn't matter which one he fixed.

Meady tried to snatch it out of his hands. She couldn't. She was too weak. She couldn't raise her body up. She was wore out from having to get up and wash both of them. And not knowing whether she fixed their bellies right or not. She just laid there and held the other one.

She heard flesh spewing and crackling in the other room. Like ham meat frying, she said. Smelled like it too—sort of. She heard something pop like a rifle. The bones. The smell and sound of a cholery hog being burnt. And she had cut the wood that burnt it.

Linus took to acting funny after that—like his brain wasn't in his head—like it was off somewhere, up in the air. He drunk and drunk. And kept on drinking till he got too much of Ad's old buckeye liquor. And it nigh got him.

He took such a spasm that Meady got scared. Got scared and blowed the fox horn. She blowed it long and loud. Three times hand-going she blowed it. So folks would be sure to hear it and come. She needed help with him.

Nigh everybody in the whole country went. I went too. I went in spite of what Ad said. But Burt, he never showed himself. Meady looked for him. She got madder because he didn't come. Said he wouldn't come if he knowed his own youngon was dying.

It took twelve men to hold Linus in bed he took such a spell. He jumped and kicked like a balked horse. He yelled about the flames. Said they were going up his nose and down his throat and in his ears. "Don't you smell it?" he asked. "Listen to it spew." He said he saw a baby before him. Then upped and told it all right there.

The menfolks tried to hold him in bed. He yelled and cussed, and said they were pulling his skin off. He said for them not to let that there God-damned flame reach him. He give one big jump and leapt out of all them men's hands. And hit the ground kerwhollop.

I reckon that was what brought him back to himself. The next week Whetsels went across the mountain after some sheep and Ad and Linus went with them. They stayed two weeks. During the while I let the youngons manage at home as best they could and I stayed with Meady and Rozella. Rozella was what Meady called the baby that lived, and Louella the one Linus killed.

Rozella got fretful and whiny one day—one day during the while that they were gone. She squirmed and went on like a drowning kitten all day. I got to taking more note of it about midday. Meady thought Rozella was dying and I had to let on like I didn't think there was much the matter. I didn't want Meady to worry any more than she had to. But I did note that it looked like it was hard for Rozella to breathe. "She breathes like she has got the thresh," I told Meady.

And that was what it was. Along in the shank of the evening them little white sores broke out in her throat. I showed them to Meady. Meady got scared and wanted me to doctor Rozella. I thought she knowed better.

"There is just one cyore," I said. "Somebody has got to blow into her mouth. Somebody that never has seen his own pa."

Of course, the only person in the country was Burt. He had blowed in the mouth of nigh all the other youngons in the country. I didn't think but what he would cure his own. It was about three mile over there, and I tried to get Meady to let me go. But she wrapped her apron around Rozella's head and started out herself. "Is there any danger in anything happening?" she wanted to know.

"Thresh don't amount to any more than a sore toe," I told her. "In nine hours after Burt blows in its mouth every one of them sores will be as gone as a burnt rag. All youngons have the thresh."

It was good dark when Meady got back. I knowed it would be. She was all out of breath. I took Rozella from her. I could tell it was nigh all over. And I knowed there wasn't anything I could do. Nothing save to take her out on the porch where she could get more air. She kept on gaping for breath. Meady followed me, asking if Rozella was going to die. Begging me to say she wasn't. And telling how Burt acted.

Meady had run nigh all the way—nigh the whole three miles. The wind was sharp as an arrow. It whipped down her throat with every breath she tried to draw. She didn't think she would ever make it. But she got in sight of the house. She didn't see Burt nor his ma anywhere. It seemed like she couldn't put one foot before the other another time. But she kept on. She aimed to keep on till she dropped dead in her tracks. She seed Burt at the barn. That was where she went, of course.

"Burt," she said, "I brought her over here. It's Rozella—and she has got the thresh."

She waited for an answer. Burt looked at her and went on pulling the yokes off the oxen. She tried him again. "Ma said the only way to cyore it was for you to blow into its mouth."

She stopped again. Burt didn't let on like he heard. "You can stop now and do it, can't you?" she asked him.

"Hell no," he flung back at her, "not now and not any other time—not till hell freezes over."

Meady stood and stared at him. She never had seen him that contrary—not ever. She didn't know what to do next. But Burt did the talking. "I heard how you and that grass-gutted brother of yourn killed one of them. Now go on and kill the other one," he said.

Meady tried to reason with him. But he wouldn't listen to reason. Said it wouldn't be the first baby that ever died. She saw there wasn't any use in arguing with him. No more use in arguing with him than with an egg-sucking dog, she said. He had his head set. There wasn't anything for her to do save bring Rozella on back home.

She tried to get in the last word at Burt. "Well, if you don't want to cyore her, you don't have to," she told him.

"I don't have to do anything save die. And not that till my time comes," he flung back at her as she was starting off.

She held Rozella close to her own body, trying to keep her warm—for the sun was going down and the wind was right keen. She tried not to listen to her gag. She couldn't help but think about Rozella, cold and stiff and not breathing.

Meady said she didn't blame Burt any more than she blamed a buzzard for eating kyarn. Burt had been good to her, she said. She could see that then better than ever before. Burt didn't look any older that evening than she looked—not a whit older. He looked young and good when he flashed his black eyes at her. He had on new unionalls and they suited him. Meady said it did her good to know he had some spunk in him. She wished he had showed it that day when she got mad at him because he had the fight with Linus. If he had, him and her never would have separated.

Meady kept trying to hold Rozella tighter on the way home. Rozella felt cold and at the same time she was sweating. A bee flew around Meady's head. A good-luck sign. She didn't see how that could be. Not with Rozella dying in her arms. Meady knowed enough about youngons to know Rozella was dying. She seed a buzzard flying around up in the air. A buzzard after sundown—another good-luck sign. She seed it was getting dusk but she wasn't afeared. Rozella still breathed. But it was mighty funny breathing.

She got on top of the hill, in sight of the house. She heard

Old Rover barking. He didn't bark like he seed anything—he just howled, long and mournful-like.

I was setting on the porch listening for Meady when he howled. And I knowed. Meady said it give her a funny feeling. I heard her coming and met her at the branch to help her across the foot-log. Old Rover didn't whine and jump upon her like general. He just stood around quiet and sorry-like.

Meady handed Rozella to me. I pulled the apron from around her head. I could tell she was choking. I took her on in the house and looked at her in the candlelight. I greased the inside of her mouth with tallow. I could tell there wasn't any use—not then. I wanted her to have air. Maybe I wanted air myself. I took her and a quilt out on the porch. Meady followed me. I laid Rozella down on the pallet. And I set down by the side of it. Meady set down too. And looked at me. "I wish there was something I could do," I said.

Rozella didn't look like she was hurting anywhere. She just couldn't breathe right. Her breath got slower. I seed Old Rover throw back his head and look toward the moon. And howl a mournful howl. I looked back at Rozella. Her mouth was shut —tight as a barrel hoop. I looked at Meady. She looked at me. I wrapped the quilt around Rozella. And toted her back into the house. Meady just set there. Set there and didn't move a muscle. Not one.

I went about. Washing Rozella and laying her out. But I took pains to watch Meady. She still set there. On the porch. Set there looking at the moon through the new morning-glory vines she had run up there on the porch. The vines she set out there so Rozella could have a shady place to play when the sun was shining hot. The shadows of the leaves made all kinds of figures on the porch. Meady begun to run her fingers around the figures.

Old Rover looked over the hill and went to barking fit to kill. I heard somebody whistling. It was Burt. And he was whistling "Can't You Love Me When I Get Old?" Then he changed. Changed to "Down by the Willow Gardens," and whistled it nigh through:

> "Why can't I take love easy
> As the leaves upon the tree?
> They only fade and wither
> So does her love for me.

> "I don't know why I love her
> For she does not care for me,
> Still I'll always wonder
> Wherever she may be."

I was right fretted with him. Whistling a song like that with Rozella laying there cold and no breath in her. And him sounding happy—happy as the mocking bird singing its own song out there in the yard. But somehow or nother, I didn't blame him for long. I couldn't. I felt about halfway happy myself. A sort of peaceful feeling—like a stuffed sow. Like something good was going to take place. I wondered how Meady felt.

"Dry up, Rover, I know who it is," I heard Meady scold.

Burt jumped upon the porch. I watched through the open door. He was shaking all over. And nigh out of breath. "Am I too late, Meady?" he got out of his mouth.

"You come in a smidgin not being," she told him, and looked at the shadows on the floor. Burt did too. They just set there.

Till they begun to talk. About the coffin. About the quiet, moonlit night. Like just one other night. The night they run off together. About where they would bury Rozella. Burt would set to making a bee-gum coffin, he said. And go along Arwoods' branch to get violets for the grave. "Remember them violets I squshed?" he asked. Meady said she did. She would go too. Take her bucket along, she said, "to pick a mess of wild sallet for us."

CHAPTER 10

GOD ALMIGHTY AND THE GOVERNMENT

Drusilla Hurst (born April 3, 1913)

I T   S E E M E D   like Pharis Drennon just didn't have any more faith in himself after he come home from the penitentiary. Before that he was counted the best boy in the whole country. And he was. I had hopes that him and Drusilla would hitch up for a life pull together. Drusilla is pretty as a speckled pup. Seems like all my grandyoungons have been. And she knows how to cook and do everything. Meady and Burt both took lots of pains in learning her things. They wanted her to know how to do everything. They said just because little Rozella died wasn't any reason they should spoil Drusilla. But they were both mighty scared the time Drusilla had the thresh, and Burt was mighty quick to blow into her mouth. They said they couldn't stand it if she should die like Rozella did. Drusilla and Pharis would have made a good-looking pair together. Drusilla had just enough of Burt's Melungeon blood in her to make her pretty—big black eyes and long black hair. And a low voice, soft as the wind rattling through sycamore leaves. Pharis knowed Drusilla had Melungeon blood in her, and he didn't care. They would have pulled hard, hitched up with one another. But it seemed like everything just never was right again after Pharis come back.

Of course, folks right around here in Cocke County don't hold that stealing against him—all of us here know how them big bugs do. How they hide behind the law and take folks's land away from them. But then, Pharis and Drusilla, not having any dirt to be rooted in, they might not have lived around here all their lives. And Pharis would have been counted a thief anywhere else.

Back when he started talking to Drusilla though, he didn't ever aim for anything like that to happen. He didn't think about ever seeing the penitentiary, much less being in it. I liked to hear him tell about it—how he was treated and all.

You see, Pharis was the oldest of Erve Drennon's thirteen youngons. They had a good farm here in Cocke County, across Reds Run Creek over there. They had a hundred acres of as good land as can be found anywheres. And they didn't have to be slaves to get a living off it. All kinds of wild berries growed on the place. Folks from all around went there to pick. The Drennons were free-hearted. And they had all kinds of fruit trees, too. All different kinds and plenty.

Pharis growed up to be honest. I know he did. He said one of the first things his ma learned him was not to ever take anything that didn't belong to him. And he said he could recollect going to meeting at Union Grove church house one time, and the preacher told some tales about how folks stole in some of the counties where he preached. And Pharis said he felt pity for folks like that. He thought they just hadn't had any raising. Of course he didn't know anything about other counties then. And he didn't know how hard it was for folks to make a living when they didn't have any land of their own.

The Drennons had that hundred acres of land that was theirn. At least it always had been theirn. Other folks around there close to them had been having to sell their land to Smoky Mountain Park folks so the Government could have it for big bugs to come and look at, and so they could kill off all the deer that folks around here liked to hold on to for theirselves. Of course, if a body wouldn't sell his land the Government just took it whether or no. And claimed they got folks some other good place to live.

The Drennons knowed that happened to other folks. But they didn't think about it ever coming to them. But it did. And it come on all fours. The place had belonged to Pharis's great-grandpa, Elishia Drennon. When Elishia seed he was going to die, he told Pharis's grandpa to go on running the place and he did. Then when he died he just left it to his two boys. That was Erve and Everett. Erve married soon. But Everett, he was sort of slow about getting married. So Erve just lived on there to raise all his youngons and Everett lived with him.

They just left the deed in Elishia's name. They didn't think about anybody ever thinking it didn't belong to Erve and Everett. They went on paying the taxes. But one day when Pharis and Erve and Everett and all of them were setting around the house telling tales and not thinking of anything much save just being content, Pharis's ma looked out and saw two men a-coming up the hollow. She said they appeared to be furriners from the way they strutted. They walked up and the fat one said, "How do you do?" He pulled off his big straw hat and kept wiping the sweat off his forehead. Then he took out his handkerchief and wiped off his shoes and brushed his britches with his hands. Then he looked down the hollow and said, "Are you the man that owns this place?"

"Me and Everett here," Erve told him.

"What is your names?" he wobbled out.

"Mine's Erve Drennon, and hisn's Everett Drennon," Erve told him.

He twisted his hat around in his hand like it was a fire coal and he said, "Where's Elishia Drennon?"

Erve told him Elishia Drennon was dead.

The man wanted to know how long Elishia had been dead. And Erve just told him, "About seventy-five year as well as I can recollect hearing my pa talk."

The fat man dug down into the ground with his heels and looked at the other man—the shy-pokey one. Then he said, "You say you two own this place. Do you have a deed for it?"

Erve told him, "Grandpa had a deed for it and we hain't never had it changed to our names. Pa never did have it changed to hisn. It come down to Pa from Grandpa Drennon, of course. Then it come down to me and Everett from Pa."

"Do you pay taxes on it?" the fat man snapped.

"Hain't never missed a year," Erve told him.

The old fat man twisted his ears around and he said, "Well, there's some folks around here that don't even know there is any such thing as taxes."

Then he looked at the little shy-pokey man and they grinned at one another. They pranced around there for a span like they didn't know what to do next. Directly the fat one said, "I'm taking in land for the Smoky Mountain Park."

"Well, you are not taking in this at any price," Erve told him. But he kept right on talking just like Erve hadn't said a word.

"Of course we buy up the land and pay a big price for it when it has an owner. But where there is no owner, of course, by rights, it belongs to the Government anyhow."

"This has got an owner," Erve told him. The man went right on.

"But in this case the land used to have an owner, and the owner has been dead for about seventy-five years. It might just as well belong to one person as another."

Erve tried to explain it to him again. But he was too busy looking at his shiny shoes and flipping a ready rolled cigarette he had in his hand.

"We can get you another place to go," he finally mumbled.

"I'm not leaving here," Erve told him.

"My name is George Caldwell. I'm from New York City. I am a lawyer hired by the Government to see that the park always gives justice to the man it buys its land from. This man with me is Mr. James Frankford. He is superintendent of the park," he spluttered. "We are put down here by the Government."

"I don't care if you are put down here by God-Almighty," Erve upped and told him, "I'm not selling this place. It always has been in the hands of the Drennons and it always will be."

But the fat man said, "It's not a matter of your selling. It is just a matter of us taking what belongs to us. We will let you hear from us. Meantime be careful you don't cut any trees or kill any animals on the place."

They got up and started off. But Erve told them they were going to promise him one thing or they weren't going to leave there without fighting it out. Pharis said it was a sight to see how both of them men looked. They looked like scared chinches. You see, they wouldn't fight a square fist fight. They had to wait till they could put on the law for a pair of knucks. But the big fat one promised Erve in a hurry that would be the last he would ever hear about the land being took from him.

And it was the last the Drennons heard for nigh six month. But Everett got married, and he wanted a new house built on tother side of the creek. So one morning him and Erve and Pharis went down there and started cutting logs to build it. Just before dinnertime that shy-pokey park superintendent come puffing it up the hill where they were. He said one of the guards heard them cutting trees and he had come to stop them.

Erve ordered him to take his foot off the place and not to ever set it on again. And Pharis said it was a sight to see how that man begun getting out of the way when Erve started walking up toward him. Seems like that is the way with all them men. They'll every one run if you shake a finger at them —just won't fight you at all. Then they hide behind the law and do you all the dirt they can.

The Drennons didn't know what to make of it. But they went on back to cutting logs that evening. Along about sundown they heard a tromping—sounded like it might be a herd of wild bulls. They just stopped and stood there. Then one of the men said, "Consider yourself under arrest." Erve nor Everett neither one didn't say anything. Two of the men grabbed Erve real quick and two of them grabbed Everett. The other two stood there with their guns cocked shaking like scared sheep. They told Pharis to go on home. So he went in and told his ma what had took place. They didn't know hardly what to make of it.

Erve and Everett both come in the next morning early. Said they had laid in jail that night. But said Frank Denis signed their bond and got them out that morning. Frank Denis is kin to the Drennons and he had been off to school and learnt to be a big lawyer. Erve said the superintendent of the park was suing him and Everett for what they called trespassing, and was trying to make them pay fifty dollars for cutting them trees. Said that big fat lawyer claimed the land didn't belong to Erve and Everett. Said there would have to be a trial in New Port to prove who the land belonged to before they could be sued for trespassing.

A month after that the trial come. All the Drennons went to New Port in the wagon. It was a big trial, Pharis said. He never had seed anything like it before. They had the arguing. Frank Denis was the only lawyer Erve and Everett had. But the park folks had two—George Caldwell and another one about like him. Pharis said both of them spluttered so fast he couldn't half understand them.

The lawyers argued and argued. First, them two lawyers argued that Erve and Everett didn't have any right to the land because they didn't have any deed to it. But Frank outdone them on that by showing a will that old Elishia Drennon had made willing the place to Pharis's grandpa for life and saying that when he died it was to go to his youngons which was Erve and Everett.

After that, George Caldwell argued that Pharis's grandpa

had signed a quit claim deed to the land twenty year ago. Frank showed how that couldn't be because they didn't have any deed to show for it. Well, they seed Frank was about to win on them and they managed some way to get it put off for another week. They claimed they were putting it off to give the lawyers on both sides time to work up their cases. They said they would have to take the case to Knoxville then.

Frank Denis took Erve and Everett to Knoxville in the car with him and Pharis got to go along. Frank got another lawyer to be on the Drennons' side—a big one. And the park still had its same two. They feared all the time about how it would turn out. Because, you see, the Government sent a man down there to decide. And everybody might have knowed he would side with the lawyer the Government had hired.

But everything them lawyers said, Frank would show how it couldn't be so. They fit back and forth for a week. They looked up all kinds of deeds. Finally, George Caldwell said that hundred acres wasn't the land that belonged to the Drennons anyhow. And he showed how, from the deed, the land Pharis's great-grandpa owned might as well be on one part of Reds Run Creek as another. He showed how a body couldn't even tell how much the Drennons were supposed to own. Pharis said Frank Denis done his best. But the judge decided in favor of the park. Then they made Erve and Everett pay fifty dollars for what they called trespassing and cutting them logs to build the house.

That took about all the money Erve and Everett had. They had always had a good living—plenty of fruit and garden things, and plenty of chickens and cows. And had just always raised enough on the place to feed the cows and horses and hogs and sech. Of course, they never had saved up much extra money. They didn't think about ever having any need for it.

It was in July they put the Drennons all out. Everett went to live with his old woman's folks. But Erve didn't know what to do. He never had rented from anybody and he said he wouldn't know how to feel, tending a crop and then hauling most of it to somebody else. The superintendent of the park got them a place to go in Morristown. Said they were putting up a knitting mill there and Erve and Pharis could both get work. So they went, thinking they could get jobs, of course.

They moved them into a little old dirty house down next to where all the Negroes lived. They didn't have room in town to turn around in. And the air was so dirty they were afeared to breathe it. Of course they had to sell all their chickens and tools and things like that. The superintendent of the park wanted Ora Drennon's spinning wheel and a lot of the furniture her grandpa had made. So she just let him have it. Said if they had another lawsuit the park folks might pen them up for big bugs to come and look at.

Erve nor Pharis neither one couldn't get a job. And it wasn't long till they spent everything they had. Of course Ora had enough stuff put up to last for a while but Erve said he couldn't figure out what would happen when that give out. So he said druther than to live cooped up there in town with no air to breathe, he would just rent from somebody.

Erve never had rented and he didn't know how to go about it. That was in September and all the good places were already rented. But he left the house one morning and said he was going to have a place before he come in that night.

When he come in he said folks in Hamblen County weren't as friendly as they were in Cocke County. But said he seed several folks that had heard of him. Some of them told him they wished they could have him on the place, but they had done already rented. The only thing that was left was to rent from Crawford Morrison's folks. Crawford had two grown boys named Rob and Shade. They had over two thousand acres about nine miles out from Morristown. But they didn't rent for part of the crop. They just give the renter a house to live in and a little garden spot and paid by the day.

They paid Erve and Pharis both fifty cents a day for the

days they worked. And on the days they didn't work they didn't get anything. There were a few fruit trees around the old leaky house where the Drennons lived and they weren't allowed to pull off enough to even make a pie. The only way they got any of the fruit was for Ora to put it up. She got half of what she put up and had to give the other half to Old Lady Morrison. But that was the best they could do since it was so late when the Government put them out.

Morrisons had about fifty regular hands and they made dogs out of them all. The trash they had working for them wasn't much more than dogs. They were just the no-accounts that didn't want, or didn't have sense enough, to shift for theirselves. That was the only sort of person that would work for the Morrisons. And that was the only sort of person they wanted—somebody they could boss and kick around.

Pharis said all the hands voted just like Morrisons said for them to. All of them traded at the Tumble Bug store house, and all of them went to the Willoughby church house. Rob paid them off on a Saturday night. Then he got the young boys in his truck and took them to Morristown. They spent a lot of their money setting Rob up to dopes and beer and stuff. What little they had left they spent on liquor generally.

Folks in Hamblen County looked down on Drennons for being Morrisons' hands. When they first went over there Pharis said he went to the Stony Road church house. And the first person he spoke to said, "You're one of Morrisons' hands, hain't you?" Then he was pointed out to all the other folks as Morrisons' new hand. Erve was done the same way. It didn't matter who they were. If they were Morrisons' hands they were counted like all the rest of them. And they were all counted rogues.

Morrisons run a regular business of stealing chickens. Rob paid the hands fifty cents a night, one night in every week, to go out to folks's houses and bring in chickens for him. Then he let Bill Cozart take them off in the truck and sell them somewheres. You see, he could always start before daylight. Bill got caught one time and was about to get locked up, but Rob just went and paid off his fine and got him out of it.

When Rob put the stealing business up to Erve, Erve told him he wasn't doing any such. Rob said, "All right, then, just go on and starve and see who gives a damn." And of course that was about what they done for a while there.

They had to get out and get the stock fed at three o'clock. Then they had to tend to the cattle and mix the slop and give it to the hogs. They had to get their breakfasts, eat, and be in the field, or everwhere they were working, by a way before daylight. They always stayed in the field till after dark too. Then when they got the teams unhitched, every solitary one of them had some little job to do—like feeding some of the stock. Pharis's job was to go with Bill Cozart and Carlous Sykes to fill the hog feeders with grain.

That is where all the trouble started. It was on a Wednesday night. They were hauling ten bushel of wheat that they were supposed to pour in the tank so it would mix with the ground feed. On the Saturday night of that week there was to be a circus in Morristown. Bill and Carlous had been talking about it for a week. It seemed like everything just worked together. That morning when Pharis and Erve went to work they had left Ora about worried to death over the baby. It was sick and she needed outing to make it some warm clothes. But she didn't have a penny to send to the store after it. Pharis said he was thinking about the outing as they were going through the field.

All the boys must have been thinking about alike, because nobody said a word till they were pert nigh there. Then Bill, he said, "This hyear wheat would bring nigh ten dollars at e'er one of the mills at Morristown." And Pharis asked him how they could get it there.

"We could haul it on over the hill hyear and hide it in that cave. Then Friday night when I'm out with the truck to bring

in the chickens, you'ns can come and set it over the fence to
me. I'll take it on and sell it," he said.

Friday night after he eat his supper, Pharis told Erve and
Ora that he was going over to Carlous's house for a while. He
told them that Carlous didn't go out on the stealing trips and
that him and Carlous were going to play set-back.

Everything went off all right. Bill didn't have any trouble
selling the wheat at the mill, and him and Carlous got to go
to the circus Saturday night. Pharis took in some croup and
pneumonia salve and some outing for the baby. Told Ora Rob
Morrison had paid him some on the next week's work, and
she was mighty proud. But Pharis said that during all the next
week he felt like somebody that had shot a deer. He kept saying
to hisself, "You're a thief." Every time he seed anybody he
thought they were looking at him and saying, "You're one of
them that steals." Said he just felt like what he was—one of
Morrisons' hands.

But by Friday night of the next week he was ready to do
the same thing again. It was ground feed this time. Bill said
any feed company would be glad to get it. He was going to
start away before daylight with Friday night's load of chickens
and with three or four calves to put on the New Port market.
And Pharis went with him. Bill told Rob that Pharis was
in with them on the chicken business and he needed somebody
along about helping unload and everything. Pharis bought some
sugar and other things to eat while in New Port. He didn't
want to spend too much money at the Tumble Bug store because everybody knowed what Morrisons' hands made.

They kept their stealing up for about two month. During
the while Pharis learnt how to drive the truck. Sometimes he
took the chickens and the feed off by hisself and Bill went
out to the roosts. That way he got fifty cents from Rob besides
his part of the feed. Old Man Morrison and Rob kept wondering why the hogs didn't do any better. But they never had had

any of their hands to steal from them and they didn't one time think about what was taking place.

They got so they would take a little feed over there and hide it in the cave pert nigh every night. Then they wouldn't take it off till it suited best. They took it to as many different places as they could so they wouldn't take it to any one man enough for him to get to the place where he knowed them. That was the way Rob had learned them to do about the chickens. Pharis told his pa what he was doing. And Erve said he didn't think any of his youngons would ever come to a thing like that. But he said he didn't know as it was so bad as long as Pharis didn't steal from anybody save the Morrisons. Said it was just what they had coming to them.

Pharis said he got to the place where he liked stealing pretty well. He still thought it wasn't right to steal from anybody else. But from the Morrisons, he thought it was different. It give him and Carlous and Bill something to talk about and it give his ma more to cook for all the youngons.

Everything went all right till one day a bunch of boys runned off from the Springvale schoolhouse and went over in Morrisons' field to go through that cave. They had fifteen bushels of ground feed in there then and were aiming to take it to Rodgersville the next week. Them schoolboys knowed the string come from a ball somewhere and of course it was plain where the ball was. Before night time, somebody told Rob. And Pharis and the other two heard it. They knowed what was up. They talked about it. Bill said there wasn't anything they could do against Rob Morrison's money.

Rob didn't say a word to the boys about it. He just went before Square Anderson and got out a warrant for all three of them. They heard about it before the sheriff come and both Bill and Carlous hid out. Slept around in the woods and in barns to keep the warrant from being served on them. But Pharis went on and let it be served on him. They summoned him to come up before Square Anderson the next Monday evening. They said it wasn't a trial, it was just to ask questions and to see if the boys knowed anything about it.

During the while Erve told Ora about the warrant and she stiffened up all over and couldn't say a word, no matter how hard she tried. She stayed in bed all that week and every time Pharis went in the house she would reach out her hand for him to come and take it. He would. And she would pull him down on the bed and try to talk. He could understand her saying something about God knowing he wasn't a thief. Something about not letting the officers put handcuffs on him. Pharis didn't say a word to a soul.

On Saturday night before the trial, the baby died. Pharis helped Erve make its coffin Sunday and that kept his mind off the trial most of the time. Monday morning they buried the baby out there in the corner of the garden. Pharis said he couldn't help but think about Drusilla and wish she was there to stay with his ma. But then he said he was glad in a way because he didn't want her to see him as a thief.

Erve and Pharis told Ora to go on back to bed. And they started to Square Anderson's blacksmith shop. Erve asked Pharis what he was going to tell and he said he didn't know. When they got there the first person Pharis seed was Rob Morrison. Several of Morrisons' hands were there. Pharis set down on a pile of lumber. Directly Sam Anderson moved over in front of him and said, "Pharis, do you know anything about this wheat that has been stold from Rob Morrison?"

"Yes, sir," Pharis told him.

"Did you steal it?"

"Yes, sir."

Then Sam Anderson said, "Was there anybody else in cahoots with you?" Pharis said that one almost got him. He didn't know what to say. He hadn't thought about him asking that. So he just stood there for a span without saying anything. Then he thought right quick. He knowed he would have to take the punishment anyhow, so he might as well lie and keep the others out of it. So he said, "No, sir." Square Anderson looked at him right straight and squinched his eyes up and said, "How did it happen that Bill Cozart and Carlous Sykes didn't have any hand in it?"

"They didn't know anything about it," Pharis told him.

About that time Pharis looked around and seed his ma setting there as white as a ghost. He knew she had followed him and Erve. And he wanted to take it all back. But he couldn't then. It took some quick thinking for him to answer Square Anderson right off. But Pharis answered him just about as fast as he asked the questions. He told him that after the boys emptied the feed out of the sacks into the tanks he went back over there and got the empty sacks out of the gear room. He told him he filled them out of the tank and toted them to the cave—a sack at a time. Then Square Anderson wanted to know how he got them away from the cave. Pharis told him that whenever Rob sent him anywhere with a load of calves or anything like that, he just left before daylight and took the feed with him. Told him he had sold about twenty-five dollars' worth in all.

"Well," Sam Anderson said, "I'll have to bind you over to circuit court. The next one will begin the first of February. Sheriff"—and he nodded to that old bootlegging Dewey Garnes—"you can care for him now." Dewey he just come a prancing up to Pharis. Like it did him a lot of good to get to say, "I'll just lock you up till somebody goes on your bond."

Pharis kind of glanced around and he seed his ma a-holding out her hand for him like she had been doing for the last week. He started to go over and take it. But Dewey Garnes grabbed him and snapped the handcuffs on him. Done it so quick Pharis didn't hardly know what was taking place. He just looked at his feet and let Dewey lead him on out like a dog. Dewey was law.

That was the last week in January. Pharis had six days to lay in jail. Erve couldn't go his bond, and nobody else offered

to. You see, in Hamblen County folks didn't know the Drennons. They were just counted like the rest of Morrisons' hands.
And folks over here in Cocke County didn't hear about it till
it was too late. If they just never had allowed them Smoky
Mountain men to have took them out of Cocke County.

Pharis said them six days seemed like half of Forever, laying
in that old stinking jail house before they got ready to send
him away. Erve went to see him one day, and told him that
during the while he was in jail Square Anderson had to go
before a jury and tell them what Pharis told him. Pharis had
already said he was guilty so the only thing they had to do was
to see if he told the truth about how much he stole. They
tried to trace around everywhere and get the mill keepers to
show where he had sold more than that. But everything the
jury could find out just showed them he was telling the truth
about it.

So finally, one day, the high sheriff—Merit Marshall was
his name—come in and got Pharis and said he was going to
take him before the circut court judge. Merit didn't handcuff
him. But Pharis said he looked like a scared chinch. Said he
had a notion to sort of walk a little fast or something to see
what Merit would do. But then said he knowed Merit was
law too.

The judge man looked at Pharis real pitiful, he said. Like
he hated mighty bad to do it. Then he picked up the piece
of paper on his desk and read it. It just told over what Pharis
had told Square Anderson. The judge looked out the window
and asked him if he pled guilty, and Pharis told him he did.
Then the judge read what he called the sentence. Pharis heard
him say he would stay in the reform school till he was eighteen
year old—one year. Then he would be took to the state penitentiary to serve out the rest of his term. That would be two
year. Pharis said the judge man didn't look at him e'er time
while he was reading it. And said the judge come nigher choking than he did himself.

Erve went to the jail house to see him that night. Walked all the way. But Pharis said hit seemed like they couldn't talk to one another. Erve just stood on the outside of the bars and looked down at the ground. And Pharis stood on the inside and done the same way. Said he wanted to ask him about his ma and the rest of the youngons and if he reckoned Drusilla had heard. But his throat felt like the wind had been blowing down it. And the inside of his nose burnt every time he started to say anything.

Finally Erve got to the place where he could talk. "They will throw you in with a lot of thieves and haul you off," he said, "but they won't any of them fight us square. They all hide behind the law. And he took out his pocket knife and went to whittling on a stick that he had his galluses fastened up with.

Pharis stood there for a while and finally managed to say, "Do you know what they are doing to me, Pa?"

Erve shook his head that he did. Then he dropped his hands down to his sides and just stood there and looked at the floor. He stood there for a while just as stiff as an iron bar. Directly he started off. He stopped once before he got out of Pharis's sight. He stood there for a minute and didn't turn around. Pharis said he couldn't help but notice how old he looked, and how—well, like one of Morrisons' hands.

The next morning Sheriff Marshall and some other men herded Pharis and seven other thieves in a truck and started off with them. Pharis didn't know much about where he was going. But them regular old thieves knowed all about it. They didn't appear to feel lowered or cowed any because they were on their way to the penitentiary. They just sung and told dirty tales and jested one another all the way to Nashville. Pharis said he stood their jesting all right save when they laughed at him about the girl that wouldn't be waiting when he got back. He swelled up like a toad frog when they jested him about that. But said he knowed they didn't know Drusilla.

He said he thought about his ma and all the other youngons. But he knowed they wouldn't ever be against him. He hoped Erve wouldn't tell Ora why he stole. Then he thought of Drusilla. And he thought maybe she wouldn't find out. Then he nearly choked. He hadn't been back over here to Cocke County to see her but once. It had been so far to walk. He never had asked her. But he had always aimed on marrying her sometime. And I just sort of wanted Drusilla to marry him too. Meady and Burt would have been proud to seen Pharis and Drusilla hitched up together.

They got to Nashville about the middle of the evening. They drove by a lot of dirty old houses and shops till they come to a big brick building. Then Sheriff Marshall, and six other men that carried shotguns, drove all of them seven men out of the truck into the building.

They took Pharis on to the reform school and kept him out there a year. They said they always learned everybody how to do some one thing. And they set out to learn him how to cook. He said he was treated all right there. The only thing was, they didn't put any trust in anything a body did or said. And the boys that were there were the sort that hadn't been brung up right.

After that year was over they took him to the penitentiary. He said the worst thing over there was, they let folks come through the building. And they showed the prisoners to them and told them what they were in there for. Pharis said folks all dressed up would come through and turn up their noses at him and talk about him. Said they looked just like the sort of folks that come up to the Smoky Mountain Park. You know, the kind that don't even know a pine tree from a sycamore. Or like them big-shot hunters that come and don't know wild turkeys and hogs from tame ones.

Every Sunday evening some preacher man come out there to the penitentiary and preached to the prisoners. The man that come one Sunday evening took his text on "Thou Shalt

Not Steal." He talked about how God-Almighty and the Government hated stealing. Said all laws were made after the laws of God. Said that was the reason we had a Government, was to see that the laws of God were carried out. Well, Pharis said he just set there and thought.

He said them two years seemed right long because the folks there weren't like the folks he had always knowed in Cocke County. But when they let him out of the pen they give him enough money to come home on. He come straight to Morristown. He said he didn't know why he thought everything would be the same as it was before he left. But said he guessed he just didn't think about it at all. When they let him out of the penitentiary he just started back the way he went.

He got off in Morristown Saturday evening. He thought he would walk on out home or catch a ride one. The first person he seed in Morristown was Carlous Sykes. Carlous didn't appear to be much friendly. But Pharis said to him, "Well, I reckon Pa is still living at the same place, is he?" And Carlous looked like the lightning had struck him. "Hain't you heard?" he said.

"Heard what?" Pharis asked him. And he said somehow or other he felt more beat than he ever had felt before. Carlous told him by the littles what had took place. Ora had got sick and died about six months after they took Pharis off. After she died Morrisons told Erve they would get him on the Government relief and he could get somebody to stay with the youngons so he could go on working. But Erve told them no. He told them he wasn't going to take any help from the Government. He wasn't willing to bow down to them even if they did owe it to him for stealing his land.

Old Lady Morrison got some officers to come out there and get all the youngons and take them off to some orphans' home. It was some state home because the county couldn't take care of them. Erve fit the officers to keep them from taking the youngons. So they arrested him and took him to what they called the insane asylum where they put crazy folks. Old Lady Morrison had done told them he was crazy and that other folks in the district were afeared of him. Pharis just stood there and listened to it all.

Carlous acted like he didn't want to be seed with him. Pharis told Carlous he didn't know what do do. Carlous said there wouldn't be any chance of hiring out to anybody around there. Said nobody would have a boy staying with them that had been in the reform school and the penitentiary.

Pharis still had a little of the money left that they give him when they turned him out of the penitentiary. So he left Carlous without saying a word and caught a bus to New Port as soon as he could. Said he felt like he just wanted to see somebody from Cocke County and nothing else. Said it made him feel as good as a rubbed kitten to get on this side of Nolichucky River again.

When he got to New Port he seed several folks that he knowed. Said they all seemed proud to see him and acted like he had just been off somewhere on a trip. Some of them asked him how he had been treated, what he had to eat and things like that. They just talked out plain about it and didn't act like it was any shame for them to be seed with him. Several folks mentioned it about how the park folks had hid behind the law to steal his pa's land.

He said three different folks asked him to go stay with them, and told him as long as they had a home he had one. So he took Old Man Arwood up on it. His place jines Burt's and Meady's place and I reckon Pharis wanted to get close to Drusilla. The Old Man Arwood had gone into town on the wagon that day so Pharis clum in and come right on home with him. He said on the way he got to thinking about it all. And he just thought. If they could have kept their land. If anybody would have just fit them without hiding behind the law.

He said he almost feared to think of Drusilla. He told himself that all kind of things could have happened. He tried to make up his mind what he would do if she wouldn't have anything to do with him, or if she was done already married. Then, and he never had thought of that before, he tried to make up his mind what he would do if she did still like him. Even if he was in Cocke County he still didn't have any place.

But one evening, after he had been at Arwoods' for about a week, he was helping the Old Man Arwood grub off the persimmon sprouts in that field right above Burt's and Meady's house. And he said once he had the quarest feeling. He thought he could see through the door and see Drusilla back in the room looking toward him. He stopped and went to looking that way. And it seemed like he seed her slip back. He looked up and Old Man Arwood was standing there grinning to himself.

When quitting time come, Pharis made a bee-line for Burt's house. He got to the barn and just went on through the hall instead of going around. When he got in the hall Drusilla was a-climbing down out of the barn loft. She had her dress tail full of eggs. Pharis stopped and stood there.

Drusilla clum on down without ever turning her head toward him. Then she looked up right quick and seed him. She throwed her dress tail down and every one of them eggs hit the ground kerwhollop. Pharis laughed. Her face turned as red as a coal for a minute. Then she bust out laughing too. Neither one of them didn't say a word for the longest span of time.

But directly Drusilla said something and they got to talking. Pharis didn't name it to her about his stealing. And she didn't name it to him. They talked for a right smart span of time about what both of them were doing, and Pharis went home.

He kept on going back. But sort of like he was going over there to talk with Burt and Meady as much as to see Drusilla. Just one time he sort of hinted to Drusilla that he wished they could marry but said he didn't have anywhere to take her.

Then both of them sort of looked at their hands and neither one of them didn't say another word.

Of course, it would have been all right if they could have stayed right this side of Nolichucky River all the time. But anywhere else their youngons would have had it throwed up to them that their pa had been in the penitentiary. It would have been bad on Drusilla, I guess he thought. And somehow or nother it seemed like Pharis just didn't have any more faith in himself. He as much as told me that.

CHAPTER 11

SQUARE BREAD

Wilbur Kanipe (born July 30, 1890)

H E LEFT here walking. Wilbur did. Said he would keep on walking. I don't guess I'll ever know where he walked. He just come home to tell me he might not be back for a long while. Maybe not ever. The other youngons said Wilbur was my pet. I reckon he was but I couldn't help it. He was the baby. The one most like Joe. And most like me. He couldn't stand it to come back here and stay, he said. He didn't know where else to go. But he wouldn't be any big bug's dog. And he wouldn't work with a Negro.

It all started on Wilbur's last day at Holiways school. He was twelve year old and going on thirteen then. Miss Omie give him that piece of paper she called a certificate and said she wanted him to go on to high school at New Port. She made it all plain to him, what high school meant and everything. Said he could get all the books he wanted to read. For Wilbur was ever wanting to read. And he said he was going to high school or he was going to bust a gut. Books were the only things he had ever cared for.

He doubled up his certificate into tiny folds and pinned it in his bib pocket. Of course the first thing he did when he got home was to show it to me. Me and him both thought it must be a mighty queer school where they wouldn't take a body's word for anything. We thought it mighty funny they had to have a piece of paper signed by Miss Omie. But thinking about having plenty of books put everything else under a basket for Wilbur.

He hid his certificate in a chink there in the wall. Then he got to thinking it might not be safe, so he hunted up one of Ad's old tobacco cans and put it in it. He took it and hid it under the roots of that old elm tree there on the side of Reds Run Mountain. He took the certificate out and looked at it so many times the next two or three days that he nearly wore it out. He kept on wanting me to go with him to look at it.

Miss Omie said Wilbur would have to have some books in high school. She had brought him all he needed to study at Holiways and heaps of others besides. She said she wanted him to bring them home with him because she didn't have any place to keep them where she was staying.

Miss Omie didn't have any books like he would need in high school. Wilbur knowed he would have to make some money to get them. He wanted to put out a crop and tend it. But Ad had sold off all the stock and what few tools me and Joe had when I married Ad. There wasn't any chance of raising chickens and making anything. Not with Ad around to sell them all off like he did everything I raised. Of course, it would have been the same with a hog or calf or anything like that.

Wilbur heard about Sam Hale over on Lick Creek a-wanting hands to help him in his crop. Of course, everybody knowed Sam Hale had about as much money as Carter had oats. He had a big farm too, and paid folks to come and help him do his work.

Wilbur didn't much like to think about it—and I didn't either. He didn't want to be beholden to anybody. But he wanted the books he would need so he norrated around that he didn't have anything to do since there were so many men-folks here at home. When Sam Hale heard it he come and asked

Wilbur to work for him. Wilbur wouldn't have ever asked for work. But he told Sam he guessed he could help him out. Sam paid his boys fifty cents a day. He handed Wilbur the pay at dinnertime Saturday of the first week he worked for him. Wilbur said he felt like a chicken thief, taking money from a man just for helping him out in his crops. But all the rest of the hands took it. And he did too. Kind of made him just one of Sam Hale's hands. And he said he felt about as ashamed as a crippled deer.

Then Wilbur thought about all them books and he told Sam he would come back on Monday. He carried his money in his hand all the way home. He said it felt like a book. He took it up there and hid it away with his certificate. That give him an excuse to take his certificate out and look at it again.

When Ad come in that night he looked like he owned the world. "Where's your money?" was the first thing he said to Wilbur.

"That's for me to know and you to find out," Wilbur told him.

"I've got to have some money," Ad stormed out.

"Well, you won't get any I've dogged for. You can set your foot down on that," Wilbur told him.

Ad threatened to wear a hickory stick out on Wilbur. Then he threatened he would just collect the pay himself after that. But Wilbur, he dared him to do it. He walked on out in the yard and let Ad cuss. Wilbur never did mind Ad fussing just as long as he didn't take the spite out on me.

Wilbur had to get up and start to work before daylight. It was a right fur piece to walk over to Sam Hale's. He never got in home till after dark. I always hid him back a little snack of what I had for supper. I didn't have much, of course. Sometimes it was sallet. Sometimes it was fatback. Ad always used up what little corn I could raise. And all I had to eat was just the few things I could grow around the house. I didn't have any seasoning for them save what butter I could keep Ad from selling.

Wilbur had to take out part of his pay in meal and flour so we could have something to eat. He said he thought it would be all right to do that. It would be the same as buying the stuff from Sam and then just helping him out in his crops to pay for it. Of course it was plaguing to Wilbur to let Hales know he didn't have any at home.

The Old Lady Hale give Wilbur some cabbage and things like that to bring home with him nearly every night. When she asked him, he told her ourn weren't quite big enough, or about all gone. Sometimes he told her we had a-plenty. Then felt like kicking himself, he said.

He started to taking part of his pay out in lard. He was ashamed for Sam to know we didn't have any at home. But it wasn't as bad to let Sam know it as it was to ask for it at the store and let all them old loafers know it.

Wilbur went to the store every Saturday evening to get sugar and salt and things like that. After he did all that he didn't have much left to put in his box. He said he just wanted enough to buy his books. Ad quit throwing it up to him about having to feed him while he worked out for somebody else.

Wilbur said he didn't think anything about it when Old Lady Hale would give him things out of the garden to bring home. But one day she come out with a budget under her arm and said, "Wilbur, I'm a-sending something to your ma. I've got more gingham dresses than I have any need for. And I'm sending her one." Wilbur said he couldn't think of a thing to say except, "Ma wouldn't care for any gingham dresses." He never did go back to work for Sam Hale any more. Sam sent one of his hands over here to see what was wrong and he told him he didn't have to be beholden to anybody. After the man left, Wilbur went up to the old elm tree and counted his money. Then he set there with his certificate in his hand and bawled like a weaned calf.

It wasn't long till high school started and Wilbur went just as Miss Omie said for him to. She told him where to catch the bus and all about it. Ad didn't say much against it at first. Wilbur told him he was going to New Port that year because he didn't have to walk as far to catch the bus as he did to get to Holiways. Ad cussed and rared a little. But there wasn't much he could say. Because there wasn't anything for Wilbur to do at home—no crop or anything.

Wilbur said they had a place there at the high school they called the library. And said there were more books in it than he ever thought there could be in the whole world. He got to set in that place two hours every day. He didn't do anything them two hours save read. He picked out all the books that looked good.

But he didn't have but a little money left after he got what books they told him to buy. What he did have he kept on spending for flour and meal. Pretty soon it was all gone. Of course we didn't have any more flour after that. I bought meal from Arwoods. Turfed and pieced quilts to pay for it.

Some of the boys at New Port took to making fun of Wilbur for bringing corn bread to school. He quit taking any dinner at all. Sometimes, he said, he would get about as weak as a baby colt. When he seed other boys eating so much, warm water would come up into his throat and he would have to swallow. Every time he swallowed he would almost choke, afeared somebody would notice him and think he wanted them to give him something to eat.

One day Bob Collins got mad because Wilbur made a better grade than he did in algebra and he throwed it up to Wilbur about not bringing any dinner. Wilbur skinned his head a little for him.

The principal, the man that kind of bossed the school, called Wilbur and Bob both into the office and asked them what they had their fight over. Bob told the principal man that Wilbur got mad because he asked him what he made in algebra and just up and hit him. "That's a lie," Wilbur yelled out right there, and he started into Bob again. The principal held him. Then he tried to make Wilbur tell. But Wilbur wouldn't do it. He didn't want to let him know he didn't have any biscuit bread to bring to school. The principal told him he would either tell or take a whipping. He didn't tell. He said he started to leave the school without taking the whipping. But he thought about all them books in the library. And he hadn't read but two of them yet. So he stood there and took it.

He kept on going to school and reading. Then one day Miss Susong, the teacher that took care of the library, called Wilbur in there at dinnertime and said she wanted to talk to him. She offered him a sandwich made out of square light bread. He didn't take it.

Miss Susong said she knowed Miss Omie well. Said her and Miss Omie had been talking about it, and wanting Wilbur to come out for football. She said the bus wouldn't wait for him but there was a woman in New Port by the name of Mrs. Reams that wanted a boy to stay with her and help do up the work of a night and morning. Said Mrs. Reams would give him his board and clothes if he would stay. She told Wilbur the principal had found out what he had his fight over and the principal hated it because he whipped him. Then Wilbur knowed.

He hadn't thought about all his teachers finding out. He never had asked anybody for help and he couldn't make up his mind to let them help him. He told Miss Susong he didn't need to stay with anybody for his board and clothes like a no-account hired man.

Wilbur didn't wait for school to be out that evening. He come a-footing it on in home. As soon as he got here he told me what had took place. I didn't say anything. I set down and let him bury his head in my lap. That night I got up two or three times and went to his bed and looked at him.

He didn't go to school the next day. The rest of the

youngons hung around the house all day and fussed. Wilbur fussed with them. It rained and there wasn't hardly a spot in the house that didn't leak. Wilbur kept coming to me and saying how good it would feel to be setting in the library reading. Late that evening Ad come in and told Wilbur he had to help tend the still that night and the next day.

Ad come to the house the next morning and left Wilbur over there on the other side of Sals King Mountain to watch the still. Wilbur slipped off and caught the school bus. When he got home that night Ad was setting out on the steps waiting for him. He grabbed Wilbur and went to kicking him. Wilbur started fighting back. They fit like two guinea roosters till Wilbur got so tired he couldn't fight. Then he laid down and let Ad kick him till he wore himself out.

Ad told him he wasn't going to have any such trash as him lolling around. Said he would shoot him if he ever set foot on the place again. Told him to hit the road right then. Wilbur said, "All right," and turned around and started back the way he had come.

I just stood there. When he got to the corner of the yard he looked back at me. My body drew up as tight and stiff as a poker. I watched him. Before he got to the top of the hill he looked back again. Then he turned and walked as fast as he could. That was the last I seed of him. The last till he come back that day, a year afterward, and told me all.

Wilbur said as soon as he got out of sight he set down to think about what he would do. His mind wouldn't work. He set there till plumb dark. Then he stretched out in the grass by the side of the path and didn't try to think any more.

The next morning he woke up and went on and caught the bus to school just like common. That day at dinner period he went in the library and got a book and went to looking through it. He knowed Miss Susong always eat her dinner in there. She brought her box up and set down across the table from Wilbur. She handed him one of them square sandwiches. "I'm not hungry," Wilbur told her, but he reached out and took it.

Miss Susong told him she was still wanting him to go out for football, and that Mrs. Reams was still wanting him to come and live with her. "I'm a-going there tonight," Wilbur told her. He said Miss Susong looked like she didn't know what to think. Directly she said she would go to Mrs. Reams's as soon as school was out and take him with her.

Wilbur said Mrs. Reams was pretty as a speckled pup. She was big and fat and had a black dress with little holes in it so you could see her naked skin. He could tell she was mighty proud and fancy. Miss Susong told her Wilbur was the boy, the one Miss Susong had talked to her about over the phone that evening. Mrs. Reams started putting on airs and asked him where his things were, and a lot of stuff like that.

Miss Susong went on back and Mrs. Reams told Wilbur to bring in the coal. Directly she told him to wash his hands and get ready for supper. She said he didn't wash his hands right so she showed him how. All during supper she set and watched him like a hawk.

After supper she asked him all kinds of questions about what Ad did and how I looked and things like that. Then she said it was time for him to take a bath and go to bed. She showed him how to take his bath and she give him a great big white gown to sleep in. Said it was hers but she would get him some the next day. Wilbur said once he stopped right in the middle of washing and started to get out and run—just run. But he thought about all them books. The bed was all fixed up pretty and as white as snow. Said he felt like a corpse when he got in it. And it smelled good too, he said, smelled like sassafras tea.

Wilbur stayed there nigh three month. Mrs. Reams faulted everything he did. She grumbled so much about how he eat that she had him afeared to eat anything at all. She didn't let him go out to play football after all. Said he had to come home and talk to her and help get supper. And helping meant getting.

She asked him the same old questions over and over till she nigh talked the daylights out of him. Wilbur said he could stand anything better than her asking if I was pretty and young-looking and if I had pretty clothes. It was just the way she asked—like she already knowed.

Every time he got to feeling girlified and shamed because he had to cook supper, he would make himself think about the books in the library. At home he never had had any good light to read by at night nor any good chair to set in. But he said Mrs. Reams had the rooms so bright they hurt a body's eyes. She had chairs soft as a feather bed. But after the first night she wouldn't even let Wilbur set down in the big soft chairs. Said she was afeared he would get them dirty. She made him bring in one from the kitchen. She had every room in the house lit up, but she made him stay in there with her. Said she was lonely. If he tried to read she asked him so many questions he couldn't get the words put together. Between the questions she wanted a drink, or her back scratched, or her shoes pulled off. Wilbur went on and did everwhat she told him to do. But he said every time he went to scratch her back he would think about me and how I used to scratch his back for him. Sometimes his eyes would drip and hit Mrs. Reams's back or neck. She would say he had been reading too much. That would put his mind back on the books. Wilbur said he liked it there in a way. Everything was nice as a fox's skin. But he wasn't allowed to do anything save just what she told him he could do. He kept hoping he would get to read some there.

Then one night he was in the room where they slept. She fixed him a bed right there with her so if she wanted anything in the night he could get up and get it for her. Then she had to learn him how to get in the bed and how to lay after he got in. She claimed he woke her up every time he moved. But that night he was back in the room where they slept and Mrs. Reams was in the room they called the setting room—in there talking to a woman that come in to see her that night. Wilbur heard her telling that woman about him. Said she felt sorry for him and she would like to see how his poor old mother looked.

Wilbur got his books and walked out the back door. He kept walking right toward home. Sometime during the night he got in sight of the house. He said he could see it good in the moonlight. The same house—pretty and fitted to the hollow, but still needing to be boarded. He kept on coming toward it till Old Shep begun barking at him. Something made Wilbur stop. He stopped and wondered if Old Shep would know him if he whistled. He said he wondered if I was cold. He wondered what Mrs. Reams thought I looked like.

He turned around and walked back toward town. He walked till he come to Sam Hale's barn. He clum up in the loft and went to sleep. The next morning he clum back furder into the hay till the hands come to feed. It was a rainy day and as soon as the hands fed they left the barn. Wilbur got to thinking about all the books in the library. He had one with him he wasn't through reading. He got it out and set there and read. Along about midday he thought about the big dinners Hales always had. Once he got up and started to go to the house. He thought maybe Sam Hale might want him to stay with him. But that would just be jumping out of the frying pan into the fire. Sam Hale wouldn't want him to go to school. He laid back down and read his book.

He got it read about the time the hands come to feed the stock that night. They never did see him. After dark he crept out and started walking again. There was something about the library that sort of drawed him that way. He walked till he got to the high school. He pulled at the door but the door was locked. He laid the book in front of the door and he went over and set down by a window where he could have seen the books if it had been light in there. He thought about all the books in the library that he hadn't read. He wished he could tech some of them one more time.

He set there and thought for a right smart span. It was the first time he had tried to think. Johnson City kept coming into his mind. That was where folks always went to get jobs. All the boys he ever knowed to go off anywhere for jobs went to Johnson City.

He had been hearing the boys at school talk about there being a new shoe factory at Johnson City. He got up and started walking again. He walked till daylight, then stopped and asked a man if that was the way to Johnson City. A man in a wagon come along and picked him up. He rode as far as that man was going. Then a man in a buggy come along and asked him to ride. It didn't take him so powerful long to get there.

They were needing hands of any sort they could get at Johnson City so he didn't have any trouble getting a job. He hated to bow down to them big bugs enough to ask them for one. But he did. They said he was little and couldn't do any work such as running the machines. So they said they would pay him a dollar a day to keep floors swept up and keep all the rooms clean of the first floor. Warmish water come up into Wilbur's mouth when he thought about toting a broom around all day, cleaning up trash. But he could use the dollars he made to buy books. When he got enough dollars he could have him a library of his own. They let him start work the next morning. Wilbur felt like a wart on a mule's hind leg, cleaning up them big bugs' cigar stubs.

The boss man told him there was a bunkhouse there kept by a woman. He said Wilbur could stay in that or he could stay anywhere else he wanted to. First he stayed at the thing they called the bunkhouse, and had to pay four dollars a week for his eating and sleeping. He said they had a plenty to eat. But the boys that stayed there were the kind that would blackgyuard a chicken roost. All they talked about was what big whore-hoppers they were, or told some dirty tale.

The boys said they had to break in every new boy that
come to the bunkhouse and they started to give Wilbur his
breakin'-in. They were going to turn him across one of their
laps and whip him. But when they seed Wilbur was going to
fight back they stopped.

Wilbur took up with Nick Nolton, a boy that worked there
sweeping up the second floor. Nick told him where he could
get board for three dollars a week. That was where Nick
stayed. Wilbur went there too. It was a filthy place. The
woman that run it didn't have any decency. Wilbur said she
was dried up and her face looked like it had already wore out
three bodies. Every time he looked at her he wondered if
Mrs. Reams thought that was the way I looked. Wilbur
thought he could bear it there. He thought he could lock himself up in his dirt hole and read as soon as he got his pay and
bought him some books.

Saturday night come and he paid at the bunkhouse for the
two nights he stayed there and then he paid Bell Jones. That
was the name of the woman he was staying with. He didn't
have anything much left. But he put it in his pocket and
started up there to a store where he had seed some books for
sale. Nick saw him going out. He said he had a girl he wanted
Wilbur to go see. Wilbur didn't have any more gumption than
to let Nick beg him into going.

All Wilbur's money went that night. And that old dirty
gal was ugly as home-made sin. The kind, he said, that just
left a bad taste in his mouth. He made up his mind his money
would go for books the next time. He didn't tell the boys
around there though. For they poked fun at books.

The next Saturday night Nick wanted Wilbur to go play
poker with him. All the boys come by after him and they
deviled him till he give in. He said all the while he was playng
poker and drinking that old rotgut liquor he thought about
what a good time he could be having reading some book. It
was hard for him to get naturalized to their ways.

He did the same trick the next Saturday night. Then he told the boys he was through. They could tell he meant it too. That Saturday night he took his money and went to the store they called the drugstore and bought him a book and magazine. Said they didn't have any books or magazines either there that looked much good. He got the best-looking of what they had. The things he got didn't have any reading in them save trash. He went on and read them. Said he thought reading trash wasn't any worse than being trash.

You see, the other boys there counted Wilbur trash too. Everybody did. Just because he cleaned up cigar stubs that them big bugs throwed on the floor. He knowed what they thought. There wasn't a one of them big bugs that would give him air if he was stopped up in a jug. That was bad enough. Let alone not getting to be with anybody save trash.

After he seed he couldn't get anything fit to read he got so he didn't care a whit whether he kept his job or not. The Old Man Whittaker got uppety. He was Wilbur's boss and it seemed like Wilbur had a grudgment against him from the first. I reckon it must have been because he made Wilbur call him Mr. Whittaker. He was forever yelling for Wilbur to empty his ash tray for him or dust his desk or hold his overcoat. Wilbur took all that without saying a word till one day the Old Man Whittaker told him to go to the drugstore and bring him two coca colas. Wilbur said to him, "Who was your dog this time last year?" The Old Man Whittaker looked grim as the devil and he said, "I'll learn you who to sass around here." Wilbur told him he didn't have to be beholden to him nor to anybody else. And Wilbur throwed his broom down and went out the door. That was on a Wednesday. He didn't go back on Saturday for his pay.

Nick knowed some boys that were working at the glass factory and it wasn't but two days till Wilbur got in over there. They put him to fetching empty boxes for them to put moulded glass into. He got a dollar and a half a day and they said it wouldn't be long till he would be getting big pay. The only thing about it was, they had a woman that always told Wilbur what to do—what size boxes to get and things like that. It was her job to send duns to all the folks that bought glass from them too. So what time Wilbur wasn't toting empty boxes or rolling a box of glass around somewhere on a cart, she had him backing and forthing to the post office with a pack of letters.

Everything went all right for the first week. But on Thursday of the next week Miss Rodgers sent him to the post office with some letters. They needed some empty boxes in the moulding room before he got back. As soon as he stuck his head in the door Miss Rodgers squalled out, "Get four number twelve boxes down here quick. You've been gone long enough to have built a glass house."

Wilbur said she nigh scared the daylights out of him, yelling that way. He couldn't do anything save just stand there. "Don't stand there like an ox," she hollered. "Do as I tell you." It was the first time he had thought about it, he said, but Miss Rodgers looked like Old Lady Reams and yelled about like her. Wilbur stood there like a bump on a log and stared at her for a minute. He didn't say a word. He just turned around and walked out. Said he didn't know what made him do it. He didn't go back any more. But the glass factory sent his pay to him in a letter and he got it that Saturday.

He went and bought another one of them no-account books. He had enough money left to stay where he was for the next week. He laid around there in his filth hole and read that book and magazine. Said lots of times he would think about me and wonder if I knowed where he was. Sometimes he thought about all the books in the library at New Port and a big lump would come up in his thoat. His body would get so stiff he couldn't move for a right smart while. He would get up and go in the room where Bell Jones was.

Nick told Wilbur that Ed McMann was going to quit his

job at the glass factory and go to Saint Charles, Virginia, and get a job working on the railroad. They were making what they called a new tramway into some of the mines there at Saint Charles. Wilbur made up his mind to go with Ed. It took them two days and a night to foot it across Clinch Mountain. They laid down by the side of a log and slept part of that night. Ed built up a fire to keep the bears away.

Wilbur and Ed stopped at a place and asked for breakfast. Ed did the asking. Wilbur told him he wasn't hungry. Wilbur said the woman he asked looked like the devil before daylight. She told them she didn't have much but she could let them have a little of what she did have. It was a little old dirty shack in the edge of some little old dirty town. Wilbur told Ed they ought to wait till they got out into the country to ask for something to eat. The woman had meat skins and coffee. Wilbur set there and tried to let on like he was eating. He could have eat the meat skins all right, but he found a big old fly in his coffee. Ed give the woman fifty cents.

Ed asked for the jobs at Saint Charles. Floyd Hawkins was the name of the big boss. Ed told him their names and how old they both were. He told that Wilbur was sixteen year old. But Wilbur wasn't. He wasn't but fifteen year old. I reckon Ed knowed they didn't work anybody under sixteen year old. They trusted Ed's word.

There was a bunkhouse at that place too. But it was full up and they put Wilbur and Ed in the kitchen to sleep. They could eat any time they took a notion to eat. Didn't have to go to the table with the rest of them. Wilbur said it looked like he was going to pacify himself with staying there. Three dollars and ninety cents a day was the least they paid. That was what Wilbur got. He said he thought about it the first night. He could save nearly all the money he made. After he worked a year he could go back to high school and live like other folks. And he would have the library and money to buy books besides. He got to thinking about where he would stay while he went to school. Said he got to thinking about how good it would be if he could come back home and stay. He could buy things and I could fix up his dinner for him. He wished he could buy a house so me and him could live there close to the school. But of course he knowed we couldn't do that.

Ed told him if he had his head set on going to school he could go there in Saint Charles as well as anywhere else. But the only sort of folks he knowed there in Saint Charles were trashy folks. And he wasn't going to have anything to do with trash when he got back to New Port. He would get to thinking about me and Amy and Meady, and all the rest. He wondered what was happening to us. Then he would get Ed started on his blackgyuardish jokes.

He stayed in Saint Charles three weeks. The first week was all right. Him and Ed worked with a whole crew, laying cross-ties. They worked right under Floyd Hawkins. Of course they were just like mules geeing and hawing when Floyd hollered. But Wilbur would think about all the books he was going to read the next year. Him and Ed went uptown after they got their pay the first Saturday night. Wilbur said street walkers were up there thick as hops. He was dodging around from them a little and he just happened to see a place where it said "Second-Hand Books Cheap." He thought he had better go in there while times were good. Some woman would soon have his money if he didn't. He found two books that he recollected Miss Susong telling him she wanted him to read sometime. He had aimed on reading them as soon as he could. They weren't but a quarter a piece so he got both of them. He read till away up into the night, and he got to thinking that he was the best off he had ever been. They just had lamp-oil lamps there of course. But that was better than Mrs. Reams's bright lights with her tongue going all the time.

When Ed come in he told Wilbur about the girl he had been with. And about the one he wanted Wilbur to be with the next Saturday night. He said Wilbur was a fool to come home and read. But Wilbur said them old women put him in the mind of snakes—they were so skinny and dried up and scaly.

Sunday morning Wilbur read some more. He aimed on reading during that evening but Ed said him and some more boys were going to walk down the tracks just to be rambling around. Wilbur went with them. Said some of the tales they told sounded right funny. I reckon if a body stays around any kind of folks he soon gets naturalized to their ways. And maybe likes them.

Wilbur said he liked that bunch of boys all right. One thing that nigh made him puke, though, was that nearly everybody they met was boogered up in some way. Some had their faces cut up. Some had two arms or two legs off. Ed told Wilbur that might happen to them when they put them back into the mines.

The next week went off about the same—save a little better. On Thursday and Friday of that week Floyd sent Ed and Wilbur away off up the tramway by themselves. He sent them up there to unload some crossties out of a lot of things they called dinkies. He didn't send any kind of boss with them.

But the next week Floyd did enough to cap it all. Ed was sick on that Monday and couldn't go to work. So Floyd sent Wilbur up there with a Negro. A Negro. Wilbur stood it the first day. Thursday Floyd did the same thing. Wilbur swelled up like a toad frog and didn't say e'er a word to the Negro all day. Said he set down on his shovel handle one time and thought about quitting. Then he thought about all the books at high school. And he thought about how he was going to board. Not just stay with somebody for his eating and clothes —but pay for a good place to stay and not be beholden to anybody. Said he thought about the Saturday nights when Ad would be gone and he could come to see me for a short span. Walk that far and come.

Then he went and did that. Friday morning when they started to work, Wilbur heard Floyd tell the Negro to see that Wilbur kept busy. Somehow it flew all over Wilbur like a flash. He said he couldn't see any mortal excuse for Floyd telling the Negro that. It was the same as making him a boss over Wilbur. Wilbur flew off the handle and told Floyd he wasn't working there side by side with a Negro. Floyd didn't say anything save, "Well, you can work or not work, just as you please."

Wilbur set to walking down the track as fast as he could. He never did look back. What little money he had was in his pocket anyway. He didn't even think about going back to get his two books. But he said he didn't guess he would ever care about reading any more.

He walked till he was wore out with walking. He rested and started walking again. And walked till he got home. It was lucky Ad wasn't here. Wilbur told me all. But wouldn't stay. He couldn't tolerate it here. He wouldn't tolerate Ad's bossing.

Wilbur set out walking again. Said for me not to fret—it was best he should. I don't know where he walked. He said he could walk till he come to the high school and the books. But his money wouldn't last long. And he wouldn't fit in there. He was rough and dirty-looking—like the trash he had been with. He wouldn't want Miss Susong to see him.

Or he could walk till he got back to Johnson City, he said, and get another job. Or to Saint Charles, and make money, maybe. Sleep with dirty women and drink pizen liquor. "But I won't be any big bug's dog," he said, "and I won't work with a Negro." And he set out walking.

CHAPTER 12

THE HAWK'S DONE GONE

Mary Dorthula White (born January 6, 1847)

I WONDER why Ad and Linus never tried to sell me off to them hunters for old things. I would be a sight for somebody to look at. Big and motley and rough-looking. Old and still strong for my age. I miss the things they have sold. These new-fangled things are weak. They make me feel weak too. But I ought not to be setting here nursing this old Bible. I ought to get out and pick some sallet for supper.

The Bible is about the only old thing I have left, though. I thought I couldn't thole it when Ad and Linus first started selling off my stuff. I hate them folks that come around hunting for things to put in the Smoky Mountain museum. And I nigh hate Linus for letting them have my things. Linus is Ad's youngest boy by his first old woman and he has been spoiled rotten. Ad is the one that spoiled him too. Ad has turned everything over to him and let him run it to suit hisself—my own stuff too.

William Wayne was the only one of them antique hunters that was decent. Him and that painted-up woman he called Miss Robinson come together. I recollect that first day when they come. I was bent over the tub washing. Miss Robinson, she strutted up like she thought she was something on a stick, all dyked out in a purple silk dress and spike-heeled shoes. The first thing she did was to commence complaining about having to walk through the mud.

Miss Robinson's old hawk eyes seed everything I had. She got around Linus and got nigh everything I wanted to keep. She picked out the things she wanted. Looked at both of my corded bedsteads. One of them wasn't in very good shape, she said, and she didn't know whether she would take it or not. I felt like giving her a piece of my mind. And I did flare up a little. I looked at her straight and I said, "Who said anything about you taking either one of them? Them is the first bedsteads my pa ever made—made them for him and Ma to start housekeeping on. I was born in this one hyear and all my youngons were born in it."

I recollect the way I said it to her. I recollect the way William Wayne looked—almost like the soldier boy looked at me that day—that first day. William Wayne had brown eyes —big brown eyes that smiled as much as his mouth did. He put me in mind of the soldier, smiling all the time and talking so gentle. But Charles would be old by now. Old enough to be dead. He was older than me back then. I was just fifteen year old and he was a full-grown man. At least he was old enough to be out fighting the Yankees. At first I thought William Wayne might be Charles's boy maybe. But then I knowed Charles wouldn't ever have any other boy. William Wayne had pity for me and he hated to take my bedsteads away.

It didn't matter who had pity, though, for Linus and Miss Robinson made the bargain. The very next day Miss Robinson would send a wagon up here with two brought-on bedsteads, pretty ones, she said, to swop for my two wild-cherry ones.

And nigh all my quilts too. That huzzy said she would take all the pretty ones. Said some of them were mighty dirty but she could have them cleaned. My "Harp of Columbia." Of course, Miss Robinson's hawk eyes got set on it the very first thing. The one I was piecing on when Charles come.

I was setting in here in the big house piecing on it when I heard the soldiers walk up into the yard—setting here in the old hickory rocking chair with Ma's red-and-tan checked homespun shawl around my shoulders. I kept it in my hand when I started to get the water for them. I held it all the time while Charles went to the spring. He looked at the quilt when he come back.

"What's that you are making there?" he asked. He took hold of it and fingered it like it was a piece of gold. "I never could handle them little squares and three-cornered pieces with my big fingers," he said. And his hands were big. But I knowed right then I wasn't afeared of Charles.

I could tell from the way he kept looking at me he thought I was pretty too. He didn't tell me till all the other soldiers went over in the horse lot to catch up Old Kate. He didn't come right out plain and tell me then. "I'll bet your name is Edith—or Mary one."

"Huh uh—Mary's just part of it."

"Mine is Charles—Charles Williams. What is the rest of yours?"

"Hit's Dorthula—Mary Dorthula White."

"It's pretty too." In that deep voice. He kept feeling of the quilt. And looking at me. "Does that little red blanket on your shoulders keep you warm?"

That "Harp of Columbia" quilt was the one I always held in my lap and worked on when anybody come to see me during the while Joe was growing inside me. I told Joe about using it to hide him. Joe thought a heap of that quilt. I think it was the prettiest one I ever made. With Joe's stitches on it. My stitches—short and straight. And Joe's over there in the corner —long and crooked. Miss Robinson didn't take notice of them, I reckon. But somebody took Joe's stitches out, I know, before they hung it up for folks to look at. Nobody else would care.

But I would rather had the hair pulled out of my head than had Joe's stitches pulled out of that quilt. The way he looked up at me with them eyes he had—Charles's eyes—and begged me to let him quilt. I couldn't help but let him do it. "And you won't pull mine out, will you, Ma?" I promised him his stitches never would be pulled out.

That night, after Miss Robinson and William Wayne left, while Ad and Linus were both out of the room, I set there on the bed and run my fingers over Joe's stitches. I reckon they wouldn't be counted pretty stitches by anybody else. I felt like getting inside the feather tick and being took off too. I couldn't sleep that night. I laid awake and squeezed that quilt in my hand.

It was lucky for me the next day. Ruby Arwood was called to straw and I had to be over there with Ruby all day. When I come in that night it seemed more different from home than ever. Nearly all my things gone—spinning wheel, warping bars and everything. Even my big bone knitting needles, and my tatting shuttle that I made myself. I didn't give up then and I am not going to give up now. Dona Fawver will be dying pretty soon and Dona couldn't stand for anybody to lay her out save me. I ought to go see her today.

I couldn't help but see the bedsteads the first thing when I come into the room that evening. There was that big old brass bed, all scarred up, setting over there in the corner, and that little old rickety bent up green one in front of the window. Both of them had the rods so scarred up they looked like they had been through the war. No telling who had used them. No telling what kind of old dirty folks had been sleeping in them. But Linus was setting in there bragging about them being so pretty. New stuff, he said, brought-on stuff. One of them was worth a dozen home-made things, he said.

I didn't look at them any more than I had to. I went on and got supper. When I turned the beds down I seed they had some big old dirty-looking gray blankets on them. I felt of them. They weren't even wool—just plain cotton. They were somebody else's old things too. I would rather sleep on the floor than to sleep on them old pads with cotton all wadded up in them. Ad and Linus said they were what all folks used that weren't old fogies. But I ought to be hunting the guineas' nestes. And I promised Mollie McGregor my receipt for corn relish.

It didn't seem right with them bedsteads in the room. And my little green and gold mug gone. It was my ma's mug. I used to think it so pretty. The time I had the measles Ma let me drink water out of it. I got thirsty every few minutes till Ma caught on and took to bringing it in the dipper.

I used to get it down and rub my hands over it. That was after Charles drunk out of it. I fixed Charles some peach brandy in it. And some wild-cherry wine one night. Charles liked that wine. I had it hid out in the yard under that rock. I dug a hole there and had it in it. The Rebels never did one time think about looking there. Charles got spoiled to it, and he wanted wild-cherry wine every time he would come back. "In that green pitcher with gold houses on it," he would say. "In that pitcher lined with gold."

I let him have wine too. It seemed like it made his brown eyes sparkle more. Charles had dark eyes, and hair all combed back slick as ice. He was tall—big and tall. That was what made me take to him. I felt stronger when I was close to him. I took note of it that first day. When he handed me the dipper his hand touched mine and it made me feel strong. His hands were big, but they weren't rough. They didn't have any big old knotty veins showing under the skin. They had nigh the strength of Letitia Edes's. Sometimes I thought Charles would mash me, the way he held me.

I was fixing to scour that second time when Miss Robinson come hunting for what she called antiques. I had sandrock beat up and scattered all over the floor and I had the water nigh hot enough to commence. What little furniture I had left

was out in the yard. Miss Robinson's eye took to the trundle
bed. She said she would give Linus a dollar for it. Said she
guessed she could pay a dollar even if it was mighty old and
wore-looking. It made me hurt inside when I seed Miss Robinson hand Linus the money. My eyes and nose stung like they
had pepper in them. Seemed like my heart was trying to swell
up and bust.

It was the bed Grandma had slept on when she was little.
Then Ma, and then me, on up till I was fifteen year old. Joe
slept on it all his life up till I married Ad. Them little horses'
heads cut out on the head and foot. I couldn't bear to watch
them tote it out to the wagon.

That little old bed seemed like it was just as much a part
of me as my own right hand. Ma used to pull it out from
under her own bed and tuck me in. "Good night, Mary Dorthula. Good night. Sleep tight. All right." I would lay there
and look out the window. Lay there and watch the witches
make tea. Lay there good and warm and think about princes
that would come riding by someday.

It was the trundle bed that me and the soldier boy piled
down on—Joe's pa. I loved Charles, and I don't care what
other folkses have said about me because I had Joe before I
married Ad. I wonder if the Yankees killed him. He said he
would come back as soon as the war was over. One of my
own brothers might have killed him, there's not any telling.
I wonder how Charles would look with his eyes shut and all
the color gone out of his face. And not able to talk. I don't
want to see him that way. I wonder how he would think I
looked that way. He talked about the color in my cheeks.

Charles wasn't like the other Rebels. I don't hold any
grudgment against him for what he did. It wasn't anybody's
fault but mine. There is not any fault to it—I love Charles.
He made the rest of the Rebels not take Old Kate, the only horse
left here on the place. And he made them shut up their mouths
when they went to talking blackgyuardish in front of me and

trying to jest me. Charles was gentle. His voice was deep as a well, and everything he said come from down in him. It didn't sound so hollow like it come out of the roof of his mouth.

Somehow or nother I didn't feel afeared of the Rebels with Charles in the bunch. Even if I was here by myself. It was the day that Belle Wisecarver lay a corpse and Aunt Cindy— Aunt Cindy was staying with me while both my brothers were away fighting the Rebels—she went over to Wisecarvers' that evening and said she would be needed that night. She said if any soldiers should happen to come by, for me to let them have everwhat they wanted.

It was along about sundown when the soldiers come. I was setting all scrooched up in that hickory rocking chair with Ma's red-and-tan checked homespun shawl throwed around my shoulders. Sewing on my "Harp of Columbia" quilt. I had got to the curve of the harp and I couldn't make the curve without puckering the thing to save my life. Them three-cornered pieces wouldn't fit together. I had just said to myself that I was going to put it up and go after the cow.

Just as I started to fold it up I heard a big commotion out in the front yard. It sounded like a bunch of cattle coming up. "Hales' blamed old cattle out again," I said to myself and raised up to look out. Instead of it being cattle, it was men— soldier men. They were already on the porch.

Seeing them made me feel like I was being stuck all over with pins. I stood there by the side of the chair and looked like a scared deer, I guess. I didn't even offer to move. They come right on in the door. And the man with the red mustache, he said, "We want some fresh water." I held the quilt in my hands and went out on the back porch after the bucket. "I'll go to the spring and get fresh water," I turned around and said. That was when I first took note of Charles.

"I'll go. Give me the bucket." He took the bucket out of my hand. "Where is it?"

"Hit's right over there under that oak tree."

"Here, you hold the dipper."

The other Rebels searched around in the house while Charles went to the spring. They wanted to take them two hams out of the smokehouse. Charles got back in time to stop them from that. "Just leave them where they are," he said in that voice. All the other soldiers must have been afeared of Charles. They all minded what he said for them to do. Then the soldier men went over there and looked at Old Kate. Held open her mouth, looked at her feet, and everything. Some of them thought they ought to take her; some thought she wasn't worth taking.

Charles stood and talked to me during the while. He run his hand through my hair and said it was the softest hair he ever seed. I've always took good care of my hair ever since then. Charles seemed to forget all the other men, and he stayed there on the back porch with me. He kept on looking at my hair. I ought to get it combed now. "Little Red Ridinghood wore a shawl like that," Charles said. That shawl come in handy to wrap Joe up in too.

Directly the other Rebels come out of the barn lot and one of them was setting up on Old Kate. They had the bridle and everything. Well, Charles went out there and pulled that man off. He opened the gate and turned Old Kate back into the lot. Hung the bridle up there on the post just like he was at home. That was another thing I liked about Charles. He did every-thing easy—just like a red bird. It wasn't any trouble for him to move around from one place to another. I didn't know anybody could ever be that big without being gawlky.

Charles went on away with the rest of the soldiers. I stood on the edge of the porch and watched him out of sight. I could tell from the way he kept looking around that he would come back to see me. He had asked me out there on the back porch who I lived with. "Aunt Cindy," I told him. "Aunt Cindy stays here with me while the boys are away fighting the Rebels. But she has gone over to Wisecarvers' because Belle is dead."

"Is she coming back tonight?"

"She'll be needed to set up with the corpse."

"Are you afraid?"

"I'm not afraid of you." I don't know what made me give
him an answer like that. I reckon it was just because I wanted to.

It was a little after dark when Charles come back that night
and there were a few stars shining in the sky. I went to bed
just as it got good dark. Before I fixed the bed I went out on
the porch and looked up the Lead Hill to see if I could see
Charles coming. I listened but I couldn't hear a sign of
anything. So I pulled out the trundle bed and crawled in. I
was still sleeping in the trundle bed then.

I was a-laying there. The stars were coming out pretty thick
by now. The bull frogs were just beginning to holler so I
knowed it was as dark as it would be. I laid there waiting.
I just had a feeling. Directly it come. "Mary Dorthula," and
then, "Hello."

"Come on in, Charles." I knowed in reason it was Charles.

"I slipped off. The others were asleep." When he talked in
the dark his voice sounded like a hen clucking to her little
chickens.

Charles kept on coming back. Aunt Cindy didn't say anything against it. For nine straight nights he come back. The
Rebels stayed around here in the mountains that long, hunting
for folkses that were hiding out to keep from joining either one
of the sides. Folkses like the ones that dodged and went over
into old Kentuck.

That was one reason I never have told anybody who Joe's
pa was. Charles being a Rebel and both of my brothers Yankees. Folks around would have hated Joe sure enough. Joe
wasn't like other bastards. But I reckon it was a good thing
he died or got killed when he did.

I never was ashamed of having Joe before I got married.
He favored his pa. At least he had his eyes and pert nigh his
voice—and his protecting ways. Always trying to save me

from something. Like the mammy hen saying, "Hide in the weeds. I'll fight the hawk."

Charles would have come back and married me if it had been so he could. That last night, he told me he would come the next night if they didn't march on. Said if they did march on he would come back soon as the war was over, or as soon as it was so he could come. I kept looking for him and kept high hopes for seven whole years. But he ain't come yet.

That is the reason I can't help but believe he was killed by the Yankees. He loved me. And he would have come back if something hadn't happened to him. He said he would, said I was the sweetest girl he ever seed. Told me that the night it was getting a little coolish and I had a fire. The fire shined against his face and I could see it in the dark. He said he liked my yellow curly hair and blue eyes.

But I liked Charles's brown hair and eyes and his dark skin better. His skin was dark as a piece of fresh sod. I liked to run my hands over it. It was natural dark. It wasn't made that way by the sun. Charles wouldn't have said he was coming back if he hadn't been aiming on doing it. He didn't talk with just his tongue.

Charles said he liked that trundle bed. "It lays so good." Every night he would sleep with me till nigh daylight. Then I would wake him up and he would go back. "I'll be back." He told me that every night. He told me that the ninth night he was here too. And I laid awake all night the next night waiting for him to holler, "Mary Dorthula, hello." I liked to hear him holler that. Like an old hen calling to her little chickens, "Come on here now, so the hawk won't get you."

I never did get to go anywhere with Charles, to any poke suppers or anything like that. We had to be sneaking as 'possums for fear the other Rebels would catch on. Maybe they did. Maybe that is the reason he never did come back.

But the third night he come he set out there on the edge of my bed and told me stories, ones he had read, he said. The

one about Bob and Julia. Robert loved Julia. "Just like I
love you." And I couldn't help but cry when Robert got
killed and didn't get to marry Julia. But I didn't want Charles
to see me cry.

That was the night I had a fire. It was the first real cold
night we had had that fall and I built a fire late that evening.
When dark come I pulled the trundle bed out in front of the
fireplace and laid down on it. It was a dark night and cold
too. I didn't know whether he would come or not that night.
Directly, the frogs begun to holler. I looked out the window
and I couldn't see but two stars anywhere. Just two stars in
the sky, it was so dark and cold.

"Mary Dorthula. Hello."

"Come on in, Charles."

"It's warm in here."

"I'm proud you come."

"I like the firelight. I can see your eyes."

"Set down, Charles."

"This trundle bed. It is soft."

Charles set down on the edge of the bed with his face
toward me and his knees upon the bed. And told me them
stories. I listened—"And Rob loved Julia just like—well, he
liked curly hair." And he said speeches to me. Poems, he called
them." I watched his face in the firelight. His mouth said,
"Whom there was none to praise and very few to love."
And his eyes looked at me and I knowed what he meant. But
he just didn't come out plain and say it. I liked it that way.

Charles tried to sing some too. But he couldn't sing as well
as he talked. I don't believe he knowed much to sing.

> "The Yankee run,
>   The Yankee flew,
> The Yankee tore
>   His shirttail in two."

Charles wouldn't have ever run from anybody or anything.

The next night was cold too. It was dark as pitch again.

I didn't lay down. I set by the fire and played the accordion
and sung. I didn't hear him come through the cow-field gate
that night. There he stood in the doorway before I knowed it.
I was just singng away:

    "Then to the wars, to the wars he did go
    To see whether he could forget his love or no.
    For seven long years he served unto his king
    And in seven more years was returning home again."

Of course, I had been singing that over and over ever since
it got good dark. I wanted to be sure and be singing it when
he come. Well, Charles, he stood there in the door. He looked
like he didn't know whether to run out the door or jump up
into the air. We looked at one another.

    "Mary Dorthula."

    "I didn't mean to be singing that."

    "Sing it again."

Charles set there on the trundle bed by the side of me and
made me sing it over and over till he learned it. "Just one more
time, and then I'll know it." And he didn't tell me till the
last night that he had been standing out there at the door ever
since good dark listening to me sing that over and over.

That was the time he made me talk all night. "As soon as
you tell me one more story I'll go to sleep." But I knowed he
wouldn't. I didn't want him to. Just some little old hant tales
was all I knowed. I told them till away up into the night,
after the fire had died down and it was so dark you couldn't
see across the room.

Charles would hold his breath sometimes. He liked the
tale about the woman making fire at midnight in that old
house. And the one about the man going to give his daughter
to the boy who could find water on his place. "I'm not sleepy."
I could tell he liked for me to talk. He set a heap a store by me.
And I set a heap a store by him, and by the trundle bed on
account of him. It was cold when the fire died out. "I'll have
to get another quilt," I said.

"Where was the one you were making on?"

"I'll soon have it pieced." But it wasn't soon. And now.

What is wrong with my eyes? No. The sun has just gone down behind Letitia Edes Mountain. It was about this time of evening when the soldiers come marching up. Time to go milk. "We want a drink of water. . . . Little Red Ridinghood . . . The squares are so little."

Of course Ad and Linus didn't think about things like that when Miss Robinson come along. The trundle bed was just a trundle bed to them. Ad knowed Joe had slept on it up till he was a great big hulk of a boy. But that didn't bother Ad any more than a flea bite.

It made me feel numb all over when I seed what Linus was doing. I went back in the kitchen and hid my face in my coattail till Ad and Linus come back from carrying it out to the wagon. I could tell them the place never would be the same without it. That trundle bed had been a part of every speck of bliss I had ever had.

All the time Ad and Linus were selling off my old stuff they were cutting logs so they could build that fine new house. A fine new house—that was all they could talk about. I heard it till the words jumped up and down in the middle of my head and fit with one another. Ad and Linus talked about it more than Barshia had back when he had it on his mind. I never did believe they would get it built till I seed them put the top on it. They fooled me one time. They finally got all the logs sawed and hauled. They took them up to Jim Heath's sawmill and swopped them for planks—thin planks made out of pine. Not good oak like the logs they cut and took up there.

I stood it all right while they were building on the house. I just didn't watch them much. They set it up right in front of my log house. Right in front of it. It covered all the pretty level part of the yard. But the house was plumb out on the edge of the bank. That made it look like a chicken coop on top of a mole hill.

I tried to keep my mind off it as much as I could while they were building it. It didn't take them any time to put it up —just two days. Little old light thing. It will just about topple over if ever the wind comes up the hollow. I won't much care. What is that I hear? Sounds like the wind blowing. I wish it would and blow it over. Cattle? Hales' cattle? Them soldier boys. That is it. "I'll go . . . here, you hold the dipper." Like a hen saying, "Let me kill the bee before you swallow it."

Both days that they worked on the house a big crowd of menfolks come to help. And a big crowd of womenfolks come in to help me with the cooking. I was proud to see them come. I listened to them talk instead of watching the menfolks work on the house. I like to hear womenfolks talk. After hearing Charles talk all other menfolks sound harsh and hateful.

The womenfolks talked about everything them two days. They were honest. They didn't wish harm to anybody. Seems like I can hear them now:

Granny, they say Penelope Courtney is going to need you again soon—you'll have to start a new life with the new house —the men are working like ticks in a tar bucket—"I'll be back." Granny, what happened to the little green and gold pitcher you had?—Have you heard about Arwoods' cow a-dying?—Sue Ella says her hens are not laying to do any good, must be bewitched—"I slipped off."—Have you heard that new song about the flying man's baby that got killed?—Do you like your new bedsteads better than your old ones?—Did you know that Brocks and Whetsels are at outs again?—What do you pack your clean clothes away in now?—"They were all asleep."—I've been sending milk and butter over to the Arwoods—Like a hen saying, "Come on out of the weeds now, the hawk's done gone."—How much did you get for your ma's three-cornered cupboard?—Wonder who will give Arwoods a calf to bring up in place of the cow that died?—Are you getting so new-fangled you aren't going to spin any more? —I seed the Smoky Mountain folks pass with your ash hopper

—Hit's a pity Joe is not here—Wonder what ever become of Wilbur?—What ever become of that butter dish Joe used to cry for the knobs off of?—"Ma, break me off them marbles, will you?"—"This trundle bed, it lays so good."

I listened to them all day. They meant well. But, of course, they didn't know everything. I would hate not to ever see any of them again. Ruby Arwood will be having a baby soon and then Penelope. Dona Fawver will be dying soon too. And I will have to lay Dona out. And Teelie Edes—I want to see if she has got any witch marks on her. No telling how long I will have to stay in this world. I will have to go on doctoring till I learn somebody else how to take my place. But it is time to put on supper now, and I meant to pick a mess of sallet. I wish I had some gumption in me. This old new-fangled chair —not like the hickory rocker I was setting in. "I'm not sleepy."

Then the menfolks tore my house down. They got me moved into the new house and Ad and Linus norrated it around they were going to tear the old one down. A big bunch of men come in one day and they set to work on it. The womenfolks come back again too. I don't believe I could have tholed it if they hadn't. They seemed like they understood more that day. They didn't make any name of my old things being gone. They sung funny songs and told tales and laughed all the time both of the days they were here. Them asking me riddles and things sort of kept my mind off the house being tore down. Imah Baines sung one of the songs I learned Charles—the one that Charles said he liked next best:

> "Come, rede us fathers, come rede us mothers,
> The Yankee tore his shirttail in two."

"Just sing it one more time. I'll know it then."

Grandma had been born in that house. Pa was born there. Ma was carried over the door sill and swept the walls down with a sage-grass broom. Charles said when he come back he wanted to live up here at the end of the hollow in that house forever.

"And slop the hogs and things. . . . Just put that ham back. . . . Raise hogs and boys."

Them things didn't matter to Ad and Linus. They tore it down a log at a time. They had a job of it too. The logs were big. I managed to stay as busy as I could. And I kept cotton in my ears part of the time to keep from hearing them tear the logs apart. I couldn't help but hear when they pushed over the stick chimney. I used to hold Joe's hand and we would stand and watch the smoke come twirling out of it. Joe would stand as still as a froze snake and watch it. "We help make the sky, don't we, Ma?"

Ad and the men had a big time when they found some notes that Tiny Brock had wrote to Joe at school. Joe had stuck them in a chink there in the wall. Linus read them out loud to all them old men. "Hello, Dern Sweetheart," they all started off. There wasn't e'er a time he didn't put in the word "dern." That meant Tiny was his secret sweetheart. He didn't want Miss Omie to know it, and he didn't want anybody else to know it. But their sparking wasn't dern at all, of course. It is hard to keep a fire smothered—the blaze will always show. Charles never did call me his dern sweetheart. But I was. He had to keep it a secret or the other Rebels wouldn't have let him come. And he never did write to me. Never had any chance to. But the way he said my name, "Mary Dorthula. Hello." And the way he looked at me and didn't say anything. Words don't mean much anyhow. You're safe as long as you stay under my wing.

The men all laughed at Joe's little notes when they heard them. They pitched them out on the ground and piled logs on top of them. They found a little speech too. One Joe had hid in there. His teacher cut it out of something and give it to him to learn and say. He used to say it over to me. "The spider wove his silvery web until his work was done." Hit was pretty. And Joe's voice sounded almost like Charles's did when he said speeches. I'll fight the hawk, Mary Dorthula.

Joe had hid that speech in the chink and it had slipped back furder than he aimed for it to. They pitched it out on the ground. They pitched everything on the ground. Joe loved the old house. I told him one day what Charles said about the house that first day when he seed it. "It is just made to fit into the shape of this hollow. No other house would look right here. It will be here when I come back. . . . It will always be here. . . . I'll be back."

"I'm proud you come."

This old new-fangled chair. Cheap. It is enough to break a body's neck. It is getting dusk outside. Time to have milking done. It will soon be dark. Time for Charles and Joe to come in from loafing at the store.

The last evening the men worked on the house, all the womenfolks went home and left me here by myself. Ad hollered for me to fetch some water. I took that old tin bucket. Water don't taste good out of it like it did out of my staved bucket— the one they sold.

I took the tin bucket and went. As I started down the steps I seed they had the house about tore down—just hadn't moved the sills yet. I sort of hoped they would let the sills stay there. I had heard Grandpa talk about them sills. The best that could be made, he said. It took six men to lift one of them. They had stayed solid even if Ad hadn't patched the roof, and the rain had come right on through. I feared Grandpa would rise up out of his grave when them sills were moved. Charles said there wasn't any such material as that nowadays. "They'll be here always. I'll be here always. Hogs and boys." I'll bet the old sow is hungry. It is dark outside. It gets dark soon in the fall of the year this way. I like long nights. I wouldn't want to be in a place where there never come any night.

I tried not to look at the pile of logs. When I got over to the spring something made me look back. I seed that big pile of logs there to be burnt. Somehow or nother, thinking about it took nigh all the strength I had in me. I set down there on the bank of the branch.

I set down without thinking. I don't know how long I set there. Then I heard Ad yelling, "What in the hell are you doing? You'd be a good one to send after water if the devil's guts were on fire." "Here, you hold the dipper." I was numb all over. I had to try two or three times before I could even drag myself up. I finally managed to pick the bucket up and start.

Listen. Yeah, that is him. The cow-field gate. Opening. Shut. Ad and Linus. It is time. Loafing at the store all day. And his shirt not patched. "Mary Dorthula. Hello." "I'm proud you come." "Little Red Ridinghood."

When I got to the house with the water I seed Ad and Linus take hold of the last sill. They couldn't budge it. Nigh all the men had to help. I was holding the bucket for Old Man Arwood to get him a drink. That strength in Charles's hands. And when I seed them lift that sill up and lay it over out of the way, something went wrong with me. I don't know what it was. But I went weak all over. And that bucket fell out of my hand. "You hold the dipper. I'll take the bucket." It hit the ground kerwhollop. I sort of went blank there for a short span.

I hear something on the porch. Them back. And supper not ready. I am a little chilly. The fire. I guess I had better punch it. My neck—it is so limber. This chair. "Just one more time and then I'll know it."

But I come back to myself before anybody took note of it, I think. Old Man Arwood said he would take the bucket back to the spring. "I'll go. Where is it?"

"Right over there under that tree."

"Here, you hold the dipper."

I reckon the men just thought I was awkward and dropped the bucket. I believe Ad sort of noticed me. I don't know though.

There are two stars. Just two in the sky. It is dark tonight. And cold. And I didn't get his overalls patched. Them frogs. They know it is time. I will punch up the fire. I'm tired of this chair anyhow—lets my head fall over like I've got the limber neck.

"Mary Dorthula. Hello."

"Come on in. . . . I'll soon have it done."

"I slipped off . . . that little red blanket . . . the others were sleeping."

"I'm proud you come . . . I didn't mean to be singing."

"Again . . . But if I touch you—"

"This trundle bed, Charles, it lays so good."

CHAPTER 13

PA WENT A-COURTING

Ad Kanipe (born January 1, 1847)

M Y WRITING looks as different from Ma's as a cow's path does from a guinea's path. But of course it was my place to put her name down here. And it was the only thing she ever asked me to do. "Amy," she said to me one day, "if anything should ever happen to me, I want you to take care of the Family Bible and keep the record up." So I scribbled her name here. Mary Dorthula Kanipe, October 15, 1939. And now I've got to write Pa's name in. I'll put it right under Ma's. Ad Kanipe, October 1, 1940. He might not care to have it in the Family Record. But Ma would want it there and still want me to keep the Bible from the antiquers. I have been careful with it. Even from Pa, I kept it hid. But he might have set something a store by it too. At the last, he might. There's no telling.

I always thought Pa was a good man at heart. All he needed was somebody to make it come out. And I guess Ma just about did that at last. I don't see why she didn't do it before she left here. Then all them men wouldn't have been laying for him. But it seemed like she never did addle her brain much over the things he did. She always tried to shield him. Of course, she shielded him this time too. But she scared him first. That was what did him good.

Folks said even at Ma's funeral Pa was glancing around at other women. Barty Franklin just swears he seed him grin at that old Tempton girl. I don't know about that. But I do know he begun trying to court again before the dirt was settled on Ma's grave. He tried to go with Rhotanna Courtney. But Rhotanna give him to understand right now that she didn't want anything to do with an old broke-down ground hog that had one foot in the grave. Looks like that would have set him to thinking. But it didn't.

Then Pa went to hanging around Zach McClann's. All them girls had been no-account. And he started going with the one called Trulie. She was that big old fat sloppy one. Pa went plumb hog wild. As old as he was. He took her to meeting and poke suppers and everything that come along. Everybody knowed all the time what was going on. And some folks allowed Zach would put a stop to it.

Finally Trulie found out she wasn't getting much money out of Pa and she started carrying on with Roy Goolen. Pa went all to pieces. He run around here like a fitified pup. And it seemed to me like his lips got thinner every day. He wouldn't open his mouth to answer anybody when they spoke to him. And you know how thin his lips always were? Well, they got so you couldn't tell he had any mouth. It just looked like a split place across his face. He would squint up his eyes and cock his head over sideways even more than general. He got just plumb quare-looking.

I dreaded to have to look at him. But, you see, after Ma died him and Linus moved over here to Sugar Creek. They didn't much want to come to Hamblen County, but they didn't have anybody to cook for them and they moved in with me and Enzor. Enzor wanted them too. He said he was going to try to get a little work out of some of the Kanipes. I knowed all the time it would give Enzor more room to fuss at me about things if they come. But, of course, we had enough room for them. We didn't have anything at all up in the loft, and we never did use that little back room for anything save plunder. It is just a little old lean-to that Enzor's pa had built on to the log part a short while after me and Enzor got married. And it wouldn't have been right not to ask them to come.

But for a whole week Pa acted quare that away. I couldn't get him to eat anything hardly. And every time I said anything he would either snap me off right short, or just not answer at all. I sort of got tired .of it. But Enzor he didn't pay it much heed. He just kept throwing it up to me that none of my folks were any account.

Pa kept on acting that way till one day he went somewheres. And when he come in that night one whole side of his face was skinned up like a willow tree. And his right eye was big enough for two eyes. He looked like he was ashamed for me to see him. And he wouldn't say ne'er a word about what had took place.

But Enzor heard it on him the next day. It was all over the country, of course, about how he had picked a racket with Roy Goolen and how Roy had jumped on him and just about beat him to death. Roy still wasn't through with him either. He allowed as how he was going to send him to his resting place someday.

For several days after that Pa shied around from folks like a shot deer. Then he got so he just held his head up and went on as if nothing had took place. Folks teased him about it but he got so he could turn the jokes off pretty well. He talked to me real solemn about it one evening when I was cooking supper. Before he started out that day, something told him not to go. Hit seemed like he could hear a voice telling him something was going to happen to him.

But after he seed there wasn't any use of trying Trulie McClann any longer he took up with Lula Mai Johnkin. He sold off some lumber on Ma's place and spent money in a big fashion after that. He bought him a suit of clothes and strutted around bragging about getting younger and younger every day he lived. He even tried to borrow some money from Enzor. And, of course, that give Enzor a chance to fuss at me some more.

And Pa told it, or it got around somehow, all over the country that him and Lula Mai were going to get married. I believe he thought they were too, because he kept talking about moving back into his new house with a new old woman —one that was young enough this time to outlast him. He said the last one was wore out before he married her. He would get as mad as a hornet every time anybody named Lula Mai. He wouldn't be jested about her at all. She was a nice girl, he told everybody, just as nice as anybody that talked about her.

But finally one day he dyked out in his suit of clothes and everything and he left home. He hollered back at me and said he would be an old married man when he got back. I didn't give him any answer because I didn't know whether he was jesting or not. But I guess he thought he was a-going to get her.

That night, a little before sundown, Pa come a-creeping up the hollow. I was milking, and I seed him coming. Hit skeered me half to death because I never had seed him look so old and humped before. He was bent away over and moseying along like an old stud horse with sore hoofs. He went on into the house. I didn't finish milking. I just milked out enough for supper and got on to the house as soon as I could.

I didn't see him anywhere when I got here so I went on in the back room where his bed was. And he was stretched out across it with his face buried down in the feather tick. "Are you sick, Pa?" I asked him. "Hell no," was all the answer he made me. He didn't come to the table for supper and I went in there and ast him if he wanted me to bring it to him. He said he didn't want any because he hadn't felt hungry all day. He didn't come to the breakfast table the next morning either.

Linus and Enzor went to the mill up at Slop Creek that morning and they heard all about what had caused Pa to act that way. Lula Mai had married a Susong boy Sunday morning. And Pa went all the way up there to see her Sunday evening. The Old Man Johnkin met him at the door and told him to come in. He went in and set there for a right smart span of time. Then finally, the Old Man told around, Pa upped and asked where Lula Mai was. And the Old Man said, "She got married to Bill Susong this morning. They got Square Anderson to marry them." The Old Man told him Bill and Lula Mai had gone over in Hancock County to live with Bill's folks. But Pa, he wouldn't believe it till he went and asked Square Anderson.

Pa just about wasted away after that. There was a month that he didn't eat scarcely anything. And he fell off till he looked like a birch sapling with britches on. I was plumb uneasy about him. A lot of folks talked it around that he was nigh dead with consumption.

Then he told me one day, real sheepish-like, that on his way over to Johnkins that Sunday evening he kept thinking he heard that voice in his ears. But he didn't pay much attention to it at the time.

He got over that spell too and finally got so he could almost stand to be teased about Lula Mai. But he threatened around that some of these days he aimed to have it out with Bill Susong.

Then he took up with Tiny Samples. She was a shy-pokey-looking little old gal without good sense. She was just fifteen year old and lived over there close to the Hog Pen church house. Pa always went to protracted meetings. Me and Enzor went over there to Hog Pen some and I recollect naming it to Enzor one day how Tiny was a-feisting around every man and boy she seed. I told him she would get out with the first boy that paid her any mind.

Then that last meeting started. Me and Enzor didn't go more than once a week, because Enzor was afraid the preacher man would speak to me. But Pa, he went every night and even took to going in daytime. I noticed how big a splut he was always in to get ready every night. But I didn't think about who he was in such a hurry to see.

One day, during the time the meeting was going on, Eva Day stopped in here from on her way to the store and she asked me what I thought about my future step-mammy. I didn't know what she meant. She told me Pa had started courting Tiny Samples. I didn't believe it. I thought he would think more of himself than that. So I didn't say anything to Enzor about it.

That night I told Enzor I was going to meeting. Of course, he wouldn't let me go unless he went too. At the supper table I told Pa we were going with him. And he didn't say a word. As soon as supper was over he jumped up and lit out like a dog after a fox. Enzor told him to wait and we would go with him. But he didn't even let on like he heard.

Me and Enzor were late. And we had to set on the back seat. My eyes nearly popped out of my head when I seed it. I still tried not to believe it, but right there in front of us set Pa and Tiny Samples all wropped up around one another as much as they could be without just being on top of one another. They set there that way all during the singing when everybody else was standing up. He had his right leg kind of wropped around her left leg and he had his arm around her.

Then the preacher man prayed and instead of closing my eyes and bowing my head, I watched Pa and Tiny. They just felt all over one another. Nobody on that seat or on the one I was setting on heard e'er a word the preacher prayed. We all just sat there and stared at Pa and Tiny. I didn't look anybody in the face for I was too ashamed. I reckon Pa thought everybody was supposed to have his eyes shut and his head down. Him and Tiny were just a show for everybody that could see them, and I seed folks from up in front looking back toward them during the while the preacher man was preaching.

Enzor got mad at Pa and said it was just in all the Kanipes

to carry on that way—even in the women, he said. He give
Pa a good cussing out that night when he got in. But it didn't
do one speck of good. He just kept right on. Everybody in the
whole country got to talking about it. It's a wonder they
didn't cowhide Pa. But the menfolks mostly just laughed about
it and the womenfolks all whispered in one another's ears and
said an old dog like that ought to be cut.

He went on the same way for nigh two month and I was
scared out of my senses nearly all the time, afeared something
was going to happen. I just kept having an uneasy feeling every
time I even thought about it.

But it all ended, finally. Pa got so he went to see Tiny
every Sunday. He stayed all day and got in about midnight
Sunday night. He had left that morning just like he always
did, except he stood out there in the yard for a few minutes
before he left. He kept his head down and appeared to be
gazing at the ground. Then he told Enzor that he thought he
eat too much supper the night before, because sometime before
cockcrow he thought he heard somebody a-hollering to him.
And then he thought he could feel hands on his shoulder and it
seemed like they were pressing against him.

Enzor told him he had better take warning, for if he didn't
he was going to keep on till he had to take Tiny. He took
umbrage at what Enzor said. He stiffened up again and allowed
he couldn't do better than to get her. I just kept my mouth
out of it and didn't say anything one way or tother.

We didn't look for Pa in that night till after midnight, just
like always, you know. But along sometime after bedtime—
a right smart span before midnight too—the dogs jumped out
and I never heard such barking in all my life. Me and Enzor
both went a-running to the door.

The moon was shining just a little and I seed somebody
coming just a-picking up his heels like he was running from
hell-fire. Enzor hollered at the dogs but they didn't pay him
any heed. They went running right on up to the man. But when

they got right up to him they stopped, so I knowed it was Pa. Well, he never did slow up one bit. It just took him about two leaps to get through the yard onto the porch. I could hear him breathing by the time he got to the edge of the yard. Sounded like a dying bull. I was still standing in the door, and if I hadn't dodged out of the way he would have runned right smack-dab over me. But I jumped back in time.

He went through the big house and into the back room. He shut the door and I heard him latch it. It has got one of these-here stable latches on it, but I reckon that was the first time that door was ever latched. I could still hear him breathing. I tried to get in the room but of course I couldn't. Then I heard him pull the window down and heard him hammering in there so I knowed he was trying to nail the window. I didn't sleep any scarcely the whole night because I feared he would smother, being so out of breath and then shutting everything up airtight.

The next morning he hollered and told me to bring his breakfast to him. So I did. He was as wild-looking as a rabbit and still shaking all over like a cold dog. He told me if anybody come a-hunting for him for me to tell them he wasn't here. He wanted me to tell them he went away Sunday morning and hadn't got back yet. I heard him fasten the door behind me when I went out.

He stayed there all day without getting out. I took his dinner and supper both to him. That night, after it was good and dark, he got up and went out in the yard for a little while. Then he went right back into the back room and fastened himself up again. He done that way for three days. I didn't know what to make of it.

But finally, one day, he got a letter. It come down to Fawvers' and they brung it up here. I took it in the room there to him, and I come on back out. He stayed around the house pretty close the next two or three days. Then he got so he went around over the place with Enzor just like he always had done. But one day Enzor was over there at the barn and he found that letter where Pa had lost it out of his pocket. Of course, it did Enzor good to find something he could fuss at me about. He picked the letter up and brung it to the house. He laid it up on the black bureau so I just picked it up and read it. Hit said:

> Hello, Dern Sweetheart,
> They hain't done nothing to me at all. They hain't done nothing save cuss you. And they aim to kill you someday. But noways shortly. They know some other folks that will want to have a hand in it. I hate Pa caught us. But he just said there wasn't anything else he could do save to make us marry. And he didn't want me to do that, and I don't either. And Ma said that wasn't her we seed come out there before Pa did. You know, I told you I thought that didn't look like her. So Pa didn't come out there, because Ma had told him we were talking low. There is something quare about it. Pa said something just told him to walk around the chimney corner at that time. They hain't even whupped me.
>
> TINY

I thought it was plumb funny, her calling him "dern sweetheart" when everybody in the country knowed how they were carrying on. And I hoped that would be enough to break Pa. I thought for a while it had. He appeared different for the next two or three weeks. Seemed so quiet and everything. Everybody wondered and wondered what could be the matter between him and Tiny. But nothing was ever said about it in any way. I don't reckon Samples ever told anybody and Pa never did, so it didn't get spread about. It soon blowed over, or I thought it did. But it seems like he just had to learn his lesson. Ma had been dead nigh a year now.

There were two old women that lived out there at Russellville. They were regular old whores—as ugly as mud pies. And the men that runned after them called one of them number 1, and the other one number 2. Pa, he took up with old number 2. She had been staying out there with Ike Lame. And I think Ike was about to run out of anything to pay her with. She had an old broke-down car she run around in. So Pa would even brag about being hauled around in a car. Folks said Ike didn't much like it at first when old number 2 took up with Pa. But I think she spent part of her time with Ike and part of it with Pa.

Pa would meet her down at the road every night. That just kept going on and on. Then Pa took a mortgage on the place over there in Cocke County and old number 2, of course, knowed he had that money and she set out to get it. He had kept all Ma's things locked up over there in the house—all the canned fruit and everything. I hadn't needed it and he kept on saying he was likely to get him another old woman and move back over there most any time.

One day, after he had been running around with that old number 2 for about three weeks, he just upped and left here. I didn't know what had become of him till the next day I heard that him and old number 2 had moved into the house over in Cocke County. I thought shore they were married, but folks said they weren't. She was just living over there with him to do his cooking for him. At least, that is what he made out like. He had started buying things on credit at the Silver City store house. And he had all that money he had borrowed too. I didn't do or say anything about it. He come over here after Old Heif. I just asked him if he got enough to eat and he said that he ought to, he had the best cook this side of Creation.

I heard from them every day or two. Everybody that knowed Pa talked something terrible about the way he did. And folks allowed Ike Lame would get him sooner or later too. Things went on that way for about nine days. And it was the ninth night that started Pa thinking.

Hit was a good while after midnight that the dogs went to barking here. They rared out big. I heard Pa speak to them.

I didn't know what to think. Well, he come on in the house and Enzor got up and lit the lamp. Pa was as pale as a slate rock. He looked worse scared this time than he did the time Samples run him in. "Who's after you, Pa?" I asked him. He looked at me like the lightning had struck him. "Granny," he said. "Granny is after me." That's what he always called Ma. He motioned for Enzor to shut the door, and then he set down there in that corner. It was the furderest away from the lamp. I thought he was going to die before he could tell it. But he got it all out.

Him and number 2 had been sleeping together every night. She always got through and got in the bed first. Then he got in. This time she had got in and kept telling him to come on, but somehow or nother he just didn't have any hankering to get in the bed. And once he thought about just telling number 2 he was tired of such doings, and that it was time for her to go back to Russellville. But then he thought he wouldn't.

He said he kept fooling around there till he guessed a quarter of the night had passed away. Then he just blowed out the light all of a sudden and jumped in. He didn't notice anything odd when he first got in. But he reached over for number 2. And he noticed she felt mighty light and soft as she rolled over closer to him. Just about that time he heard number 2 say, "Hain't you going to love me any tonight?" He said he never had such a quare feeling in all his life. But he thought right quick, and he thought maybe he had the quilt in his arm. So he just answered back to number 2, "I thought I had you in my arms."

"You have got me," he heard Ma say right in his ear. He said it was Ma's voice just as clear as a whistle. So he started to jump out of the bed, but Ma just rose right up over him and he couldn't move. So he laid there without saying a word.

Number 2, she begun wanting to know what it was, and she riz up in bed to see. Then she went to screaming, "What is it? Ad, hit's an old woman." Ma never did say a word to number 2. She just talked to *him*. Number 2 grabbed the pillow and throwed it at Ma, but the pillow landed over on the floor and appeared to have gone right through Ma without ever teching her.

Then Pa felt Ma get back over in the bed between them, and felt her pull the quilt up around her shoulders. He riz up in bed too. There was number 2 setting up over on one railing of the bed and him on tother. He was afeared to look at the bed but something kept telling him to go on and look. So his head finally just turned that way.

And there was Granny laying there just as plain as the nose on your face. He thought she was a little palish-greenish looking the best he could make out, not having any light. But she was there and he could see her head and he could hear her breathing just like she always done. He started to climb out of bed again. When he did he felt her pulling him back. "Who is it?" number 2 kept wanting to know. "Hit's Granny," Pa told her. "Just like she was—it's her." Then Ma turned her head over toward number 2. Pa knowed Ma must have looked right straight at her because he was watching number 2. And she just looked like a scared guinea. Then she jumped out of the bed and yelled like one.

Pa, he started to get up and see which away number 2 was going but he felt a hand on him pulling him back. The hand was on his shoulder pulling him, and yet he looked and Granny was still laying right there not moving or anything save just breathing.

Pa said he laid there for what seemed to him like all of Forever. But directly he heard the roosters begin crowing, and he seed Granny get up and back out the door. When she got to the sill she said, "I'll be back, Ad." And she went on out the door as natural as a hen flying to roost.

Pa was about half scared to death when he got here and by the time he got the whole tale told he was scared worse. He was shaking all over like a leaf in the wind. He wanted to know if I would sleep in the back room and let him sleep with Enzor. I told him I would and I went on back there and slept for the rest of the night. Nothing didn't happen.

All the next day Pa looked scared. But he laid around and slept most of the day. Me and Enzor, we got to talking about it. And I told Enzor that I didn't believe Ma had come back here to earth. I didn't believe dead folks could come back. I just allowed Pa's conscience had got to hurting him because he was running with that old woman since Ma died. Enzor said he didn't know. So I just didn't think much more about it.

That night Pa set around like he hated to go to bed, but me and Enzor went on and crawled in and just acted like nothing uncommon had took place. Finally Pa went on to bed in the back room. He tried to make Linus come down out of the loft and sleep with him, but Linus wouldn't do it.

I had got to sleeping sound when I heard Pa holler out like a buzzard had him. I jumped up and went running in there. Pa was jerking the cover up over his head. All of a sudden I looked at the foot of his bed. There stood Ma. And Ma looked plumb pretty. She was standing there looking right at Pa's head. She had on some kind of a thin, loose robe sort of thing. It was a kind of a whitish thing that looked like a green light was shining on it. And her hair was hanging down like it always did when she was combing it. I stood there and looked at her for a right smart span, but she was just gazing at Pa. She didn't seem to notice that I was in the room. I listened to see if I could hear Enzor getting up and I didn't.

So I just said to myself, "Hit is Ma. She is here and I am going to speak to her. She won't harm me." I pulled myself together and I said, "Ma, hit's you. What are you doing here?"

"Hit's you, Amy," she said, and she turned around toward me. Her whole body turned when her head turned. She looked right at me. I could see her eyes and they sparkled like they always did. "I just come back to warn Ad," she said. "That woman was about to run away with all the money he had and what's left of my quilts and things too. She was aiming on leaving with what few things I had left from the antiquers. She was going to do it tonight. I just thought I had better put a stop to it while I could. She was aiming to take them up to Ike Lame's."

"Hain't you peaceful, Ma?" I asked her. "Where are you?"

"I am in a world of Spirits," she said. "Spirits. Spirits. All I ever see is Spirits. And I get so tired of Spirits. I want to come back once in a while and straighten out things. I see what goes on and I want to help. I wanted to come down here and run that woman away. But I am at peace."

Then she walked up to the head of Pa's bed. "I'll come one more time before you die, Ad," I heard her say. And then she drifted out. I didn't see her leave. "Ma," I said, and I kept on hollering for her. "She's gone, Pa," I told him. And I went on back to bed knowing she was at peace.

Pa, he got up the next morning and come to breakfast. He didn't look scared but he looked like he was in a deep study about something. He set out here on the back porch for a right smart while after breakfast. Then he got up and went walking off.

I didn't see him any more till after sundown that night. I was worried to death when he didn't come in to dinner. But along a little after sundown that evening he come a-moseying in. I looked at him and I didn't know what in the name of Creation to think. He was as pale as a berry blossom. And yet he looked different somehow. He didn't look bothered about anything. I didn't know what to make of it, so I just ended up by asking him where he had been all day.

He said he was a changed man. He started out to walking that morning and every step he took he heard a voice calling to him. But he wasn't able to make out what the voice was saying. He tried to keep right on going and not give it any heed, but he couldn't because every step he took it kept calling to him. He just went on walking. He didn't know why nor where he had started. But by the time he got down there to the Headed Woods he was about half give out. And for some reason he turned there and went on up the rail fence till he come to that reed patch. Something just made him set down there, and he kept hearing that voice over and over. He said it sounded just like Ma did that night. Once or twice he started to run, but he knowed there wasn't any use in that for the voice come to him as much one place as it did another.

While he was setting there he went back over his whole life, how he had treated Ma and all. And every time he thought of something he had done, he could smell sulphur a-burning. And meat of some kind. Then a hot flash went all over his body and he thought he was on fire. Just about that time he got up on his knees. He never had prayed and he didn't know how, but he just went over all the low-down things he had done. And he burnt with shame when he thought of the Lord knowing all them things.

Once, while he was on his knees there, everything sort of went blank for a minute, and he seed Roy Goolen and Old Man Samples come up to him from one side and Bill Susong and Ike Lame from tothern. It seemed like they grabbed him and throwed him off some kind of big cliff. He said it seemed like it took him forever to fall, and while he was falling he could see a big fire below him. And he could feel bolts of lightning going through his whole body.

That falling feeling made him sick as a pizened rat, and he puked all over the ground there. He thought sure he was a goner but he just said out loud, "Lord, I hain't never going to do ne'er another thing wrong." Then he said he had the quarest feeling. His body felt so good all over that he could feel his flesh tingling. Like it does when a body is about half drunk—plumb good. And he knowed then he was a changed man.

That night, again sometime in the night, I woke up and I heard Pa a-talking. I didn't know what to make of it. I thought he was talking in his sleep. So I slipped out of bed again and slipped in the back room.

There stood Ma at the foot of the bed, and she was looking square dab at Pa. Pa, he was sort of raised up on his elbow, and I heard him say, "I guess they'll get me, but I feel content now." And Ma, she just walked up to the head of his bed and I seed her lean over and kiss him right on the lips like you do a child before you give him a good dose of medicine.

Other Stories

SHIN-BONE ROCKS

IT was about eight o'clock Sunday morning and the first bell was ringing for the Sunday School folks. Shorty Fuller just happened to be passing by the Rocky Point church house. He had been up on Bay's Mountain to get him a little peach brandy. Nobody could make peach brandy like Noah Sutherland could. Shorty never had seen sech a morning as this. His hands was froze blue. He didn't reckon it would be a bad idea to just stop and git warmed up a little. Maybe none of them boys would steal that stuff out of his saddlebags. Everybody was pretty glad to git hold of everything they could around about Christmas time that away. But he guessed they wouldn't be likely to steal stuff from a stranger. He didn't reckon he knowed a single soul there, excepting Preacher Hale, and he liked Uncle Pat, as everybody called him. Uncle Pat preached at the Rocky Point church once a month, just like he did at Low Land. And at both places he was a mighty well-thought-of, humble man as preachers go. There wasn't nothing too good for him to do for a person. He was not only a right noisy preacher, but a good worker with the sinners too. Uncle Pat could pert nigh draw the heart out of a hollow log.

Shorty tied his mule up to a cedar tree and looked at the little log church house. There was something about it that made him think he would sorta like it. It was low and looked pretty near buried under with snow, and all the trees around it were weighted down with snow too. Everything looked so clean and white. The sky was bluer than he ever seed. It never seemed that blue at home. The little stick chimney was bending over the roof at the top and was covered with snow too. The smoke coming out of it looked friendly. He liked to see it curl around for awhile and then be wafted up into the clouds. That smoke put him in the mind of— well—in the mind of Uncle Pat. It was friendly just like him.

He went on and got him a seat on the right hand side of the church where the rest of the men folks were. It was good and warm in there because the fireplace was big and they had on a great big hickory backstick. The mantlepiece had pretty little notches cut in it. It was bright in there too, even if they did have to have the windows all shut up on account of the cold weather.

He wondered what that red-headed boy in front of him was staring his eyes out at. He guessed it was ill-manneredly, but he believed he would sorta look around toward the left too. So that was what that fool was gazing at—that girl. Well, she didn't look much different from other girls to him. She had yellow hair and blue eyes just like all girls. But somehow or nother she did look like she would be the kind of a girl he would like pretty well. He wondered if that pop-eyed jackass in front of him tried to spark her. He didn't see what she wanted with a hog like that. But she did look pretty good in that brown-colored homespun dress. A lot of prideful girls he knowed thought they was too good to wear anything excepting store-bought clothes. He bet she had made that funny ruffly bonnet she had on. But he wished it wasn't so big—it kept her face hid all the time excepting when she looked around that away. He wondered if she cared anything about that pop-eyed boy.

When Uncle Pat finished making the Sunday school talk, he told the congregation they could have a few minutes recess. Shorty thought he just wouldn't get up and go out. That way he could find out what kind of a girl that girl was. If she was a nice girl, she wouldn't git up and run out during recess. That was just the cavorting kind of girls that done things like that. He didn't know why it made any difference to him, but somehow or nother he just wished she wouldn't git up.

She didn't get up and go out and he was glad she didn't. He noticed that that boy in front of him didn't get up and go out neither. He wished the devil he would. He thought it didn't look becoming in men to set around in the church house at recess. It was a pretty sure sign of something—that they was lazy or that they was trying to set up to some girl, one. But this fool didn't look like he had no harm in him. There come Uncle Pat towards him.

"Well, Shorty Fuller! What crooked wind blowed you away up here?" the preacher greeted him.

"I just come by here. I've been up on the side of the mountain to do a little hog-swapping. I left home this morning before the crack of day."

"I'm proud you stopped in. There's some mighty good Christian folks up here."

"Yeah, I like it all right here—pert nigh everybody spoke to me when I come in. Everybody seems to be right friendly."

"You don't have to git on back after meeting, do you?"

"Yeah, I reckon I'll have to mosey on."

"I'm a-going over to Brother Arwood's for dinner. You better just come and go along with us. He'll be proud you come."

"I can't go today, I reckon. You better just go down with me."

"I'll have to stay around here, I reckon. I've done told Brother Arwood I would go with him."

"Well, you're coming around to our house week after next, I reckon? We'll be a-fixing for you."

"I guess I'll be around. Don't put yourselves to no trouble. I always get plenty to eat. How are all the folks?"

"They're all as well as common, I reckon—they're all still a-kicking."

"Yeah, there's always two places I like to eat—that's you all's house, and Brother Arwood's. Brother Arwood has got some mighty good cooks at his house. That's one of his girls right over there—the youngest one. The other one run off the other day and got married."

"Where? Which one?"

"That one there with that brown frock and pink bonnet on. The one that runned off and got married was older than this one. They're both mighty good girls and their daddy's mighty tight on them. Well, I reckon hit's about time I was tapping on the bell and getting them all in. We're starting a meeting up here the next Sunday after Christmas. You ought to come up some if it hain't too fur for you to ride."

"When did you say you was starting it?"

"The Sunday after Christmas—three Sundays from today, it is."

"Yeah, I'll try and git up some, shore, if nothing don't break no bigger than a shoe string."

"You better just stay with us today. Brother Arwood treats a person right when they go around him. He knows how to have the grub set out too."

"Well, I guess I ought to git on back and water the mules. I could stay, I reckon, but I don't know none of the Arwoods."

"They're mighty common people. The old man Arwood will be proud you come. They don't live fur—just about a whoop and a holler up the Shin-Bone Road here."

"Say, Uncle Pat, who is that red-headed boy on that bench right here in front of me?"

"That's Red McMann. He's the most bashfullest boy that ever walked the face of God's earth. He don't never speak to nobody save when they speak to him first. Then he acts like a scared rabbit. I don't guess he ever looked at a girl. They say he hides behind the bureau when anybody goes there. He's a mighty fine boy but they say he's a little grain techy."

When Uncle Pat had gone on to the door, Shorty decided he would make that fellow talk. He moved up on the bench beside him. "Do you live around here somewheres?" he asked.

Red looked out the window. "Yeah," he said, "I live down the Hollow Lane here."

"I hain't never been inside this church house before," Shorty went on. "I come up here one night with a crowd from Low Land to help protect a boy from down there. A bunch of boys around here had made it up to rock him. He was a-going to take the Franklin girl home. I come along to help him out. But I don't memorize seeing you nowhere."

"You helped him run, didn't you?"

"A little. Was you in that?"

"No, but I heard George Arwood telling about it. I think everybody else was. George said they wouldn't a-kept on rocking them till they made everybody run if you'ns hadn't brought your guns along. The way everybody does around here is, if they have any guts in them, they stand and take it, and if they don't have, they run and then git devilled about it the rest of their lives. The crowd keeps on throwing till they git out of rocks or till they make the fellow run. All they're after is to see him run. Nobody never gits hurt, and the one that gits rocked never gits mad about it."

"Do they always tell a fellow around here when they're going to rock him?"

"He generally smells a mouse from somewhere. Somebody generally talks too much."

"Did you ever git rocked?"

"Yeah, I got rocked one night during the time of the last protracted meeting. I waited up here at the church till Walt— that's one of my brothers—took one of the Bewley girls home. They rocked him a little that night and I was with him."

"Did they hit him?"

"No, but they did me—right on the leg."

"Did he run?"

"No, but I did."

"What did he do?"

"Him. He hid behind a bank. They didn't nary rock come anywhere near him. I tell you, when the rocks begin to fall around you like hail, I think it's time to take your heel in your hand. Rocks don't have eyes, you know."

"Did they think it was him a-running?"

"Yeah, they still think it was. Lee Hurst cut a big gash in his overall jacket when he tried to argue he didn't run. Lee thought Walt was just trying to lie out of it and make him out a liar."

"Did you ever git rocked when you was out by yourself?"

"I hain't never took no girl home yit."

"You ought to get you a bussy."

"I hain't a-going to spark none. I'm just going to blaze right off when I git set on fire."

"Have you got you a woman picked out?"

"Yeah, I've had her picked out for a tolerable good while now. She don't know it yet. Or I don't reckon she does—I hain't never told her. Penelope Arwood is her name. That's her over there. Everybody calls her Neppie for short."

"Ha! ha! that was a good one, Brother Arwood. Know any more catchy ones?"

"Yeah, twenty-four sticks and a back stick—how many sticks?"

"Why, twenty-five, of course."

"Well, by my way of counting, twenty *fore* sticks and a

back stick makes twenty-one sticks. Hain't that right? Ha! ha, ha!"

"I guess you're too sharp for me. But let me try you one: 'What rooster was it that crowed and everybody in the world heard him?' "

"Everybody in the world heard him?"

"Yeah, and there hain't no trick in this one neither."

"Well, there must be a trick somewhere. I can't rede it."

"Can anybody else rede it? . . . Well, I'll tell then. Why it was the rooster in Noah's ark. I knowed I'd catch you on a Bible one. I'll bet Neppie there knows some good ones, don't you, Shorty?"

Shorty looked at Uncle Pat, startled. He thought he heard the preacher call his name. He wondered what it was he said. He had been busy watching Neppie take up the bread and pass the things. Waiting on the table didn't look like it was any trouble to her. He guessed she was used to it. Then everybody was looking at him. So he guessed Uncle Pat had asked a question. "Was you talking to me, Uncle Pat?"

"I said I bet Neppie knows some good riddles, don't you bet she does?"

"Yeah, I bet she knows some good ones. Try us out and see how good we are, Neppie."

Neppie's face turned as red as fire. "I don't know no good ones," she said. "All I know is little old silly ones."

"That's all right. Give us them," Shorty begged. "Maybe we can guess them kind."

"All right.

> There was an old man
> That didn't have but one eye.
> But he had a long tail that he let fly.
> Every time he went one gap,
> He left a piece of his tail in a trap."

"Whew—" Shorty whistled. "Who do you take me to be? Solomon?"

"I think we all have to give up," the preacher told her after a while.

"Why it hain't hard. It hain't nothing but a needle and thread—that's all."

"I never would have guessed it," Shorty said. He looked up at Neppie and smiled. She was just like he had her figured out to be. Asking a riddle about a needle and thread. He bet she sewed up that dress she had on. That little boy there beside of him—Neppie called him Bud, he believed—had a nice looking patch on the knee of his britches. He bet she was a good patcher too. He watched her passing the things back and forth. He bet she was good at throwing the shuttle backwards and forwards. She just looked like she would be. "Ask us another one, Neppie, will you?"

"If I could think of ary one. I know one about

> Fruits of England, flowers of Spain,
> Met together in a shower of rain.
> Bound with a napkin, tied with a string.
> Guess this riddle and I'll give you a ring?"

"I believe you're too good for us," Shorty told her. "What's the answer?"

"A sack of flour is the answer to that one."

"A sack of flour? You don't expect all us men folks to be cooks, do you?"

So Neppie knowed all about cooking.

"I know another little old silly one too:

> As I went up the bunker's hill,
> There I met my brother Bill,
> With a hammer with a nail,
> With a cat and nine tails.
> Through a riddle, through a reel,
> Through an old spinning wheel,
> Through an old horse's bone,
> Such a riddle has never been known."

"Well, Neppie, you are right sharp, hain't you?" Uncle Pat said.

"Yes, sir, I guess I'm about sharp enough to stick in the ground."

"And green enough to grow, and fool enough to try to blossom," Bud added.

"Bud, I believe she's done already blossomed, don't you? That bonnet she had on this morning made her look like a big pink flower."

"For Heaven's sake don't tell her that," Bud said. "She's proud enough already—she tries to make her hair pretty by sousing it in sap from wild grape vines, and she cuts off pieces of her hair and puts it under a rock in running water, and she carries a hornet's nest in her dress bosom to make some boy fall in love with her, and she—"

"Shet your mouth, Bud, before I mash it as flat as a flitter," Neppie said.

But Bud went on deviling her:

> "Oh, Neppie's mad and I am glad,
> And I know what will please her
> A bottle of ink to make her stink,
> A bottle of wine to make her shine,
> And Red McMann to squeeze her.
> That's all it'll take to please her."

Shorty noticed how red Neppie's face turned. He liked to see her beat. "You hain't a-going to let him plague you to death, are you, Neppie?" he said.

George Arwood gave Shorty a hard look. He didn't like for boys to be so spry around his gal. There wasn't any sense to gals jowing and carrying on with every stinking boy that come along. He didn't aim for her to ever spark anybody. If she had to marry, she could just up and marry without all that tomfoolery. Red McMann would be waiting for her. Red was bashful and never did say nothing, but he would pluck up all right when the right time come.

"What is that thing hanging up there on the wall, Neppie?" Shorty wanted to know, directly.

"It's a fly brush," Neppie told him.

"It shore is fancy. Where did you git sech a fancy thing?"

"Me and maw made it last summer. We made it out of an old catalogue. We took the fluting irons and curled the ends that a-way."

George pushed back his chair. "Well," he said, "if you'ns hain't a-going to eat no more, I reckon there ain't much use in just setting here. But I wish you'ns would eat more of what little we've got. Why, you, Shorty, you hain't eat enough to keep a cat alive. You must be afeared our grub's pizen."

"Me? I wouldn't care for any more—I've had a-plenty."

"Well, you don't eat nigh as much as I do. My maw's about like a rat hole. It's pretty hard to fill up."

"Mine too," Uncle Pat said. "My old woman always has to git the almanac to see when I'm going to full. Sometimes she threatens to yoke up the oxen and pull me away from the table."

Neppie came on in the other room to help talk to the preacher. Maw had tended to the baby while she waited on the table. Now it was her job to tend to the baby and help talk to the preacher while Maw eat her dinner and washed up the dishes.

"Do you play the organ?" Shorty asked her.

"I hain't good, but I kindly bang around on it. My sister that got married could make it talk right well."

"I heard you singing alto plumb across the aisle this morning."

"How do you know it was me?"

"You don't think I'm blind and deaf, do you?"

George Arwood looked at Shorty again. "You're a stranger around here," he said. "Let's all go out and let me show you over the place. I've got several good walnut trees up there on the hill."

"You and preacher Hale go ahead. I never do feel much like walking after I've eat a big dinner," Shorty said.

When the two men had gotten out of hearing distance, George asked Uncle Pat: "Say that boy's from Low Land? Do you know him pretty well?"

"Yeah, I know him as well as the bark knows the tree. He's a mighty clever boy. The whole family is that a-way. There hain't no commoner man living than old man Fuller."

"I don't reckon he means no harm by jowing with women folks, does he?"

"No more harm than a news bee. That's just his way. He'll talk to anybody. He don't mean nothing by it. He's done got him a woman picked out to hitch up with. A right nice girl. She lives close to him."

"Just the same, I don't like the way he tries to carry on with Neppie. My other gal runned off and got married, and I don't aim for this one to pull the same stunt—particularly one she don't even know nothing about. I'd run him off if I thought he was a-trying to spark her."

"That's as fur from his mind as Heaven is from Hell, Brother Arwood."

"Well, it better be. There's more than me that's got a claim on Neppie. She don't know it yit, but I've been seeing it for a long time. And there was a butterfly in the house last summer, so that means two weddings during the winter."

After a while, George and Uncle Pat walked on back to the house. They found Neppie playing the organ, and Shorty singing to the top of his voice. George just heard the last verse of the song:

> "And that young couple got married,
> And married let them be.
> And that young couple got married,
> So why not you and me?
> Oh, why not you and me?"

"I don't think young folks has got any business singing sech songs as that, do you, Uncle Pat? It don't do them no good— do you think?"

"Well, I don't know," he said. "I don't reckon it looks so good on Sunday. But I guess—"

"That's just what I think about Sunday, too," George broke in. "I think some church song would be better. Why don't you'ns sing, 'God Be with You Till We Meet Again'?"

"I don't like that," Shorty told him. "Pick out something else."

Red McMann pushed the window door open and looked inside the church. There set that Low Land bird—right there with Neppie Arwood. The meeting had been going on four nights now, and he had took her home every night. That was just about as much as he could afford to take off of that stuck-up devil. He had a good notion of calling him out of the church house right then and just whaling the life out of him. He didn't want the woman he married to be fooling around with nobody else—most particularly one of them Low Land devils. He never had seen one of them jackasses from down there that had sense enough to pour water out of a boot —not even if it had the directions on the heel.

He just had a good notion to take her away from him tonight. But then he would have to take her home himself, and he never would know how to talk to her. He did wish there was some way he could make it known to her that he wanted to go with her, without telling her. He just never did like to tell nobody nothing. He never had hardly spoke to her. He just couldn't do it somehow or nother. But it was more easier to talk after a person was married. They had the crops and the dogs and the youngons and things like that to talk over. Her pa had always seemed mighty common and friendly. Red didn't believe he would pick a row—he believed he would just git him a big crowd together and give that upstart a good rocking. That would scare him so bad he never would come back around Shin-Bone no more. All them Low Land fellows was afraid of their shadows. Yeah, that was just what he would do—he would give Shorty Fuller a good rocking.

He went over to the tree where a whole bunch of boys were standing. "What you'ns say? Let's rock that Low Land bird tomorrow night."

"What bull's that a-bawling?" somebody asked. "It's not Red McMann, is it?"

"Pon my word, tain't nobody else but," another boy said. "The wind will blow, even if it is cold enough to freeze it, won't it?"

"Rock him, the devil," somebody else laughed. "Red wouldn't harm a flea, even if he could."

"Naw, Red's as soft as a wild snow ball," another put in. "His mamma would be afeared he might throw his arm off. And it might give him the croup to stay up so late. The night air ain't good for babies, you know."

"I think it would be funny to see Shorty Fuller run, though, don't you?" somebody asked.

"Yeah," somebody else added. "Let's do it. I ain't seen a good race in a coon's age. Reckon we can git him to light the rag?"

"Yeah," Red said. "I'll make him run or bust a belly band."

George Arwood came walking up. "What you boys up to now?" he wanted to know.

"Nothing much," one of them answered.

"Aw, go on and tell him," Red said. "We don't care. He don't even like him. He don't want her to go with him. What we're planning on doing, is rocking that Low Land devil tomorrow night. You don't mind that, do you?"

"It would tickle me into a franzy. I'm with you, but I didn't know you ever got into such devilment, Red."

"I never did before, but I would just like to see that bird run."

"I thought you was too bashful to get close enough to a stranger to hit him with a rock."

"I just want to have a bushel of fun for once in my life before I marry and settle down."

The whole crowd laughed. "But it better not get to him," Red told them. "If it does he'll bring a bunch with him that don't mind using their shooting irons."

"Well, we can use shooting irons too, can't we? I want in on this thing. I'll bring my old double-barreled shotgun. It'll shoot a dozen buckshots, and a dozen buckshots will do a lot of torment—just in case, you know." George seemed to be frisking for a fight.

"Somebody told me that ever since you'ns rocked that other fellow, everybody that comes from down at Low Land brings a crowd along with him, though," Red said. "But I don't want to have no row or nothing. I just want to see him run a little."

"Yeah, what did I tell you?" Every boy in the crowd began hollering. "I knowed Red would back out. He couldn't no more throw a straight rock than the devil can count sixpence."

"All right, I'll show you. I'll bring Pa's old cap-and-ball army pistol," Red said. He was surprised at himself when the words came out.

"All right. See that you do it," one of the boys told him. "And we'll carry our end of the load."

"I'll get up the crowd," George said, "and see that they bring ammunition. We want plenty of ammunition so that just in case he does happen to bring a crowd of shooters along, we'll be looking for them. I sorta hope he does. I don't see much fun in throwing a few rocks at him just to make him run."

The second bell was ringing for meeting now, and fifteen boys were busy piling up rocks on a little bank near the end of the Shin-Bone Road. George and Red had gone on to meeting. It wouldn't do for too many of them to stay away from the church house. Somebody might smell a mouse. If any of the old fogies caught on they would try to put a stop to it, and if Shorty Fuller got wise, he might not take Neppie home that night. Several of them that wanted to be in it could slip

down through the cedar thicket there after preaching, and nobody never would know that they didn't go home.

George came slipping through the thicket followed by about
twenty boys. "Good God! What a pile of rocks. You must
have hauled a wagon load up here. Who's this coming sneaking
around? Why, hello, Red! You still in it?"

"I ain't in nothing else. But I don't think we're going to
need anything save rocks. He don't seem to have nobody with
him. I don't think he even has a scent—"

"They'll be the last ones to come along. What you say to
making little piles of rocks all along from here pert nigh to
the end of the road? We want to just keep letting him have it
as long as we can reach anywheres near."

They had their rocks all stacked up in little piles now.

"Shh—I think that's him and Neppie coming up the road
now. It's as dark as pitch tonight—a person can't hardly see
his hand before him, but I think that's them."

"He's a-singing," Red said. "I don't believe he smells nothing. Just listen to him sing." They all listened.

There was happiness in the words that came up from the
road:

> "And now we are married, we are, my maw.
> Now we are married and you can tell Paw
> For he can't help it you know, my maw."

"Shh—right here he is—get ready! I'm a-going to throw the
first rock," Red said. "I believe I can come pretty close to him."

"All right," George whispered. "One for the money, two
for the show, three to make ready, and let her go." The rock
whizzed down to the road. George saw Shorty jump and look
around. "Let him have 'em fast and hard!" he said low. "Let
him think it's hailing rocks around him."

He saw Shorty come half way to the ground, and then start
running again. George noticed he wasn't running quite so fast.
But still he wasn't surrounding the gouted-out places, but leap-

ing them like a cat. "God damn!" he said, "somebody got him
on the leg!"

"But don't try to hurt him," Red begged the ones around
him. "Let's just see a good race."

"He's at the end of the road now," George said. "We can't
reach no furder—shh—good! God! I can't see good but I
believe he's stopped. Keep on throwing. Maybe a few will
reach him."

"No, don't, boys," Red begged. "We might have hurt him.
Do you—"

Ping! ping! came from the end of the road. "God damned—
a thirty-eight!" George said. Then from the same place came
ping! again, then ping! ping! ping! "He's got it emptied now,"
George told the boys. "He can't shoot no more for awhile, so
keep giving him the rocks!" But then another gun began firing,
and another, and another, till that whole hillside at the end of
the road was covered with streaks of fire and smoke.

All the boys huddled together around George. "Don't call
none of your own crowd by name," he told them. "If you do,
they'll git shot. He's got a whole damned bunch hid over there.
Be careful. Git behind some God damned tree or something and
then fire fast as you can. Don't stop for nothing save to reload.
Look out there! Git you a place—give it back to 'em. I'll start
it." He raised the old shotgun to his shoulder. Bang! sounded
all over the mountain side. Bang! Bang! came back from the
other side. The noise was deafening as thunder. "Oh Lord,
my hand!" Red yelled. "I'm shot! oh, Ma! God! I—I—" For
about three minutes the whole hill belched smoke and lightning
and thunder. Fire answered fire from one side to the other. Then
there was a minute of uneasy silence. "They're having to reload," George whispered to them that could hear him. Then
at the end of the road Shorty Fuller's voice broke the calm.
"I'm right here on this stump," he said, "right here on the
top of this little rise of earth. You needn't mind for Neppie,
for she's done gone to cover. Put all the damned bullets in me

you want to—my pa's got plenty of money to have 'em picked out. So let 'em rain or let 'em hail, I'll stop 'em for you."

Red peeped out over the rail fence. He just barely could see a man standing on that stump. It was a right smart piece but he believed he could shoot his legs out from under him. He hadn't aimed on trying to hurt nobody, but one of them devils had put a shot in his hand. He aimed carefully and pulled the trigger. "Take another one," Shorty hollered back. Red pulled the trigger five times without changing his sight. Then for another minute thunder roared and fire flashed from both sides. There was nothing to be heard save the bang of guns and the thumping of bullets as they rived the trees and rails all around.

Then Shorty's voice came again:

> "Well here I stand on this stump
> It's where I set with my sweet sugar lump."

Just then George Arwood pulled both sides of the old double-barreled shotgun. He hadn't aimed to use it again but that fool verse was enough to make him and Red both mad. He aimed to kill Shorty Fuller even if he had to follow him to Hell for doing it. The gun made one sudden big bang. George thought he heard somebody yell out hurt and fall down. He was still surer he heard Shorty Fuller holler, "I'm kilt!"

Everything was quiet a while. Several of the boys came out from their hiding places. They gathered around George. "Do you reckon they're still over there working with him?" one of them asked.

"No, I don't think so," George said. "Give me your gun and I'll see." He emptied the pistol. "No, they're all gone," he told them. "I guess we're safe now. Come on out fellows. Is anybody hurt?"

"Hell, no," about fifty people answered, "not over here."

Red stuck his hand out to George, "I–I–I—"

"No, you're not," George laughed at him. "You've just got

one grain of shot a little piece under the skin. You can take your knife and pick it out easy."

The boys laughed at Red's scare, and continued the conversation. "But I'd hate to see the shape Shorty Fuller and a few others are in right now, wouldn't you?"

"Yeah I'd hate to be the doctor that picked all them shots out."

"I don't guess he'll have to have them picked out," George said, trying to sound calm and steady.

"Why?"

"Buckshots hain't so easy to pick out."

"Do you reckon?" Red asked as if this was the first time it had entered his mind.

Everybody was quiet. George finally broke the silence: "I think we better all be moseying along. I think we've had enough fun for one night."

All the way home Red thought of his victory. He knowed he could win her. That shot in his hand was close to the skin. He could pick it out, but he didn't believe he would. He would just let it stay in there where it could be seen under the skin. He could show it to his boys and raise them up to be men. He could tell them that was the way he got his wife—he fit for her. He didn't just set around and try to out sweettalk somebody; he got out and out-fit somebody. He wouldn't be blowing when he told his boys how he fit for the woman he got. He could just see them looking at him with their eyes stretched wide open. What kind of a pappy would Shorty Fuller have made anyway?

Red knew he was a little early for meeting tonight. But he wanted to hear what had been said, and if anybody had any idea who done it and everything. He met George Arwood out in the yard.

"Red, I saw Shorty Fuller this morning."

"Saw who?"

"Shorty Fuller."

"You're just scared, hain't you? He ain't had time to get to Hell and back yet, has he?

"No, he ain't never been."

"Wh—?"

"He's just as much alive as a three-year-old colt."

"Why—er—I thought sure—how does he look?"

"There hain't a grain of shot in him. But he was hopping a slight bit—I guess that was from that rock that hit him on the leg."

"Where did you see him?"

"He come over our way this morning."

"How did he know you was in it? Did he cuss—"

"I don't reckon he knowed it."

"What did he have to say?"

"He didn't have nothing to say to me, but I had a-plenty to say to him, and to her too."

"What did you say?"

"I made her meet him at the road this morning. I wouldn't let him come inside the yard. I told him never to put his foot on my place again, and I told her that of course I couldn't help it now that it was done done. But I told her that when she found out how hard she had made her bed, she could just keep on laying on it."

"Neppie done what? When?"

"Him. Last night before preaching. They—Howdy do, Preacher Hale."

"Well, sir," Uncle Pat greeted him. "Your girl got a mighty clever man, a mighty clever man, Brother Arwood. You ought to be proud. And Shorty got a mighty nice girl too."

"Yeah," George answered and looked down at his trigger finger. "And somebody said he got a nice rocking last night. Have you heard anything about it?"

"There's nothing to it, I don't think. I heard a little something about it this morning at meeting. But I asked Shorty about it this evening and he said it wasn't nothing excepting a few boys throwed some clods over the fence at him. He said he wouldn't have minded if they had give him a big rocking. That's one thing I'm thankful our young folks don't carry on."

"It's a pretty dangerous business, I guess."

"It is, shore," the preacher agreed. "Rock's don't have eyes, you know."

Uncle Pat went on in the church. George looked at Red. "Bullets don't have eyes neither, do they, Red?" he grunted sheepishly.

"No, I guess not," Red mumbled. Then he opened his knife and started picking that shot out. "And damned girls don't neither," he said from the bottom of his throat.

THE PIECE OF SILVER

PA told folks George went back to the mine up in
Virginia after Cathey Hancock died. When anybody
asked him, that is what he said. But Ma, she never
did say anything save that she didn't know. "I just don't
know," she would say. And then say it another time to herself, "I don't rightly know." Even when I took the piece of
silver to her she didn't say much. She just looked at it and
said, nigh like she was saying it to herself and I wasn't there
to hear her say it: "Hit is back in the shape of the neckpiece,"
and she took it, handling it gentle-like, as if it was a baby,
and put it in the washstand drawer where George had kept it.
The next day she asked me, in a low voice and anxious seeming, if that deer I seed looked fat and healthy.

George, he was three years older than me. And him and
Cathey Hancock played together more than me and him did,
for she was tomboyish and rough, and tough as a pine knot,
always. With this withered right side of mine, and one leg
shorter than tother, I wasn't given to playing as hard as they
did. They played a heap over there in the old hollow oak that
shaded the big spring. Cathey liked it there, and George did
too. He liked to set in the hollow of it and come out smelling
of the doty wood and to hear Cathey brag on him for being

a real woods man. That's why I went there looking. I recollected them spread-out limbs of the tree and the picture of
George and Cathey in the clear water. I thought about it in the
daytime and at night time I dreampt about it. And it come
into my head to go look there for George.

Cathey did the climbing, the biggest part of it, she did,
when they was playing. She would holler back to George
from limb to limb. "Look how high up I am," she would
say, for she was ever a better climber than George. And a
better runner. She would climb, easy as a squirrel, to the top-
most limb of the tree and sing back down to George, for he
nigh always crawled into the hollow trunk and set—just set
and looked at her like he would give his right hand to be
like her, maybe. I would scramble up on the stump on the
bluff close by and watch them and listen to them and wonder
in my mind at Cathey's ways.

> Possum up a simmon tree
> Raccoon on the ground
> Raccoon says to the possum
> O, shake them simmons down.

That's what Cathey would sing. And she would shake the
spread-out limbs of the oak and George would crawl around
the tree ducking his head down to make like he was picking up
persimmons to eat them. I had seed him around the tree and
in the trunk of it so much, when he was little, ducking his head
up and down and leaping on his all fours, that it nigh seemed
natural that morning when I thought I seed his eyes a-shining.
But somehow a queer feeling took holt of me and I stopped.
Stopped and whistled when I got in good sight of it. And the
buck jumped out. Jumped out of the trunk and looked at me
and nigh started toward me. But then went running off up
the hollow. I couldn't help but note the eyes—they were so
gentle seeming, and almost spoke. I stood awhile. Then went
on to the tree.

George set a heap a store by Cathey. From the day she was born, he did. Ma named it often. "He just dotes on her," she would say and sometimes seem sad when she said it and hold her hands tight in her lap. Cathey's pa and ma lived on our place, off up the hollow there in the little log house, and Ma was granny-woman to Old Lady Hancock when Cathey was born. There wasn't anybody else to be. Pa was out in the field when Old Man Hancock come for Ma, so she, of course, couldn't leave George at the house by himself and had to take him with her. And he seed Cathey soon after she was born. He was two year old then and cried like a weaned calf to hold her in his arms. And always afterwards wanted to hold her in his arms, Ma said. She sometimes said it, and Pa laughed and jested George about it.

As soon as they was big enough, George and Cathey took to playing together. Cathey would come down here soon of a morning and stay the day—the whole day long. And always she had her own way about what they should play. Or shouldn't. She made George set in the playhouse with her, and he would do it, no matter how much Pa teased him and called him girlified and threatened to make him wear dresses. He would make cornstalk dolls when she told him to make them and would rock them to sleep in his arms and try to sing the songs she told him to sing. Or he would help her stick thorns into the heads and hearts of them to kill them dead so they could have big funerals and buryings for them.

But she liked most of all to play with that old iron kittle— the one that had a crack nigh the top of it from the water freezing in it. She would put two forked sticks into the ground and put the kittel on a stick that retch from one fork to tothern. She would fill the kittel to the crack with muddy water and splunge chips and leaves down deep into it with her hands and watch it close till she said it was done enough to eat. Then she would play that she was eating. She would tell George to eat some too, and he would dip and blow and sup and make out

he was putting victuals into his mouth and maw. Cathey would
say, sometimes, "Hyear, George, you stir the stew whiles I run
to the woodpile to fetch the wood. Now say the rhyme. Say
it nine times and the stew will be done." And she would hand
him the stirring stick.

George, he would stir the muddy water round and round
in easy motion and say the rhyme and stir and keep on saying
it some more.

> Onery doury dickory day
> Halibone crackle bone tenderlay
> Whiskey brandy American thyme
> Humble bumble twenty-nine
> Oory ary ockery ann
> Mulberry wax and tarry tan.

That's what he would say nine times. Then Cathey, she would
take the stew off and they would set the table, with them
pieces of broke dishes that Cathey brought, and they would
make like they was eating.

Sometimes, in the springtime and in the summer, they would
play over in the first hollow of the cow field, amongst the
clover and the persimmon bushes, and George would stand still
as a stone and watch Cathey catch the honeybees from off the
white clover blossoms. "They won't sting," she would say,
"if you will hold your breath, or if you will charm them—
like this." And she would hold her breath and catch a bee that
wouldn't ever sting her. Then she would catch anothern, just
walk up to the clover blossom it was lighted on and say out
loud, as she wove her finger round and round it in circles,

> Johnnie jizzer jacket
> You can make your racket
> But you can't no more sting me
> Than the devil can count sixpence.

And George, he would look at her and seem pleasured at her
ways. But he wouldn't ever offer to touch a bee hisself.

Sometimes they would ask me to play with them when they

were playing and twice I did—before the time I got afeared of Cathey. I never had set much a store by her nor cared much for her ways, but I never had feared her till that day I seed her running. Her and George had been carrying on in the playhouse all the day long, till they were tired and wore out from gathering wood and making stews and washing dishes. And so they took to running. They run a race down the road. Cathey made the mark in the dust to start from and said the rhyme, "One for the money, two for the show, three to make ready, and here we go." And they started. But before they got halfway to the first apple tree George stopped and stood still as a post and watched Cathey. I watched her too and took note that she wasn't ever hitting the ground with her feet—nigher flying than running, it was. She went all the way to the mark and turned and come all the way back to where George was standing without stopping. And she wasn't panting. George didn't name the running to her but he took to begging her to sing and kept on a-begging, saying to her a blue million times or more, "Sing 'Tam Lin,' Cathey, about the Queen of Fairyland."

"I don't care to," Cathey said.

"You sing better than a mocking bird, you do," he said and kept a-begging. But Cathey just shook her head and laughed nigh fit to kill and kept shaking her head, her hair a-flying wild in the wind.

"I know what let's do," she said. "Let's play cat."

"Play cat?"

"Play like we're turning into cats."

"I don't know how," George said. "Sing 'Tam Lin' for me."

"This away," Cathey said. And she got down on her all fours and took to meowing. It sounded for all the world like a real cat. I looked at her and thought her ears stuck up and I kept on a-looking. I took note of her eyes too. And her mouth. Seemed like—to me it did, I didn't name it to George—they got littler and rounder. And I took holt of George's

hand and helt it tight, for I somehow felt afeared of Cathey.
"I don't want to play cat," George said.

"You're lazy as a cow bird," Cathey said, and shook her
head and looked sullen. "I'll get my bonnet and go home."
But she didn't go, for George begged her not to then. He got
down on his all fours to pacify her, and she took to laughing
and singing.

> Ha ha—There was an old man lived on a hill, ha ha
> If he hain't moved away he's a-living there still, ha ha
> Ha ha ha ha ha ha ha ha ha ha, ha ha.

But George, he was awkward at the crawling and meowing,
not seeming naturalized to it like Cathey seemed. I named it
to Ma when I got to the house. And Ma just said, "Cathey's
bounden to a-learnt sech from her Ma." But afterwards I took
note that she looked bothered in her mind a little and that she
tried to keep George from playing with Cathey so much. But
it was like trying to keep a mule from kicking. For George
was nigh twelve year old then.

He was nigh twelve and Cathey was going on ten; and they
took to the woods. Pa didn't make George work in the field
much; so him and Cathey played in the woods nigh all the
time, climbing trees and chasing after butterflies and bees and
such as Cathey wanted to chase after. Cathey knowed heart's
ease, and sang too, and all the flowers and herbs and where
they growed and what every one was used for; and her and
George gathered them for Old Lady Hancock. And once I
seed her make George cut a limb from off a thorn tree and tote
it to Hancocks' house. I told Ma again, and she asked Pa if he
reckoned Cathey knowed love weed and might feed it to George
when he was older. Pa laughed and poked fun at her and said
he didn't believe in any such weed. And she didn't name it to
him any more. But just said she wished Old Lady Hancock
wouldn't ever talk to George. And was proud when Pa started
making George go to the field.

George sometimes jested Cathey about eating the grass and bushes. But she did eat them—sweetgum and sassafras and sheep sours and things I didn't know—bushes and leaves and roots. Just eat them raw. And sometimes George would eat them too, when she begged him. He would chew them up and spit out the spit or swallow it. Whatever she told him to do.

Till George was nigh about fifteen year old. Then he quit playing and took to working all the week without Pa having to make him or to ever tell him to. And on a Sunday evening —every Sunday evening—he would put on his suit of clothes and go to court Cathey. He took her to a poke supper down at Low Land and to the Saturday night singings over at Campbells' and to a cake-walk down at Springvale and had a ruckus with Pal Hawkins over her because Pal asked her to cake-walk with him. And Ike Thompson had to hold George to keep him from getting into a fight with Pal.

At first Ma fussed at George and told him Cathey wasn't his kind and that some folks were dubious of her ma. She named other girls that he could pay his court to. But she soon give up her talking, for George was logger headed as a sow and said he set a heap a store by Cathey and he aimed to marry her for his wife if she would have him. But Cathey, she wouldn't hear his talk about marrying. She would start running. When he named marrying to her she started running. He would start talking to her about it and she would up and flounce out of the room. And if he followed her she would run, skipping along over the rocks like the wind a-blowing, not looking back at him. Or she would shake her head, letting her long thick hair fly through the air and not make him any answer. But he kept on a-asking her. I watched him practice on the bank of the creek, holding his arms first one way then tother and working his mouth up and down and shutting his eyes and groaning it out: "Cathey, will you—I'll make money by the bushels—my wife—why won't you marry me?"

He set around and talked about it to Ma and sometimes to

me when we were doing up the work at night or early of a
morning. And sometimes he laid the blame on Ma, saying she
didn't like Hancocks because they didn't own land of their own.
He fell off till he was slim as a rail almost and took to groaning in his sleep and singing love songs about hard-hearted girls
and every day he sung that one about

> You should have employment then
> And to her your wages lend
> When you ask a girl to leave
> Her happy home.

He said he believed Cathey wanted to marry a rich man and
he was going to make himself rich so she would have him.
That's why he took out to Virginia. Him and Cathey had rid
the horses two or three times on Saturday evening and gone to
Russellville. And George talked with Abe Drennon out there.
Abe had a map that he claimed was made by them men—
Swift and Munday, their names were—that had found a
silver mine up in Virginia. Abe got it, he claimed, from his
pa, who had got it from the man that stole it from Old Man
Swift at an inn somewhere when the old man was coming out
from finding the mine. It was drawed on something that looked
like paper but wasn't.

So George, he told Abe he would go help him find it.
George said the map was nigh wore out—just ready to split
at every place where it was folded. And it begun cracking up
into little squares—twelve of them—every time they tetched
it. But they could read it clear, and George set his head on
finding the silver for Cathey.

He went to see her the evening before he started. Right after
dinner he went and didn't come home for supper. He didn't
come home till it was time for Ma to get his breakfast for him.
She got his breakfast and filled Pa's old saddlebags full of
victuals for him; and him and Abe got a soon start.

They walked fast as an ant, George said, and made it to

the first hog drover's shelter by midnight or before, maybe, and
rested there till daylight, sleeping. Then went on their way
again. The next night they slept in a sheep shelter nigh the top
of Reds Run Mountain. And there were two other men that
come along and spent the night there too, in the shelter, and
slept on the floor with them. Claimed they were mule traders
from South Carolina. But George said he never named e'er a
word about the mine when he talked to them. What little he
talked.

Him and Abe parted with the stranger men the next morning and set out on their way again. They come to Four Hills,
up in Virginia, before nightfall and seed and talked to a man
there that asked them to stay the night with him. They did,
and he put them off up in the loft by theirselves and they felt
safe up there and like they were nigh to the silver and could
almost feel it in their hands. They whispered back and forth
to one another and lit the candle and propped the door fast
with a chair so they could look at the map to tell which way
to go from there. And Abe pulled off his right boot.

He took out the map and started putting the pieces together.
But all at once he jumped up so high he nigh hit the ceiling
with his head and yelled out to the top of his voice and kept
a-yelling: "The balance—the balance—where is the the balance
of hit?" For there were just six pieces to be found. He took off
all his clothes and turned them wrong side outwards and shook
them and took the insoles out of his boots and still the map
wasn't there—the other six pieces of it. And he set in on George,
saying George had told them men; but George said he hadn't.
And Abe and George took to argufying back and forth and fussing with one another and got dubious of one another and sullen.
But neither one of them was willing to turn back towards
home.

So they set out to find their way through the woods without the map. They couldn't tell much with just having half
of it. And at nighttime George was afeared to sleep sound for

fear Abe would kill him. For Abe took to claiming he believed George had stole part of the map out of his boot whiles he slept in the night. George stripped off naked as the bare ground to prove he didn't have it, but still Abe was dubious of him and was short in talking to him. Then he took to saying he believed Old Man Swift's ghost come and took the map and he told George such tales till George got so he seed ghostes and empty caving-in mines in his sleep—when he slept. But he kept his heart set on the silver for Cathey.

George stayed with Abe in the woods for a whole year and wandered around in the wind and rain and slept in caves and hollow trees. Till one day he found a lump of something— something he thought might have silver in it. He marked the spot somehow and in a branch that runned there close he found another lump. He put both of them in Pa's saddlebags and fastened them in there tight as skin, telling Abe he would be back, or maybe would, as soon as he married Cathey. That would be enough, he thought, to show her he could be a rich man for the asking. So he left Abe up there and set out to find his own way home. And didn't have any trouble a-getting here.

He set by the fire three days straight hand-going—the first three days—and piddled with the lumps before he went to see Cathey. He melted one of the lumps and got the silver—for sure enough they both were silver—from it to make the chain. He melted it and drawed it out into a wire and quiled the wire up in little round rings and made the chain to fasten the other piece onto. It did make a pretty neckpiece, and he set out up the hollow with it, strutting like a turkey gobbler in the springtime, thinking on how proud Cathey would be. "I'll tell her there's more than this that I'll go back for. Hit'll look pretty on Cathey's white throat, won't hit?" And he strutted and strutted—with his long legs. And told me to keep mum about the lost map and not name it to Cathey.

But he come back soon. And yelt out at me, and dared me

to talk to him or ask him any questions. And he wasn't ever the same afterwards. Ma named it several times about him being changed and about him not going to see Cathey. Nor making any mention of her. Then one day he told it. Me and Ma was setting a-picking out walnut kernels when he told it. He just kept a-staring at the kernels.

"Do you want some of these?" Ma said. And handed him some picked-out boy's britches.

"No," he said, "I don't want anything—I don't know what I want."

And he set into talking and told it. The silver piece scared Cathey. He handed it to her and she retch out her hand towards it saying, "Hit is pretty, hain't it?" Then the wild look come into her eyes, like in the eyes of a scared deer, he said, and she drew back her hand and never tetched it.

"Hit's yourn," he said. "I will go back for more—some day, when we need it, I will go back."

"George!"

"That's why I went."

She started to open her mouth and didn't. And run out of the house and up through the pine thicket like a streak of lightning, by leaps and bounds—so quick George couldn't think to try and follow after.

He didn't go back to spark her on Sunday any more. And Old Lady Hancock, when she come to help Ma make apple butter, named it about George not finding the mine. "Did he tell you he didn't?" Ma said. "No," Old Lady Hancock said, "I just thought maybe part of the map got lost or something —I didn't know."

But soon Cathey took to coming here again. Ma made note of the way she feisted around George when she come. And George, he appeared to like it whiles she was here. He would ask her in and set a chair for her and tell her her dress was pretty. She did have pretty clothes, Cathey did, that she made; always with low-cut necks that showed her white chest; and she was proud as a king with her long hair slicked back and shining. George, he would set and look at her and smile, and when she rubbed herself up against him he would feel all over her with his hands. But he never named her after she was gone. And never made offer to walk a piece of the way home with her. Just set and stared at her leaving.

When she was gone, if it was in the wintertime, he would set and look into the fire. Or if it was summer he would set on the front steps staring at the sky or at the bull bats darting down toward the ground. Or at the calves over in the horse lot playing. And not say anything or answer me or Ma when we spoke a word to him. Till Ma took it into her head to tell Old Lady Hancock she didn't think it looked right for Cathey to come down here feisting around George, and Cathey didn't come any more.

Then George took to working and kept hisself busy as a bird all day every day. He took all the feeding and wood-chopping off Pa and stayed in the field from daylight till dark in crop time. During the winter days he was ever busy piddling in the barn or in the tool shed, till Pa was proud of him, saying his trip to the silver mine had done him good—made him know that the only way to get what a body wanted was to dig for it, and to dig in his own ground. Him and Pa cleaned out the fence rows and fixed the porch and Ma, she looked contented in her mind. And peaceful.

Save that Pa kept seeing a deer that come nigh and played around close to the house late in the evening, nigh every evening. The prettiest deer, he said, that he ever seed in his born days, with a white breast. But he had a feeling that it somehow boded bad luck the way it kept a-coming. And he set his mind on killing it. He took to setting out behind the smokehouse a-watching for it. Eight different times it come close up and he shot. But somehow he couldn't ever kill it. He was a good shot, Pa was, and said he knowed he hit it. But every time he shot, it lept into the air and kicked its heels high and went running off so fast Pa just stood with his mouth open a-looking at it.

Till after the eighth time, when he got more dubious of it, I reckon, for he looked in the washstand drawer, where he knowed George's silver piece was at and took the neckpiece from off the chain. He melted it in the ladle and poured it into the bullet moulds like it was lead. And didn't name it to George and I didn't either. Nor Ma.

Pa loaded the rifle with the silver bullet and set out behind the smokehouse every evening watching. Then one evening the deer come—right up to the rail fence, held up its head and looked across. Pa, he took good aim at the white breast, and shot. The deer fell over. He went running up to it. It was heaving its sides up and down a-dying, and he called George to come from the barn and see it. George, he looked and somehow, I don't know how, got the bullet out of its flesh. Not thinking, I reckon. But instead of dying, it jumped up and run away as hard as it could run. And Pa said the blood was dark and thick and not bright like deer's blood was wont to be. And Ma, she took to shaking like a cold dog when she seed the blood on George's hands and made him wash it off quick. And she looked uneasy and troubled in her thinking.

Soon the next morning, Glen—he was Cathey's brother—brought word down here that Cathey was dead. Said she died from a big boil that come on her chest and when the core come out it took to bleeding and wouldn't ever stop bleeding —no matter how much spiderweb and devil's snuff they dusted on it.

Ma went to help lay her out. George, he went over there too. And Ma come home and told about it—told me. Said whiles she was washing Cathey she had to go back through the room where George was setting and that Old Lady Hancock was setting square dab in front of him, eyeing him up and down from toe to head a-staring. And then when she was through with Cathey the old lady said to her: "You thought him not her kind, didn't you?" And Ma said she reckoned it must a-been in her own mind's eye she seed it but said she thought she seed the devil a-working in Old Lady Hancock's eyes. Thought she seed some kind of picture there.

After the burying George just set with his head bent low and his hand in his pocket. He nigh quit working. No matter how much Pa fussed at him or cussed. Then at times he would take something out of his pocket and stare at it full half a day, setting out under the sugar tree or behind the smokehouse, one. Then one day when Pa had gone to the mill, and Ma to Old Man White's burying at Cedar Knob, George made me go to the kitchen and set with the door closed, not giving me any reason for it. I peeped through the slats anyways to watch him. I seed him before the fire melting something in the ladle. But I didn't tell Ma.

Pa, of course, tried to make him work and George took umbrage at it and took to going away from home. At first it was just from meal time to meal time. Then it was from daylight till dark; and Ma said she hoped he wasn't asking victuals from Hancocks; so she left something on the table for him and his plate set, day and night, all the time.

He sometimes talked to Ma in the kitchen when he come in and soon he got to making wild talk, about finding a silver mine on our place and about talking to a deer in the woods and what the deer said to him. And about Cathey. Strange things about how he could still see Cathey. And how she run from him. Once I laughed when he was telling it and Ma shook her head at me and frowned. And when he left again she threatened me to box my ears if I should ever laugh at him again.

Then three days went by when he didn't come in. Me and Ma took victuals and set them around here and there. And everywhere, almost. We took some bread and meat and put it on that old flat rock up there on Slate Hill. The next day I looked and all the victuals was gone. And I took to thinking about the old tree by the spring. And couldn't ever get it off my mind.

George come in and stayed one day and left and didn't come back for a week. Then he come in during the night, early in the night, and come on into the lean-to where I was sleeping. Ma heard the racket. And she run in with a lit candle. "Hit's you," she said to him. And I riz up to speak to him and seed that he was trying to pull off his clothes. But he was awkward as a blind buzzard at it. Seemed like he couldn't straighten himself out or that he was stiff all over and drawing toward the floor. But he kept his fist, his right fist, closed tight as a turtle's mouth.

Ma asked him if he didn't want something to eat before he got in bed; and he went to the kitchen with her. I heard her talking but never did hear him say e'er a thing save "uh-huh" and "huh-uh," grunting the words out to her. When they come back into the lean-to I asked him if he wanted to sleep in front and he just looked at me like maybe he didn't know what I meant; but I moved over and ater a while he crawled in. I took note that it seemed hard for him to stretch out straight; but Ma took the candle on out and I went off to sleep.

And slept till it was nigh daylight and I heard a racket. I riz up quick and got a glimpse of George going out the door. I seed his clothes still on the chair round and I yelt for Ma. She come running; but it was done too late, for he was quick away. And gone out of our sight. Me and her and Pa tried to track him; but it was dry weather and we didn't have any tracks to go by.

Ma took me with her the next day and we went up to Hancocks' to ask them if they had seed him; and the old lady just set and grinned at us and said over and over and didn't say anything else, nor answer Ma what she asked, "You thought he wasn't Cathey's kind." So we kept on a-takng victuals to the woods and looking for him. But we never seed hide nor sole leather of him again. Ma didn't name it to Pa about the clothes on the chair and Pa said George had gone back to Virginia to look for the mine and told everybody that: that George had the wanderlust and had gone back to find more silver. But Ma, she didn't say anything, and I took note of the piece of slat, the piece of ash wood, nailed with three nails and tight across the washstand drawer. Me and her kept on taking victuals to the rock and leaving them there.

Till winter come and the big snow started falling. Early on a Sunday morning it got dark as night; the clouds were down so low, and Pa said we were in for a snowstorm. He made me hold candles for him whiles he laid feed by for the cows and horses, and Ma stuck a pine torch up in a tub of ashes and carried in wood by it, filling the big house full and stacking it on the back porch and in the kitchen.

Then the snow commenced to fall and it lightened up some. I looked at Ma and she looked at me and we set out in search. I yelt and whistled and looked in every fence corner and brushpile. And the snow soon started laying. Then it got dark and we couldn't tell whether the clouds was low again or if it was nighttime.

But it come light again in the morning and we started our searching over—save that the snow was sticking to briars and trees and bushes and nothing looked the same when it was covered—till the first thing we knowed we was going around and round in circles and stepping in our own tracks. The snow kept getting deeper and Ma took to lagging behind and panting. And it was away up into the shank of the evening before Pa come with Old Shep and the horses and found us.

It was two weeks before the snow melted much. Ma and Pa, they both just set and looked at the fire and first one and then tothern went to the window. And once Pa said, "If George finds a cave he will stay in hit—George is good at telling weather." Ma didn't say anything, and every time Old Shep moved on the porch she run to the door. And at nighttime I dreampt. Seemed like every night I dreampt. About

Cathey and George mostly—how they played. And about the
tree. They would wake me up from hollering at one another
and I could hear her singing down to him:

> Raccoon said to the possum
> Shake them simmons down.

And I could see him jump out of the hollow trunk and start
running. I would wake up just as he got out of my sight and
not ever get to see him good. But it always seemed that he was
somehow different. It bore on my mind so that I told Ma
about it one morning. She listened. Then she just said, offhand
like, "And you hain't et your breakfast yet." And she didn't
say any more save to ask about the tree. "The hollow trunk
is big, hain't it?" she said. I told her it was. And she seemed
eased in her mind a little. And not so jumpy.

But the snow melted fast when it started. And soon as it
was off the trees enough for me to tell my way I set out—
without the rifle. And stopped and whistled. The deer jumped
out—a buck, it was. And looked at me. I stood awhile. Then
went on up to the tree. And there it was in the trunk a-shining.
The piece of silver was. And I retch in and got it.

A FEELING OF PITY

SHE says she understands, Cora does, and she's not going to hold it against Eli. Other folks—all folks that know her—feel pity for her; but she takes umbrage at it. She says she's not in the need of pity. At first it even made her mad when anything was told on Eli. It was a tale-idle, she said. Till she seed it with her own eyes she said that. Now she just says she understands or that she feels pity for him or just don't say anything; and there's no changing her.

I told her the first time she ever set with Eli how his pa was, that he was lower down than the devil's footstool. Old Noah. That's what folks called him. He didn't raise Eli right, Cora says. But I don't see why that calls for Cora to put up with Eli's ways. She ought to have better. Now that old Noah is dead looks like she could manage Eli. She worries more than she lets on she does. I know that for a fact. Else she wouldn't talk about it to me, making excuses for Eli.

Her and Eli went right on over there to Noah's place in Hamblen County that Monday evening as soon as they got married. The first thing that Noah did was to start fussing. He throwed it up to her about her pa a-making liquor. And he told her he didn't have any faith in me as a granny-woman. He allowed as how Cocke County folks didn't act like Hamblen County folks. Said they acted more like somebody wild or trashy. And Noah had a lot of room to talk, he did.

He would set there and draw his lips in and fuss. Even in front of anybody that come in he would fuss. He would suck them thin lips away in. And that slanting mouth, always dirty—with tobacco and spit. I don't see how Cora bore it. Nobody else does. He looked like the devil, or worse maybe if that could be. But he thought he was plumb pretty. Got that into his head and couldn't ever get it out, not even after he bought that fine newfangled looking glass so that he could see himself—with his bald head and his shoulders bent away over like they were. Folks talked about the way he looked. Folks that knowed him did. Said he had just been so contrarious all his life that he was going to turn into the devil, maybe. If he hadn't already.

He fussed and kept on fussing till Cora didn't know what to think. She didn't say e'er a word. And Eli didn't either. Not till Noah throwed it up to Cora that she used to go with Will Hamblen. When he did that Eli got up and left the table. He looked back at Cora. That look, Cora said. She couldn't help but notice that hurt look.

Cora took as much that time as she could bear. Then she got up from the table and commenced washing the dishes. Narcie dried them that night. Narcie is Eli's youngest sister, and she thinks she is something on a stick. She dried the dishes and mumbled about how hard it was on her pappy and Eli since all the other youngons had got married.

Cora got through with the dishes. Then she asked Narcie where hern and Eli's room was. Narcie barked it out like an ill pup, about it being the little old room up in the loft. With a hypocrite bedstead, and everything dirty. It made me feel like a wooly worm was crawling on me when Cora told me how it looked. Of course it was nearly as good as she had been used to here at home. But it wasn't as good as Noah had. They had another room besides the company room. But I reckon they just thought Cora never had been used to anything and they would put her off up there. Looks like Eli would have kicked for his own sake. Cora wasn't used to dirt. But she would take up for Eli. She said it was because Noah never had let him have any fun when he was growing up. Eli's ma had died when he was little, and Noah had always been hard on him. Nigh like he hated him.

Noah kept his fussing up. All the time he grumbled about something, one thing or another. What time he wasn't fussing, folks said, he must have been worrying over what he was going to fuss about next. He grumbled about Cora eating so much, about her being so lazy. He fussed if she made big biscuits, and he cut a through if she made little biscuits. It didn't suit him if she wore a pink dress and it didn't suit him if she wore a green one. And of course she never got any new ones. Eli, after so long a time, bought one of Narcie's old ones for her. Then Narcie took the money Eli paid her and got her a new dress.

Eli cut a regular through when Feeona took one of her dresses over there for Cora to wear to the baptising down at the bend of Nolichucky that Sunday. He said Cora's sisters needn't try to let on like they had to help keep her up. And he made her wear that same old black wool dress he had bought from Narcie—on the hottest day I nigh ever felt.

Noah traipsed around—made special trips over here to Cocke County to find out every little thing that any of us did. Then he throwed it up to Cora. It makes my blood bile every time I think about it. He started it on me that I was a witch. Claimed that Cora owned up I was. But I know Cora didn't. And started that Feeona was a whore. He was jealous because Feeona was better looking than Narcie. And he fussed at Cora all the time about that. Tried to get other folks down on Feeona. Of course, I didn't get to see Cora much—still don't. Noah made Eli not hardly ever let her come home. Said she would just carry idle tales.

Noah harped on Cora about her pa being a Democrat instead of a Republican. Said all Democrats were dirty whores and whorehoppers. And he would go around singing that verse about fried rats and stewed cats being good enough for Demcrats. Him and Eli made Cora say she would be a Republican. And Cora, she went down there to the election polls and voted for all the Republicans just like Noah and Eli told her to. Everybody said it was pitiful the way she looked when she went down there. After being raised up in such a hotbed of Democrats.

Then Noah put it into Eli's head that a body couldn't live right unless they belonged to the Hog Pen church. Eli told Cora to jine. She went down there and jined that mess. After that they fussed at her all the time and threatened to have her churched, claiming she wasn't good enough to be a member.

Noah was the cause of trouble between Eli and Will Hamblen too. I know he was. Noah kept telling him that Will was liable to come in any time and take Cora away from him. Said it was his bounden duty to take things like that in hand.

Then one day Will was passing there and he said "Howdy do" to Cora. She was out there hanging out clothes and of course she spoke back to him. It was just a few days after that that Eli kilt Will. Said he had to do it to keep Will from killing him. Got by with telling that. And Cora, she swore to every lie Eli told. Stood up on the witness stand and swore it.

When Noah would get tired of fussing at Cora, he would fuss at Eli for marrying her. Then Eli would take the spite out on Cora. Eva Day says she has passed there as much as five times and heard Noah upbraiding Cora. She told me herself that he slapped her one day because she didn't have the beans cooked right.

Narcie was nigh as bad as Noah. Or worse, if that could be. She didn't fuss. But she didn't say anything. She just turned up her nose and grinned that stuck-up grin. And wouldn't have anything to do with Cora. She wouldn't go anywheres that Cora went. But I reckon she wasn't too good to eat Cora's cooking. It's a wonder she ever left—even when she did. After that first night that Cora was over there Narcie never turned her hand to do a lick of work. She couldn't think of anything save how pretty she was. And Noah thought she was too, even if nobody else ever accused her of beauty. She stood in front of the looking glass nigh all the time, Cora said. Nigh all the time that she wasn't galavanting off somewhere or laying up in the bed. She wouldn't even do a hand's turn when Cora was down flat of her back and couldn't.

All of Eli's brothers looked on Cora the same way. Looked on her as a hired girl. They still pour in there on Sundays with all their youngons. Cora has to cook dinner and wait on them. But she says she understands Eli. She knows he means well. At first she said she couldn't stand it if it was so what folks were telling around. But she said she knowed it wasn't so. She even got mad at Eva Day for telling her that Eli was running around with the McClann girl. She was just not going to believe it, saying it was a tale-idle—like she was having to argue with herself about it. Like she was having to argue with her own common sense and knowing.

Noah even fussed about Cora eating the things that he said he worked hard to raise. Of course he never made mention that Cora worked like a regular hired hand. She went to the field when Noah and Eli did. No matter what the work. Then she come in and got dinner and went back to the field when they did. And chopped out corn or throwed up hay. None of the other women folks around there worked over a half a day at a time. They took note of how Cora done and they told her she ought to leave Eli and she kept saying she was going to. But she never has. She owned up to herself after she married him that she had jumped out of the frying pan into the fire. And she didn't mean to go on living with him over a month. But she claims every time she has started to leave he would look up at her and there was something in his look that made her turn around in her tracks.

She kept it a secret as long as she could about Junie a-going to come into this world. Finally she was so proud that she upped and told Eli. I reckon she thought it would make him different. I don't know. Of course Eli had to go and blab it to Noah. He always told him everything. And always added to it, I guess.

The first thing that Noah took to grumbling about was that Cora would want to have me for a granny-woman. He allowed as how I couldn't ever set my foot in his house. Him and Narcie talked and talked. Right in front of Cora, they talked. They talked about who they would have for the granny, what they would name the youngon and everything. Of course Cora didn't have any chance to get me the word and I didn't know a breath about it till Eli come over here that morning looking like a sheep-killing dog that had been caught in the fold. But it was bound to be hard on Cora to hear them talking so when she wasn't feeling fit to kill. She said there was two or three times along then when she started to leave Eli sure enough. But she couldn't help but think about how pure and seely he was and how he had been raised.

She said the baby was all they talked about. Noah and Narcie. They just set and talked about the baby. And Cora just got to the point she didn't care. She told Eli if they was going to have the baby she would just let them go on and have it.

Noah and Narcie had Eli doing everything they told him to do. He kept telling Cora over and over that they weren't going to have me for the granny-woman. Told it all over the country too. Cora spoke up one day and told him that she would just come back home and have it. And she started. But he looked at her that same way and she didn't go any furder than the big road before she turned back.

Noah and Narcie finally made up their minds that they

wouldn't have any granny-woman at all. They thought it would be big-looking to put on style. So they said they would have Dr. Wright from Morristown. Narcie had been to him to have a boil lanced and she was in love with him from top to toe. She wanted to get to see him again and thought that would be a good way. She said they would have the doctor and she would do the rest. They had it all fixed in their minds. But Cora argued with Eli, and he said he aimed to have Dr. Wright too. Said Cora could have him or none at all. Right then Cora made up her mind that she wouldn't have anybody with her. She would be as contrary as they were. After that, till she was called to straw, she just minded her own business and said nothing about it.

When the time come Cora didn't let on to a soul. She said she believed anybody could have drove nails into her head and she wouldn't have raised a finger. The funny thing to me is that they didn't catch on to what was up till it was done too late to go to Morristown after the doctor. Eli run and got Eva Day because she was the closest one.

Save for one little gown, Cora hadn't made any baby clothes. I didn't even know she was called to straw. It was during the winter time and with not much passing I never seed anybody from over in there. And of course Cora didn't know anything for herself. She just talked to Eva Day one time after she thought there was something wrong with her. And Eva told her what it was and a lot of other stuff too. I think Cora would have been better off if she hadn't been told. Eva said if she clum up into the barn loft it would cause the baby to be born dead. Said that would pull the cord tight around the baby's neck and choke it to death. Since Eli was having her climb up in the loft twice a day to feed, she just allowed it would be born dead and she didn't make any clothes save the one gown for it to be buried in. Different folks around there in the district sent over a few things that they had used when they had youngons. But Cora just took them and throwed them down in the bureau drawer. That night when the baby come she couldn't tell Eva Day where anything was. Eva said when she begun to ask her, Cora looked up and said, "Well, hit's dead, hain't it?"

Noah and Narcie said the boy ought to be named after its grandpa, and so they named it Noah Eli. But folks around thought that wasn't fair to Cora. So nobody has ever called him that. Eva Day started calling him Junie. And that is what everybody in the country calls him because he looks for the world like Eli.

But the awful thing is how Noah acted about me. I heard it from all sides. He had told everybody in the country that I shouldn't set foot in his house. Well, when Noah and Narcie and Eli got up the next morning after Junie was born, there wasn't any Cora down there to get breakfast for them. Cora said she reckoned Narcie finally did knock up a little snack for Noah and Eli. But nobody brought her anything. And she was so weak she couldn't hardly tend to the baby. So it throwed all the work on different folks that come in to see Cora and the youngon. Everybody that come in got mad at Eli. They wanted to put Cora in a wagon and bring her home right then. But sick as she was, Cora took up for Eli. Said she knowed other folks didn't understand.

Finally Eva Day just upped and told Eli he had to come after me—like he ought to have done in the first place. Eva was staying down there pert nigh all the time. And Narcie was letting her do all the cooking. There was a heap of folks that said they wanted to come in and help Cora and the youngon. But they didn't aim to wait on Narcie and Noah to boot.

Eva told Eli the folks of the District was going to tie him up to a post and give him a good flogging. That word got a hustle on him, and he brung hisself right over here after me. I didn't know at first what could be the matter. But I dropped everything here at home and went. I stayed two weeks and did the work—the cooking and washing and everything. I did it for Noah and Narcie and all the rest.

Then one day we was all there at the table eating when Noah complained that he had to keep up Cora. Said it in that snarling way he had. And besides that, he said, he had to keep up her ma too. I thought that exceeded the measure. I told Cora, and she said me and her would go home the next morning. But when morning come and I named it to Cora she said I could just go on by myself. She said she got to thinking about Eli being left over there without anybody to do any- thing for him. She said it seemed like he had already had a token of her leaving and that he looked at her that way again, the way he had of looking when she named it about leaving him.

Then straightway Old Noah got sick. And I reckon he was more contrarious toward Cora than ever. She had to wait on him and tend to Junie too. She had to do that besides doing the rest of the work. Narcie just set around trying to look pretty and didn't even offer a hand's turn for her pa.

Noah wanted a drink now and a biscuit then and something else at another time till Cora nearly trotted her legs off. You know, he didn't have any teeth and he liked apples better than anything. So he commanded Cora to stay right with him all the time and scrape apples for him.

But I reckon bad things come to an end sometimes too. Some bad things do. Like Noah. Cora was nursing Junie that day when Noah called to her to bring him a drink of water be- cause he felt like he was choking. She took it. And he said for her to set down there. He looked up at her. Like a scared chinch, Cora said. "Well, I believe Katie is going to borrow the dough," he said. That was the way he always said it when he meant somebody was going to die. Then he walled his eyes back and begun to retch and choke. The covers was sprayed with sour puke. Cora run out on the porch and hollered for Eli to come from the barn. But the devil couldn't wait till Eli scraped the manure off his shoes.

Some few days after Noah was buried Eva Day gossiped to Cora about what Eli was doing. Said she seed him with her own two eyes—down at McClanns' Saturday evening when she went to the store. Of course Cora couldn't leave him at a time like that. Or it would be bad to. That is what she thought at least. Or claimed she thought. And after that she vowed she didn't believe a word that Eva told.

But the next Saturday come and Eli went to town as usual. That evening Cora said she had the quarest feeling when he left the house because he just looked like he was in such a splut to get away. Still she wouldn't let herself believe it. She had set her mind not to, I reckon. Yet she couldn't help but think on how he had been acting of late. The last five or six nights he had taken to sleeping by hisself. Said he told her that her and Junie got in his way. But he hadn't been fussing any lately—just hadn't been saying anything. And she thought it was on account of his pappy dying. That's what she tried to think.

It got good dark. And still Eli didn't come in. Cora couldn't keep her mind from wandering off to Trulie McClann. At that time Trulie was just fourteen year old. All her sisters had already left home and become whores. All the older ones. When Cora went to the barn to feed the horses, Old Rover stuck his nose through the cracks in the crib and whined. He had been up all day and hadn't had his dinner. Eli had put him up that morning to keep him from running up to Newberrys' after that young bitch of theirs. Through the cracks Cora seed a pitiful look in Old Rover's eyes and she felt pity for him. So she opened the crib door and let him out to run where he would.

She said after that she shucked corn for she didn't know how long. Then she fed the horses. Maybe twice as much feed as common. A weak feeling of pity had come over her.

She felt sorry for animals that wanted for anything. She recollected how much she wanted Eli. Leastways how much she had wanted him at first. She could understand, she told me. She said she didn't hold any grudgment against Eli for being the way he was.

FOR THE LOVE OF GOD AND
SAM SCOTT

I TURNED around and around, like a chicken on a hot rock, trying to see Sam—to tell him much obleeged again for taking me to where the root was. But hide nor sole leather of Sam wasn't to be seen. I was on the front steps. I heard the old speckled rooster crowing for daylight and went on in. I listened. Long Boy was still a-breathing. I chunked up the fire and put another piece of wood on. It hadn't burned down much since I left.

"Hit is getting up time," I said to Dora. She come out of the lean-to. And I took note of her hair. Then I looked toward the trundle bed and squeezed the root tight.

I wanted to go on and give it to Long Boy without talking to Dora. But I didn't know how to fix it—whether I should make a tea out of it, and how strong the tea should be made, and how much of it I should give Long Boy. And I took to blaming myself for not asking Big Sam, with Long Boy laying there, not eating or nussing. Dora had poured bean soup down his throat and held his nose to keep it from running back up. He was too weak to swallow.

Then I noted Dora staring at the root. "Hit's just like what

Little Sam had before," she said. "Big Sam made a tea out of it. In the mug, with the spout." Little Sam was what she kept on calling Long Boy.

I stood like the lightning had struck me. "Hit was a root?" I said.

"Big Sam biled hit—till it was red as the blood next a body's heart."

I grabbed the mug out of the three-cornered cupboard and let the root fall into it. "Get some water," I told her. "Fetch the bucket here." I put two gourds full in the kettle, watching it like a cat at a mouse hole. Long Boy whimpered and twisted and turned. I tried to hurry. But seemed like I didn't have any mind of my own. Like somebody else's head was onto my body. Making me move when it said move.

Dora poured the red stuff down Long Boy's throat and looked at me; but still I didn't tell her where I got the root. I thought she might start off on her rigamarole about God a-guiding them that had faith in him and that Big Sam was a man after God's own making and God had sent him there to care for her and all such stuff, till I might get mad again.

I never would a-left Dora in the first place if she hadn't harped so much about how good Big Sam was. Always naming him and God in the same breath, it seemed to me, like there wasn't any difference in them. Ma had warned me and talked against me traipsing off over here in Crockett County to marry Dora. But I wasn't able to help myself. Any more than a bird charmed by a cat. I reckon what first did it was Dora's hair. It was her hair I noted most and thought most on after I seed her the first time—at Happy Hollow church House. I was sparking Sara Martin. And I went with Martins in the wagon to meeting that night.

It was experience-telling night. Just happened to be. And Dora—of course I didn't know her at that time from Aunt Froney's goose—but Dora, she got up and told her experience. Said she wanted other folks to know what one good person could do.

She told as how her pa was an ill-tempered, contrarious man and how she took after him when she was a youngon and paid no heed to things her ma said to her. Till the Lord, when she was twelve year old, took her ma away from her. She made the Lord a promise that she would live right. But three year afterwards her pa died too. And left her over here on the hillside by herself with the woods all back of her and in front. Still she trusted in the Lord and wasn't e'er a bit afeared to stay—till Old John Toms come along and tried to harm her. After that she was afeared and went to live with her Uncle Sidney. Till he took to treating her like John Toms did, and she went back home.

But since she had seed meanness, she feared to live by herself any more and asked Bill Campbell and his woman to come live with her. Bill was good to her, and she somehow—she didn't know what made her do it save that she felt obleeged to him for his goodness—she took to laying down with Bill when they was out in the field together or in the barn loft.

Bill's woman, Lou, she caught on, and she raised Cain, of course. Bill moved away—away off somewhere where he hadn't been heard tell of since—and Dora was left by herself to have a youngon. Or would a-been if Sam Scott hadn't come along. Sam come along about three months before the youngon was born. He was a lone man in the world and had spent the last ten years of his life up in Virginia hunting for a gold mine that he had heard tell of. He hadn't found the mine but he had learned a heap of things from being off up there by hisself and he was a knowing man about herbs and animals and such.

Sam just happened to come by her house and stop on his way out of the mountains, not knowing where he was going. She seed that he was hungry and she set him down to the best she had—corn bread and cress sallet. And the first thing

she knowed she was telling him everything there was inside
of her to tell.

Sam looked like he didn't hold her to blame. He told he she
couldn't go on living by herself, and he made offer to live
with her—as long as she should have a need for him. And he
stayed. He was a crafty man and waited on her whiles she was
called to straw. The baby was born dead. Sam made a box and
wrapped it up and buried it for her, and she believed God sent
him—believed God had a way of working through some folks,
and Sam was one of them.

Every time Dora seed him help up a calf or work with a
sick sheep she thought on how good he was and she felt mean
and unpure herself, she said, and thought on her sin. Then
one day she was out hunting turkeys' nestes. She was crossing
that old rail fence—the one that cuts the Red Ridge off from
the deadning—and she seed a pile of leaves in the fence corner.
She thought maybe her old bob-tail turkey might have a nest
there. And she got down on her knees to look. There wasn't
any eggs, but after she got down it was hard to get back up.
So she just stayed. And begun praying to God. She kept her
eyes shut, but seemed like something passed over her face and
she seed God. And she couldn't help but note how much Him
and Sam favored one another. Sam and God.

She could tell from the look in God's eyes that He seed her
side and wouldn't hold any grudgment against her. She got
up and felt happy and hopped around over the rocks and
stumps like a fairy. And begun singing,

> O, glory, glory, glory,
> O, glory to the Lamb.
> Hallelujah, I am saved,
> And I'm so glad I am.

Till she found the turkey nest with eleven eggs in it and
went on back to the house. She had been at peace with God
ever since, she said, and felt like singing nigh all the time.
Then she started out,

> I'm happy when it's raining,
> I'm happy when it shines,
> I'm happy now in Jesus,
> I'm happy all the time.

The meeting crowd, they took it up and sung with her:

> O, glory, glory, glory,
> O, glory to the Lamb,
> Hallelujah, I am saved,
> And I'm so glad I am.

I was a sinner, of course, and was prone to laugh two or three times whiles she was talking; but something kept me from it. It was the way her hair shined and the way her voice sounded, I reckon. I punched the boy in front of me. "What's her name?" I asked him.

"Dora Hawkins," the boy said. "But she's a Christian now." And he giggled.

"She won't spark no sinner," the boy by the side of me said. "But I don't know whether it's for love of God or Sam Scott."

I don't know everwhat made me, but I took it into my head that I wanted to spark Dora. A feeling of hate for Sam Scott run through me every time I thought about it, and I thought about it all the next day.

I went to meeting again that night. Rode Old Doll and went by myself. But I didn't hear e'er a word the preacher man said, for all his yelling. I just set and stared at Dora, at her hair, the way it shined in the lamplight, like the dew in the sunshine of a morning, and the way it crawled around over her shoulders when she moved her head one way or tother. And the way her eyes looked when she was singing, happy as a bird and content:

> The widow was there and the orphan;
> God heard and remembered their cries.
> No sorrow forever in Heaven;
> God wiped all the tears from their eyes.

I stood by the door when the meeting was over. Dora come out behind most of the crowd and I caught her eyes.

"Howdy," I said to her.

"Howdy," she said back to me. And said it friendly.

"Is somebody with you?" I said.

"We rid in the wagon with Thompkins. Where's the balance of you'ns?"

"I rid horseback and come."

"I've heard Sara name you," she said. "How do you like hit over here?"

"I like hit a sight in the world."

"Hit was a good meeting tonight."

"I liked hit last night."

"You come back some more," she said.

That was all the talking we had with one another, but I was cross and contrarious as a hornet the next day—all day, and couldn't keep my mind on anything save on Dora. I kept seeing her hair shining in the lamplight—red. And I took to hating Sara, or almost hating her. When night come I went back to meeting. The preacher man did hard talking to the Christians that night. Told them they had to work with the sinners like the devil a-whipping out fire if they aimed to do any good with the meeting and have any professions made. So when he called for mourners all the Christians stirred theirselves about like tadpoles. Old Man John Swab made a bee line for me and asked me if I was a Christian. "No, sir," I told him. And the old man lit into talking. Then Sara, she come and took holt of my hand and set in on her spiel.

I hung my head down like a sheep-killing dog and let them all talk to me that wanted to talk. Till directly Dora come. "I allowed you was done already a Christian," she said. "Don't you want to be? Hit makes a body happy." I retch out my hand to her and looked at her hair. "Won't you just go give the preacher man your hand," she said, "and ask to be prayed for?"

I went. The preacher man showed me the mourner's bench
and tried to push me down on it, but I didn't take the mourner's bench that night. I waited till two nights afterwards—
after Dora talked to me again. Her hair breshed against my
face, and I thought of what the boy said about her not sparking a sinner, and I went.

I sat on the mourner's bench three nights straight hand
going with head bent down. Then got up and shook hands
with the Christians standing round and made out like I had
got religion. Sara run up and grabbed my hand and shook it
till I felt like a broke-winged hawk. Old Lady Martin shouted.
She jumped up and down and flopped her arms around like
a dying buzzard and screampt till you could a-heard her in
hell. "Praise the Lord! O, praise God!" she yelt. "My prayers
are answered. God answered my prayers. I knowed he would.
Glory! Glory! he's saved." Dora, she shook hands with me
and smiled. I smiled back at her. And everybody set into
singing:

> On Monday I am happy,
> On Tuesday full of joy,
> On Wednesday I've got the peace
> The devil can't destroy.
>
> O, glory, glory, glory,
> O, glory to the Lamb!
> Hallelujah, I am saved,
> And I'm so glad I am.

I sung it with them and got louder and louder and throwed
my head back and felt like I had got religion sure enough, or
almost got it.

When meeting was over I asked Dora if I could take her
home, and she said I could. I meant to say that little verse
about "Star light, star bright, May I see you home tonight?"
but I couldn't get it out so I just said, "May I see you home?"

I took holt of her arm and walked across the field with
her, talking about the meeting and the weather and how hot

it was in the meeting house at nighttime. Sam, he went on ahead. And when me and Dora come to the fence between Dora's field and Old Man Crockett's field, I turned my back till she could get over. But I heard the wire a-rattling and heard her say real low-like, "Aw, heck," and I couldn't help but look. I didn't mean to. But there she was—with her petticoat all cotched on the barbed wire. And her on top the fence a-rocking backwards and forwards. Seemed like it took me half of forever to get her undone.

I was plagued and didn't take holt of her arm any more. I just walked along, and she walked along. The moon was up—big and round and full. But I looked at the ground. Most of the time, I did. Save when her hair glittered in the light and I peeped up at it. Till we had gone a right good many paces. And Dora, she sort of laughed. It wasn't so bad being a Christian, I thought. I liked to hear her laugh. And I laughed too.

Ma took a tantrum when she found out I was sparking Dora. She allowed as how the pappy of her bastard youngon might kill me. Said it might not even be the man she laid it on, that Sam Scott might a-been hunting his mine in Crockett County instead of Virginia.

But I set my head on Dora and kept on courting her. Till the next protracted meeting. And then I asked her to marry me. I didn't name it to her about hating Sam, for Sam had always been mannerable and treated me right when I went there courting. I just asked Dora if she would have me. The night the meeting broke, when I was taking her home across the field, I just upped and asked her if she would. "I hain't never wanted to marry anybody else," she said, "save you." And sort of laughed. And we got Square Hawkins to marry us.

I come to live with Dora, and Sam lived on here too of course. He kept his mouth out of things and there wasn't any reason why I should have a grudgment against him. But I just somehow couldn't help being fractious when he was around.

Then one day Sam told Dora in front of me that he felt like he was a hindrance, and should maybe leave. But Dora told him she couldn't do without him. She needed him to draw water for her and to feed the chickens. She would need him worse than ever when the baby come, for she was called to straw. And she thought the time was nigh, from the way she felt.

It rubbed me the wrong way—her talking did. For I thought I was the proper one to hear such talk first. And somehow, I don't know why, I took to thinking on things Ma warned me of and I hated Sam Scott worse than a dog hates a snake. And glared at him and didn't say e'er another word to him.

Dora went on to bed. At first she slept sound. And then was restless. It come a storm soon in the night. A regular gully washer, with lightning and thunder. Dora didn't pay any mind to the storm, but a short while after midnight she woke me to say she believed the baby was coming. Somehow it struck me queer and made me mad too, her having a youngon on such a night. I couldn't go after Gertie Cocke, away over in Boone County, with the branches up. I couldn't even go after Old Lady Moore.

"Water is all over Creation," I told her. "Can't you put it off till daylight?"

But the baby come and Sam did the doctoring. I just stood and felt useless as a kitten and hated Sam worser.

I kept thinking on Dora's everlasting religion. And the way she spoke of God and Sam Scott. And the way she sung all the time about being happy on Sunday and Monday and Tuesday and Wednesday and Thursday and Friday and Saturday, Glory, Glory, Glory. And I couldn't help but think on the bastard youngon. I told myself that Dora had got religion since then and wouldn't so much as let me kiss her before we got married. But I claimed I had got religion too and hadn't. Ma might be right, I told myself—I would go home and talk to Ma. As soon as the branch went down I would go.

The next morning I went. Just told Dora I would go let Ma know about the baby and would be back. She looked up at me, and her hair fell down around the pillow, long and curly. Curly all over and frowzy. "Fetch me the comb afore you go," she said. I handed it to her and went out the door. I am proud—now I am—I didn't tell her to let Sam get it for her. Then I set in to wishing I could watch her comb her hair. I told myself Sam would set and watch her. Maybe comb it for her. Maybe he would. He would! Run the comb through it. Run his fingers up under it and feel the softness of it.

Ma, she was proud to see me come home, of course, and sided with me. Said the youngon might not even be mine. Said a dog never got too old to get pups. And she was proud I had enough gumption in me to come on back and let them and their religion have their way. After that, seemed like I couldn't handily go back as I had aimed to. Or half-way aimed to. So I stayed on.

Ma waited on me hand and foot, and I didn't ever want for anything. But soon I got restless as a jay bird. And couldn't be still. I couldn't work. And I couldn't stand to hear Ma talk, for it was forever something about Dora and Sam. Soon I took to drinking hard.

Then Sam Scott come a-riding. "Your baby's sick," he said.

"Why don't you and God cyore hit?" I asked him.

"Nigh to death," Sam said. "Or has been. And Dora, she's a-grieving." And he didn't say any more for a span. I didn't either. We just stood there looking at one another till Sam said I could ride the mule back and he would go through the fields, just take it slow a-walking. I stuck my head in the door and told Ma I was going and jumped on Old Beck and set out.

But I didn't know what to say when I first saw Dora. It was work doing up time, and she was out slopping the hogs. Had the baby in one hand and the slop pot in tothern. She poured the slop in the trough and stood and stared at me. Then she started towards me. I got down off Old Beck but couldn't say anything. Her hair. It made her look different—like a picked gander, almost.

"Is he—?" I said.

"Feel how fat he is."

She handed the youngon to me. I squez it tight as a turtle, for fear I might drop it. "He is so fat," I said. "What is the matter with him?"

"Hit was a breaking out. Gertie Cocke didn't know what hit was. But Big Sam cyored him."

I scringed when she said it. The same as throwing it up to me that Sam had and I hadn't, I thought. Sam and God.

"He's fat as a mud ball," I said. "And healthy looking."

"Who is that, Little Sam?—can you say 'daddy'?"

"Little Sam?" I said.

Dora didn't say anything.

"Is that his name?" I asked.

"That's what I call him."

"Dora," I said, "your hair."

"Hit was hot," she said. "And Big Sam hurt hisself getting the root—must have clum high and fell."

I didn't like Dora's crap-tail looks and I didn't like the way she kept on naming Big Sam, but I gritted my teeth and nussed the youngon whilst she got supper. I took note that she kept looking across the hill and down the hollow. And she kept on saying she felt uneasy in her mind about Big Sam. "You're going to stretch your neck off if you hain't careful," I told her. But still she kept on looking—till night come and she begun saying she heard death bells ringing in her ears. I didn't have a mind to go out in search of Sam. And we never did hear tell of him after that night.

I didn't have any short words with Dora for nigh six months and got so I set a heap a store by the youngon. I told Dora I didn't like Little Sam for a name and I took to calling him Long Boy, for he took so to growing. Dora called him Long Boy too. Sometimes she did. But she kept on naming Big Sam,

telling as how he come back after he had started off, took Little
Sam up in his arms and told him not to cry, he wouldn't ever
let harm come to him, and she went on talking about God working through Sam and how she still felt Sam nigh her. Till I
took to thinking she was grieving for Sam Scott and I took to
drinking again. Then one day I come in and found her setting
down in the floor singing to Long Boy:

> The gambler was there and the drunkard
> And the man who had sold them their drink;
> They were all surrounded together,
> Together in hell they must sink.

I took umbrage at it. I told her I didn't care any more for her
kind of religion than I did for her, which wasn't much.

She could take her God and go with Him, I told myself. I
could get notice from other women. And I started going back
over in Boone County and laying out with Sara. Two nights at
a time. Of course things went to wrack. Long Boy got to looking peaked and not being very anticky. About all he ever had
to do with me was to stare at me and say, "Where been?" It
made me mad to hear him say it. Seemed like every morning
when I come in from being over at Martins', then Long Boy
would stand and stare at me and say, "Where been? Daddy,
where been?" Dora went dirty and her hair stayed short and
stringy, like a crap-tailed hen, and she took to letting Long
Boy go ragged and dirty too.

Till I got sick of it and nigh puked everytime I set foot
in the house. "If you tried to be anybody," I told her, "you'd
keep the youngon decent looking and keep his nakedness
kivered."

"If you'd mend your ways and help some—"

"Who are you to be mending my ways?" I yelt at her.
"Don't everybody know what you are? You stood up in Happy
Hollow church house and told it to the whole country. Don't
deny that, do you?"

She didn't say any more to me. And never named it about me going to see Sara. Till I got to thinking maybe she didn't know it, so I upped and told her that night—when she said Long Boy was needing something, had been fretful for two days and dauncy about his eating.

"Get your God to come down and cyore him," I told her. "Or Sam Scott. I've got to meet a woman."

I come in a little before midnight and hadn't much more than got to sleep good when Dora woke me—just as I was dreaming. I dreampt that I was sick—bad sick and Katie was nigh ready to borrow the dough. The devil with a blazing stick was standing over me a-grinning. Just waiting for the last breath to go out so he could set the fire to me. The last breath was going— when Dora woke me.

"Hit's that breaking out again, Earl."

I didn't know what to do, for I somehow feared to fuss at Dora, after the dreaming. I told her she needed sleep—to go on to bed in the lean-to and I would watch after Long Boy. I set my head on keeping awake, of course, so's I would be ready to jump up if the breathing should change. But I couldn't help myself; and the first thing I did was to go off to sleep. It wasn't a real sleep either. But sort of an Indian sleep.

I was laying there in that shape, about half asleep and half awake, when I heard what sounded like somebody walking— coming in the door. But I wasn't awake enough to stir myself. "What the—" I said to myself sort of low down in me.

I could still hear Long Boy breathing. His breaths was coming and going and coming again. But still there was something that made me sort of just not easy in my mind. And I I opened my eyes. I fought to keep from opening them, for I was somehow afeared. I looked at the wall. Seemed like the firelight on the wall looked quare. I wished Dora was in the bed with me. I stared at the wall for a span. Then turned my head to look over in the direction of the trundle bed. And there it stood! I couldn't make out what it was. It wasn't exactly the shape of a man. But still it was almost—just a sort of cloud—like a body sees sometimes in the sky. Almost forming something—then breaking up, and almost forming something else.

All kinds of feelings went over me. I thought maybe Long Boy was dead. And this was a token of his death. Still, I could hear Long Boy breathing. Then my mind got all bumfuzzled, and before I could tell exactly what I was doing, I said: "Who are you?"

Right before my eyes, but so quick I couldn't see it, the cloud-looking stuff changed into a man—Big Sam. "I've come," Big Sam said. And his voice sounded like maybe it come from up above somewhere.

"What do you want?" I asked him.

"To cyore Little Sam."

"Hit's none—" I started to tell him—but caught myself. "I'll be much obleeged to you."

"There's a herb."

"Where?"

"I'll take you to it."

"I can't leave here," I told him. But all at once it seemed like the feathers in the feather tick begun moving around and around under me—like they was changing places with one another, and every time they changed places they left a space where they had been before and the space was filled with air and the air was pushing me up. And in a short span of time the side of the feather tick next to the wall was higher than the side I laid on. I felt it pushing me out by the littles. Till my feet was on the floor, and without taking e'er a step or doing anything save trying to hold back, I was going, following Big Sam.

Till we come to a place up above Mulberry Cliff. Away up high. But it was easy to climb the steep rocks. Sam went in front and I followed—my feet going to the right places without me having to make them go there. For when I looked there was no place for my feet to set. Till we come to the top. I looked back down, and it seemed if I should fall I couldn't stop till I hit the bottom of hell, it was so high and steep, with nothing sticking out on the sides of it but sharp pointed rocks. I seed the devil coming up the bank, jumping easy from one sharp rock to tother, looking at me and grinning. Then a man —Big Sam, it looked like, with a stick, keeping the devil pushed back.

But Big Sam was there with me. I looked at him. He pointed to a plant. It was a small, tiny plant. About like heart's ease, save that it had sort of star-shaped leaves instead of heart-shaped ones, with red veins running through them.

"Leave the plant," Big Sam said. "Just take the root—the big one thar." I pinched the root off—easy like. Big Sam started back down the cliff—like a feather floating in the air. And I found myself going after him. Sliding, or sort of sliding.

"Sam, I'm much obleeged to you," I said.

"You're quite welcome, I'm sure," Big Sam said. And that was all. And I hadn't asked him how to fix it.

But I poured the red stuff into the mug and took it over to the trundle bed. Dora come too. "To the spout," she said. "Just like Big Sam." I didn't take umbrage at it. She poured it down Long Boy's throat, and I took note of her hair in the lamp-light. "Hit's getting long again," I said, "hain't it?"

A WASP STING

I RECKON it has about all died down now. And I don't never aim to say e're a word about it. And I don't aim to nuss any grudgment against Elzie and Froney. But I'm just glad I didn't pick up that broom like I started to. If I had I don't know what might have happened. Ad would have been glad, I reckon. He would like to claim that I am a witch.

But I couldn't make out what in the name of creation Elzie wanted with me when I hyeard him holler that night. It was away after midnight when he hollered. I had been awake two or three times during the night and I thought it must be getting up towards midnight. I hyeard the dogs tear out at something. I hyeard Elzie scolding them and telling them to shut up. I tried to make out what could be wrong. I knowed Froney's time wasn't up for three weeks yet. And it come to my mind that she must have run into some bad luck. I had told Elzie that I would come when the time was ready but that if anything should happen beforehand that he could come after me. I was willing to do all I could for him and Froney, even if I did know Elzie didn't have any use for me. None of Ad's youngons by his first woman don't have any use for me, to hyear them tell it. But when they want something they always come to me. That just goes to show that they think more of me than they let on they do.

Then I hyeard him holler, "Hello." Ad, he knowed who it was and he got up and went out. I hyeard Elzie tell him that Froney wanted me to come over there that night and that she might want me to stay for a span. So I got up. Ad ast him if anything was about to happen. He said he didn't think so but that Froney just wanted me to come over there. Just wanted me to come.

He had brung along Old Beck for me to ride. I got on her and went back with him. I didn't ask him any questions on the way and he didn't tell me anything, save that Froney had got hurt a little by a cow. I thought he seemed mighty shut-mouthed about something. But I didn't keer to talk much either, so I just kept my tongue to myself too. And kept it still.

Hit was away up in the morning when we got over there. I got down offen Old Beck and went on in the door. Well, just as I started to step over the door sill I seed a broom laying right across in front of it. I started to stoop over and pick it up but somehow or nother something like a cold chill run down my back. It seemed like something just told me not to pick it up. So I stepped right on over it. I noticed Elzie kind of watched me like a cat when I went in, but I didn't one time think about them trying to test me out. I knowed that too was a test, or should have knowed, but I just didn't think.

I couldn't make out what had gone wrong. I went on over to the bed where Froney was. I thought she looked kind of sheepish like. But I didn't know for what. So I just said, "What's the matter, Froney? It hain't time yet, is it?"

She kind of looked up at me like she didn't know exactly what to say and she finally mumbled, "No, but a cow kicked me yesterday morning. And I thought I had better stay in bed for a span." And I seed that her face turned red and she looked like she thought she had done some harm to me and was sorry for it.

"Is that all that has took place?" I ast her. And I noticed
that she was mighty slow about making answer. But she finally
got it out. "Yeah, we just wanted to see what you thought I
ought to do."

I looked at her right straight like and I said, "Now, Froney,
there hain't no use in lying to me. Tell me what has took place."
So she upped and told me.

Froney and Elzie both ought to know for sure what ball
the thread was coming from. But I never am going to tell them
all I know. There hain't no need in telling them just for the
sake of making them know it for sure when they already just
the same as know it for sure. It would just make them feel bad
for me to go and tell them the whole truth. Of course they
done me low-down. But Ad brung Elzie up to be that way.
And poor Froney don't know any better. She is a half-breed
Melungeon and she don't have much mind of her own. She just
does what Elzie tells her to do.

But it was right funny—them thinking it was me when it
was Froney's own sister Mallie. Or I don't have any faith in
signs and eyes if it wasn't her that was causing the trouble.

Froney told me how it had all started. On a Monday morning she went out to milk Old Heif. That was just three weeks
before time for her to go to the straw. And that morning about
the time she had milked three or four streams, Old Heif turned
around and butted her over.

Well, she just went on back into the house and didn't try
to milk any more. She said she was afeared she might be hurt,
so she just stayed in bed all day. Well, when Elzie come in that
night Froney told him how Old Heif had done and he went
to milk. But Old Heif wouldn't let him come nigh her. She
just throwed her tail up in the air and bounced around over
them hills like a leaf in a whirlwind. He chased her till pert
nigh dark and finally he had to go down to the Collins's and
get one of the boys to come up there and help him with her.

They finally got her hemmed up in a corner and he started

milking her. He was just milking away not paying any attention when he looked down and seed that the milk was reddish. Then he tried all the tits and seed that she was giving bloody milk out of her left front tit. He stopped. He didn't know what to think. But that Collins boy told him Old Heif was bewitched and they would have to get the witch doctor. Elzie got on the horse and rode plumb down to old man Gulley's to get him to come and see the cow. Folks say he's a right good witch doctor.

Old man Gulley come and looked at Old Heif. They hemmed her up and he looked at her eyes. He said she was bewitched. That was it. So he shaved up a piece of silver money real fine and put it in a gourd of water and drenched Old Heif with it. He told them to milk the milk out on the ground for the next nine days. He said they could begin using it again on the tenth day.

He told them that during the meantime they mustn't loan anybody anything they had. And he said for them to make some bullets out of silver money and keep the rifle loaded with them so they could kill any kind of varmint that come around in the night. So Elzie and Froney got to thinking about it. They wondered who could be a witch and want to do them harm. And the first person Elzie thought about was me. Froney didn't tell me they thought it was me, but she told me all the rest of it and of course I could see that the broom had been put there to test me. Elzie just about recollected hearing Ad say he was leary of me. And Froney told me she recollected hearing her ma say that one way to tell a witch was to put a broom down across the doorway and a witch wouldn't step over it.

That was the reason Elzie come after me that morning. He wanted to see if I was the one. I am glad now that I didn't stoop down and pick it up like I started to. I don't know what might have happened.

The broom laid there for three whole days. Two or three men folks come during the meanwhile and there didn't any of them appear to take note. I just went on and done Froney's work for her and let on like I thought that was what they had come after me fur. Acted just like I hadn't cut my colt's tooth yet, I reckon. And that was what Elzie thought. But I couldn't help but notice how close they watched me every time I went out the front door. They watched me when I was setting by the fire too. That is another test, you know. If sparks jump out towards a woman who is setting around the fire, that woman is a witch. But neither one of them never has even to this day said a word to me about it.

But that morning of the ninth day, Mallie, Froney's sister, come up there. And when she got to the door she stopped dead still. Then she just retch down and picked up the broom and set it up in the corner on its handle. She ast Froney how she was and Froney told her she was feeling better. I never did say anything to Froney about it—about Mallie a-picking up the broom. Froney hadn't been looking that way when Mallie come in and she didn't notice her stooping down and picking it up. After Mallie ast all about Froney she said she had come to borrow the sifter if we done had the bread on for dinner. Froney told her we hadn't got it put on yet. Mallie just kept on wanting me to go on and get my meal sifted so she could take it home with her, said a hole had come in theirn. Froney made all kinds of excuses and directly she just out and told her that the witch doctor said for them not to loan anybody anything.

Mallie didn't seem to pay Froney no more heed than a deef man. She just went right on talking. Then Elzie come in and he wanted to know who picked up the broom. Nobody didn't said a word. Everybody just stood there and looked at one another.

I went on out. I didn't want to tell on Mallie. I would have almost druther had it packed on me than to have told on somebody else. But Mallie just kept a-staying and asking to borrow things. After the sifter she ast for salt and then meal and after

that she wanted some of them peaches that was ripe on that
tree out there in the corner of the garden. But Elzie and Froney
told her they were afeared for her to take them. So directly she
got up and started home. And for some reason or nother Elzie
got up and stood in the back door to sort of watch her out of
sight.

As soon as she got to the corner of the garden, she grabbed
a limb of that peach tree and was pulling it down so she could
grab a peach when Elzie hollered and told her not to. She sassed
him back but he went running down there and told her he
wouldn't mind her a-having the peach but that the witch
doctor said for them not to let anybody take anything off the
place, nor to loan anybody anything. So she just kind of looked
at him and he stood and watched her till she got onto her own
place. He come back into the house and looked at Froney real
quare like and Froney bust out to crying.

But I seed something I don't know whether Elzie seed or
not. I come might nigh a-asking him. But just as Mallie went
away from the peach tree all the wasps in that nest there in
the boxing of the house eve went to flying around and around
in a circle and followed her. They just went right along with
her, circling around her head.

Elzie told Froney it kind of looked like they had found the
witch, but Froney argued there wasn't anything to them tests.
But when Elzie said he thought there was something to them
Froney didn't say anything. She just laid there and cried. She
said anybody was likely to stoop down and pick up a broom
when she seed it laying in the floor in her own sister's house.

So neither one of them didn't say anything about it any
more. But that night just a little after the chickens had crowed
for midnight, we hyeard an awful commotion in the chicken
roost down there at the wood pile. Elzie grabbed his gun and
went running down there. He shot and he said he was pert nigh
sure he hit the varmint but it went running off. Said it looked
like a fox to him. He shot it with that silver bullet he had in the

rifle because that was what the witch doctor had told him to do. So he said whether it was just a common varmint or a witch, it looked like a silver bullet out of that old thirty-eight ought to kill it. And he believed it would go off somewhere and crawl in its hole and die. Or we might find it around there in the weeds close to the house somewhere where it had fell dead in its tracks. Elzie said he thought it was just a common animal, just a hungry fox like any other hungry fox.

The next morning Roy Collins, Froney's half-brother, come up there and brung the news that Mallie was dead. He said she had died a little after midnight. A wasp had stung her the day before and the only way he could make it out was that the pizen from the sting had went to her heart. Said the back of her dress was split and a wasp lit on her skin where the tore place in her dress was. And when she went to brush it away it stung her. The spot was at the edge of her right shoulder blade. He wanted me to come down there and lay her out. I hated to go and do it, but I went on and didn't say anything. And nigh her right shoulder blade there was a hole, big enough, it looked like, for me to stick my little finger into. And there was blood all around it. I didn't wash the blood off. I just washed around it. I got her burying clothes fixed as soon as I could and put them on her and never did say a word to a soul about it.

They took her up there on top of the hill and buried her the next morning. Nearly everybody in the country was there. And I don't reckon anybody ever one time thought anything. If they did they didn't name anything about it. They opened the coffin before they put her in the grave and let folks look at her. You know you hain't supposed to open up the coffin of a witch and let folks look at her. But Elzie and Froney was the only ones that didn't look at the corpse. They didn't budge an inch from where they was standing. Froney cried a heap when they put her in the grave and Elzie stood there with his head down and didn't look at anybody. I tried to get his eye.

But I don't believe he moved, even his eyes, the whole time they was burying Mallie.

Froney went on back to the Collins's to stay all night that night and Elzie caught up the horses and took me home. He didn't look at me nary time all the way there, and he didn't speak a word. When we got home he still didn't say anything, so I just clum down off Old Beck and said, "If you ever need me to help you out again, just let me know." He said, "Much obleege to you," and rode on off.

The Collinses never did have a funeral for Mallie. And everything about the cow being bewitched soon died down. I went back over there the night the baby come but there wasn't a word said about anythng like that. Elzie and Froney neither one wouldn't look me straight in the eye. They put me in the mind of chicken-catching cats the way they done. But I don't ever aim to tell them so. Hit does me a world of good that they don't know for shore.

THE PICTURE FRAME

CLAUDE talked about the pretty he would have for Annie when she come back. "Annie Lee will come back—she's bounden to," he said. "And bring the powder horn of money with her." And he kept on a-talking. He would have such a pretty for her, when she come, she never would want to see another Yankee flag. "For hit will be pretty —prettier than the picture—when I am done with it."

But he didn't name what the pretty was; and I didn't ask him. I didn't know—not for sure, I didn't—till that morning, when I found him—setting in the rocking chair by the side of the bed, holding the picture frame in front of him, in his hand like he was handing it to somebody. I seed the size of the empty square in the frame and knowed right off, or knowed in reason.

Ever since Annie Lee went off, Claude had worked up in the loft. I heard him hammering and sawing. But long as I was able to climb the stairsteps to make up his bed he kept a lock on the chest, the big one made from oak planks he lugged up the stairsteps one by one. He kept it locked all the time save, I reckon, when he was up there working, till I broke my hip and couldn't get up the stairsteps any more. Or thought I couldn't. Till that morning.

From time to time, and that right often, I seed him taking cedar—always it was cedar, I noted—roots and limbs and the little blue balls from off the trees up the stairsteps with him, and I heard him at nighttime, late into the night nigh every night, sawing and hammering. And on Sunday mornings I knowed he always, or nigh always, went down to the Diamond Hill, hunting the little glassy rocks, or ever what they were, that he called diamonds. And he would come in with his pockets full and take them on up the steps with him, whistling, thinking he was being dern about it, I reckon. Sometimes at night, all through the night, I would wake up and hear him hammering.

Then that morning I called and called and still he didn't answer and I set into climbing. There he was. With the frame. The diamond one just done, for the paste wasn't dry yet. I felt to see. And the others, all hanging round, covering up the wall almost and packed high in the corner. I retch my hand down into the powder horn, and there it was, the picture of the bird, with the flag in the corner. The Yankee flag marked out with the charcoal, and the Rebel flag drawed over to the side of it, crooked and ugly. I tried it in the frame. It fit exactly.

Dave Cocke is the only one that seed the frame. When he come to help me tote Claude down the stairsteps he seed it. And after I fastened the picture into it he put the frame in the coffin with Claude and fixed his hand on it.

Claude didn't ever say he wanted to marry Annie Lee or that he aimed to. And he didn't appear to grieve over losing the money out of the horn or hold any grudgement against Lep Callis even. He just talked about Lep turning her into a Yankee by his fancy drawings. That was what was most on his mind, seemed like. He was so sure he had her raised right. He would set and talk on it and blame hisself for flying off the handle about the picture, saying when she come back, as she was bounden to do, he would have the pretty for her, such a pretty no Yankee could ever equal. And it was pretty, with the diamonds, big and little, stuck into the cut-out places to make the

stars—and them a-shining. He said she would look at it, not
ever naming what it was, and turn into the Rebel he thought
he had raised her to be. As strong a Rebel as he was hisself,
he said, or maybe stronger.

For Claude was a real Rebel. A hot-headed one, Dave Cocke
called him. He was young—fourteen year old—when the Civil
War was fit. And he was Ova Russell's only youngon. His pa
went off a-fighting with the Rebel soldiers and Claude, somehow, he got restless as a jaybird at home, and he set out and
jined up too, with the same side, lying about how old he was.

He stayed in the war the whole time through and was six
more months a-getting home. He never did say why. But his
pa got kilt soon after he jined up and was buried off somewhere.
I don't know where. Ova got word of her man's death but she
never did hear anything from Claude. After three year went
by and still she didn't have e'er a word from him, she married
Josh Meigs. Josh had been off a-fighting too. On the side with
the Yankees.

Then Claude come in—six months after Ova and Josh got
married. It was hard for him to get it all into his head, so much
had happened unbeknownst to him and he was tired and wore
out and crippled in his right leg; and he somehow held grudgement against his ma for marrying Josh, he had took such a hate
to them that fit for the Yankees.

But him and Josh lived on in peace together till summer time
come. And one day Ova—not thinking, I reckon, or maybe not
knowing—hung Claude's uniform out on the garden fence to
air and hung Josh's blue one by the side of it. And Claude and
Josh, they took to jesting one another about the fighting. Then
they got mad, the both of them, and took to quarreling. The
first thing Ova knowed Claude was going at Josh like a biting
sow with fists a-flying and would maybe a-kilt him if Ova
hadn't got herself in betwixt them. Claude, he come on here
and stayed the night and talked to Ma. For Pa and Dave Cocke's

pa was about the only ones around here anywheres that fit on the same side Claude fit on.

Ma needed a man on the place, of course, for Pa wasn't fitten for work when he come home from the war, and in seven more months he died. So Ma told Claude she would be proud to have him come. She told him she would pay him fifty cents a day for the days he worked. And of course he would just live here like her own boy if she had one.

He went back home and told Ova what he aimed on doing. And when he started off she give him his pa's powder horn with the money in it and his pa's picture. "Hit's what your pa left when he went off," Ova said to Claude. She handed the things to him with his clothes and uniform in a meal sack, saying to him that his pa was keeping the money for Claude to start out on—to buy land of his own, to set up on, when he was ready for marrying. And told him how she hid it—in the churn—from the soldiers when they come by—the Yankees once, and the Rebels twice, she told him, both a-stealing.

Ma give Claude the room in the loft. And soon as supper was over at nighttime he went up the stairsteps, or generally always. And didn't have much to say. He didn't pay me any mind even if I was the only one left at home and was about twelve year younger than he was, but was in long dresses. He talked to Ma about the stock and the crops and sometimes about the weather. And clum the stairsteps.

Till Annie Lee was born. She was born about three months after Pa died. I had gone up the branch to the bend to pick a mess of cress sallet when Ma took sick. Before she could much more than get herself to the bed Annie Lee was coming. She knowed Claude was working on the fence over in the horse lot and she yelt to him. He come running to the house. "What's a matter?" he asked her.

"The baby's a-coming," she said. "Hand me the scissors from off the fireboard." He handed them to her and watched her cut the cord. Then he pitched in and did the rest. Like he was used to it, Ma said. He tied the navel cord and carried out the afterbirth and washed Annie Lee and put her hipin and her nightgown on her and stood and stared at her so that Ma asked him what he wanted to call her, and he named her Annie Lee. He put the Lee into it, he said, because Lee was the man he fit for in the war and Annie because she was the only person that ever made him feel needed. And then Claude claimed Annie Lee as his own. He nussed her on his knee at nighttime and changed her hipins and washed them and toted her around on his hip till I jested him about it, calling him a grannywoman and threatening to norrate it around through the country so he would be sent for. He didn't pay my jesting any mind and went on doting on Annie Lee. And bragging on her. He said she would be the Rebelest little Rebel in the whole world and the prettiest.

Annie Lee was pretty. When she was about nine year old she had hair that come down nigh to her knees, and was a bunch of rings around her face, and hung in rolls all down her back till she could set on it. It was red, light red, nigh the shade of copper, and her eyes was big and brown and trusting. Maybe if she hadn't been so trusting she wouldn't a-gone off with the wandering penman, if she went off willing. She had brown freckles across her nose and cheeks, but Claude said he liked the freckles because they put him in mind of the little Rebel girl that brought him the acorns when he got hurt off in the fighting. And he wasn't ever willing for me to put buttermlk on Annie's face for bleaching.

He was all the time learning her something. How to march like soldier men marched in the war or how to play eleven hand or club fist as his ma had showed him when he was little. At dinner time, nigh every day, instead of resting whilst the horses eat, he drilled Annie for soldiering. So I guess she stood the marching good when she went off. And he showed her all the ways he knowed to kill a Yankee, if she should ever have need to kill one. He named it after she left, saying she would manage Lep Callis and would come back, he knowed she would.

Annie Lee wasted nigh all her time a-following Claude—here and yon—like a pet deer; me and Ma didn't ever make her work in the house much. She liked to watch him make things—singletrees and axe handles and the little horses and baskets and dogs that he whittled for her—out of wood sometimes, and sometimes out of peach seeds. All his Sundays he wasted making things for her. She would stand and watch him and brag on him, on how pretty he made them out of wood. And I didn't think about her ever taking up wth any other man, from the way she talked to Claude and talked about him, bragging on his ways like she thought the sun riz and set in him.

At nighttime he played games with her and made her learn the counting-out rhymes even if there were just three of us to be counted out:

> Wire brier limber lock
> Three geese in a flock
> One flew east and one flew west
> And one flew over the cucoo's nest
> O-u-t spells out
> Stick your nose in a dirty dish clout,

he would count. And he always seed that I—I never could tell how—was the one to get counted out. Annie was always left to be It.

When Annie Lee tired from playing club fist and eleven hand, Claude took her on his lap and told her tales about the war till she went off to sleep, tales about how he marched in the rain for four days straight hand going without e'er a bite to eat save hackberries and black haws that he grabbed here and there from trees and bushes and how men lay a-dying when he passed by and would cry for a drap of water on their tongues and he would have to leave them there and keep on going. And about how Annie Lee put him in the mind of a little girl that come to see him every day whilst his leg was healing. He was in a big house somewhere with a lot of men that was groaning and cussing and dying around him. Once a week the doctor man come. And women folks that lived thereabouts brung things for the soldier men to eat. Other women and girls come to see all the men, but Mary Elizabeth Cain, that was the girl's name, she just come to see Claude. She brought acorns to play hull-gull with him and he set in the rocking chair with his leg stretched out in front of him whilst she told him about things she heard folks say, of how the war was going and where the men were hiding.

"Was she pretty?" Annie asked him.

"Pretty as a speckled pup," he said. "And a real Rebel."

"Did she have curly hair?"

"She had hit done up on the top of her head in knots."

Annie Lee jumped down and run off into the parlor, sulking. Then the next night when she come to get on his lap she had her hair done up on top of her head, tied here and there all over with calico strings, them sticking up blue and red and white. And an ear of corn to play hull-gull. He played with her. And learnt her to count. When they was tired of playing she put her arms around his neck and hugged him till she nigh choked the breath out of him and said to him, "Is my hair pretty done up?" He told her it was pretty and picked her up and toted her to the bed.

Claude kept the horn hanging above the bed, and every Saturday when Ma paid him he stuck the money down into it. He never touched it save when Annie begged him to count it with her. Then they would set down on the bed and pour it out into the place she patted down for it, and they would count it piece by piece, him making her learn what each piece was called and making her count it up in her head when they had it all poured out. "Hit hain't enough yet, is it?" Annie would say, like she feared it maybe would be. "Hit hain't enough yet to buy a place of your own, I know hit hain't."

And he would say no, it wasn't enough yet but soon would be. And Annie would say, "You don't want to go, do you?"

"Not and leave you here," he would answer, and she would run around him singing and jumping:

> Put my uttermoger in
> Take my uttermoger out
> Give my uttermoger a shake shake shake
> And turn myself about.

Claude didn't ever go off the place save sometimes hunting and sometimes to Jockey Town on the first Monday to bargain for a mule or cow Ma needed and sent him for. And he didn't ever buy hisself any clothes. Me and Ma patched for him and patched till his clothes was nothing but one patch on top of tothern. Once, shortly before Ova died, she come over here and spent the day and brought him a shirt and a pair of jeans britches she made. He put them on and took Annie Lee to meeting at Hollow Ground church house the next Sunday morning. They got there early, before anybody else got there. He led her up the aisle and set with her in the a-men corner. Directly the Knox girls, all three of them, come in and they sniggered, all of them did, and sniggered and spoke to Claude and took their seats behind him. Julie, she was the youngest one, she asked him if that was his little granddaughter he had along with him. And they all set into sniggering again. And giggling. Claude didn't give any answer. He just upped and walked out of the church house with Annie Lee and brought her on back home. He told Ma about it in the kitchen, saying a body couldn't expect any more from Knoxes for their pa fit with the Yankees and wouldn't a-fit with either side if the Rebels hadn't been about to catch him, and he got scared a-hiding out.

Annie never did go anywhere after that either. Nor spark any boys. She never did know any to spark. Nor go anywhere to see any. She just stayed at home, following Claude around in the field, taking him the hammer or the nails or the water jug or whatever he had need for. And standing in the gear room on rainy days watching him whittle, a-making things. Or gazing at birds. She liked birds and flowers. He took her on Sunday evenings a-walking in the woods and fields and they come back telling what they seed—the ivy, and the laurel and the cucumber trees blossoming. It was a sight in the world the way she liked the flowers. And pretty sunsets. And pretty dresses. Me and Ma never did get store-bought cloth for our dresses—we wore homespun; but we made Annie's of store-bought cloth. And always when I picked the calico for her a new dress I got a bright red or blue or something with pretty figures in it. And that was the only time she ever left Claude alone, was when me and Ma were making a new dress for her. She would stand and stare at Ma a-cutting and sewing and not take her eyes off it till it was done. Then she would grin and say, "Wonder what Claude will think of it?" She would put it on and run to meet him when she saw him coming. "Look," she would say, "hain't hit pretty?" And always of course he said it was pretty and told her she was pretty in it. And she would twist and turn. But she never would go to the store with me, not even to pick her own dress when she knew I was going for one. She wouldn't give any reason. "I just don't want to," she would say. "I hain't a-going."

And she didn't pay any mind to women folks that come to see us and asked her when she was going to start setting with the boys. She just grinned and shook her head and said she didn't know. She just kept on following Claude around, making him wait on her; for all she ever had to do to make him try to pull the moon down for her was to tell him he did it better than anybody else could do it. Claude would say, "A Yankee couldn't do hit, could he?" and she would say, "Not like you can—not nigh so good as you can do hit." Then Claude would laugh and pull her hair and call her his little red-headed Rebel girl. And try to find her strawberries in January if she asked for them.

Annie was fifteen year old when Lep Callis come to make the Family Record. He called himself a wandering penman, Lep did, and he toted a little pack on his back. In it he had a whole heap of pen staffs and pen points and pencils and a blue million jars of ink—all different colors. And different sizes of heavy paper to make his markings on.

Lep went through the country, from house to house, a-walking, and asked folks to let him make a Family Record for them. Ma, she let him make one for us. And it was pretty. It was so pretty Annie Lee left off following Claude and stood behind Lep, watching him all the while he was drawing on it.

He got it from Ma that Pa had fit in the war, on the side with the Rebel men. So in the middle of the paper, at the top, he made a flag, red with broad blue stripes running catacornered and crossing in the middle; and in the blue stripes he put thirteen stars—one big one in the middle where the stripes come together to make a square and three little ones running four directions out from it. Claude seed him working on it before he started off to his ma's, after he had got word Ova was bad off sick. And he named how pretty it was and said he would make a frame for it out of cherry or cedar maybe, when he come back. Then he went off and was gone six days, for the burying and all, before he come in.

At the left hand top corner of the paper Lep drawed a bird —a dove it looked like with a letter in its mouth—and writ the word LOVE on the letter in the place where the backing generally goes; and in the right corner he made two hands a-clutching one another. Down to the left side of the paper he put the births in pretty writing and in the middle the deaths so far. Down the right hand side he wrote the marriages. Wrote them in the fancy long-tailed writing. And in the right hand corner at the bottom he made a big bird carryng a baby by the hipin so that the Record was the prettiest thing Annie ever seed, and she just set and stared at it and stared. And he kept on a-talking to her.

He asked her when her name was going to be writ on the marriage side, and it plagued her. But I could tell it pleasured her too, from the way she laughed. And he named it about her hair being red. Said he liked red hair. And he took to asking her riddles. Asked her the one about the old woman that didn't have but one eye and Annie couldn't rede it. But she wanted to show off in front of him, I reckon; and she asked him that mixed up one about going out to view her hicktickle, hecktickle, pracktickle present, and Lep laughed all over hisself he thought it was so funny and told her she was smart. "Sharp as a razor," he told her, and she come back into the kitchen smiling, saying what pretty words Lep used. Once she even said Claude didn't know as many funny things as Lep knowed to tell. She also said the side Lep was for in the war won the fighting.

Lep kept on a-staying. He stayed four nights after he was through with the Record. Ma didn't say anything to him, but she named it in the kitchen to me and wondered what he was staying for. She said she had begun to take a dislike to his mustache, so short and so black. And I don't reckon she noticed herself, but she took to singing the last verse of that little old song:

> Now girls beware of my sad fate
> And do not be so rash.
> Just leave alone those gents who wear
> A little black mustache.

But Lep kept on a-staying. He named it several times about Annie Lee's hair being pretty, and her eyes. He said he would like to draw a picture of her. Said he could do it for ten dollars and make her hair and her eyes both the color they were. Annie wanted it made, of course. And she took to begging Ma. But Ma put her foot down against it, saying she couldn't afford to have it done that year but maybe could the next year when Lep come through, if he come through.

Annie, she set into bawling, right in front of Lep. He run

his hands through her hair and said he would make it next year, for she would be more prettier next year. "Prettier than you are now even," he told her, and said he would draw a picture of a bird and give her to recollect him by. And he set into drawing.

Annie watched him whilst he worked. I kept around in earshot. "Get up here closer to me," he said to her. "So I can draw it better." And Annie stood up close. Once he stopped and put his arm around her—around her waist—and didn't hold it there long. Annie, she didn't offer to move away from him. I didn't ever tell Ma. He begged her to go down to the spring with him but she wouldn't. "Why?" he said. "I just don't want to," she said. "I hain't a-going."

When he got done with the bird and handed it to Annie she stood with it in her hands smiling and saying, "Wonder what Claude will think of it?" Then Lep took to teasing her about the way she liked the hired man. "He hain't no hired man," Annie said back to him. "He's got a whole powder horn full of money to buy hisself a place with."

"I'll bet he keeps his money hid in the ground?"

"Keeps hit in a powder horn his ma give him with his pa's picture in the bottom of it—a horn his great grandpa toted to King's Mountain. And he keeps hit over his bed. With heaps of money in it."

Then Lep took to talking to her about going off with him. He didn't say anything about marrying her, not in my hearing. He just talked to her about going away with him when he went. Said he would take her away to his big fine white house—he didn't name where it was—and she would have a new dress every week and wouldn't ever have to turn her hand to do e'er a lick of work. She set staring at him in wonderment, her eyes wide and blinking; and the words, the way he put them together, they did sound pretty. I didn't tell Ma, for I didn't think of her going and I feared Ma would get bothered and make Lep mad or something.

As soon as Lep got done drawing the bird he went into the parlor. He put red and green and blue and all colors of feathers on the bird and made it with its bill open and one wing flopping down like it was preening itself in the hot sunshine. Annie was proud of it, of course. In the top left-hand corner of the paper he put the flag. A pretty flag with red and white stripes and a blue square in the corner with white stars in it. I didn't think about it being a Yankee flag. And I reckon Annie didn't either. She was proud as a peacock of it and went running to Claude that night the first thing when he come in the door. She went up to him with it in her hand and said to him, "Look, hain't hit pretty?" He just stared at it. "You'll make me a frame for hit, won't you?" she said.

"Did little black mustache give hit to you?" he stormed out at her.

"Lep made hit for me," she told him. "You'll whittle me a cedar frame, won't you? With fancy doings on hit—maybe diamonds?"

Claude didn't answer. He jerked it out of her hand and whirled around and went stalking up the stairsteps like a mad boar. And Annie set into bawling again. Lep called for her to come in the parlor and talk to him. She went.

Claude didn't come down the stairs to eat his supper—just hollered back and said he wasn't hungry. And the next morning when he come down me and Ma done already knowed, and Ma looked up and told him. "Annie's gone," she said. And he just stood there stiff as a poker.

Then he set out to searching, far and near. But all we ever heard was that two men out tracing their trotlines below Grangers' on the Nolichucky River had seed a boat go down the river some time after midnight.

The next day when Claude went to put the pay Ma give him into the powder horn he found the balance of the money gone. The horn was hanging with just his pa's picture in it. He said he took the bird and stuck it there too. He told me that. He never did tell Ma. And I didn't either, for she blamed herself for not waking when Annie Lee got out of the bed with her.

Afterwards Claude wouldn't take his pay on a Saturday evening. Ma tried to force it on him. But he just said he didn't have any need for pay. And he didn't seem e'er a bit bothered over losing the money. He just mumbled about Annie being a traitor and a turncoat and blamed hisself for flying off the handle and grabbing the picture, saying she wouldn't a-left if he hadn't.

Then he took to talking on how things would be when she come back. And him and Ma seemed right eased in their minds from the talking. He told Ma about the pretty he would have for Annie when she come back, something prettier than the picture, such a pretty she wouldn't ever want to see anything made by a Yankee.

But soon Ma died. And Claude lived on here with me. I didn't name any trade with him and he didn't name any with me. He just stayed on and did the work as he had been a-doing. And late in the evening, nigh every evening, he would stand out on the porch looking up the hollow, like he expected to see her cross over the stile in the woods lot. Sometimes he talked about her. Even when he got old and I got old, too, he kept on talking. And blaming hisself. He just worked and come in and looked up the hollow and went to the loft.

When I got so I couldn't climb the stairsteps I sent clean sheets up for him to put on his bed and he seemed glad, almost, I couldn't come. Once I asked him what he was working on so hard at nighttime, and he said: "Something Annie will think prettier than the picture, something that will make her a Rebel again soon as she comes."

Then one morning I yelt to him and yelt and yelt and still he didn't answer. So I got up the steps by the littles. There he was in the rocking chair by the bed. And all the frames. And the one in his hand still, with the diamond stars a-shining through blue balls. The place in the middle, the square where the big star belonged, was empty. The picture fit into it. And it was pretty, the frame was—a sight prettier than the picture.

THE TURKEY'S FEATHER

EVERY time I think about the feather I take to giggling. Even with Jake in his grave I still giggle. Aunt Mayme said it wasn't the feather that charmed Jake, it was the giggling. But I don't know. I just know he wasn't bothered with the witches any more and wasn't ever sorry for marrying.

For I set my head on marrying Jake from the first time I seed the log house, here at the head of the hollow, with three oak trees a-shading it and the rock-lined well built up high and covered. And I tried everything I knowed to try on Jake, from baking cakes and pies a-plenty to wearing a red and yellow dress with neck cut low. Aunt Mayme said it was a waste of time, for Jake wasn't a marrying man. And it did look awhile like she was right· for the more sweet things I cooked and the more I put cow piles and cucumbers on my face for bleaching, to make him talk on marrying, the more he talked on the weather, and crops, and witches.

I never had seed Jake till the day Aunt Mayme brought me over here when his ma lay a corpse. He just stayed back at the head of the hollow and didn't ever get out save to go to

Golden Gate store sometimes, I reckon, and that not often. He kept hisself busy waiting on his pa and ma, and age slipped up and he was old before he knowed it. Leastwise three times as old as I was. But his pa died, and then his ma, and left him here with just the witches, or what he thought was witches. And me on yan side of the hill.

I was fifteen year old and hadn't seed any boy I wanted to marry or e'er a one that had asked me to. But I didn't like it living with Aunt Mayme. I had had to live with her ever since Pa got killed off fighting against the Rebels and Ma took sick and died. So when I saw the house with the white ash chairs and iron cooking vessels in it and the beds with the spokes all carved out fancy and the washstand with the little rooster cut out into the drawer, I set my head on keeping it and cooking in it, it was so pretty.

And after the burying I went up to Jake and told him not to stay over here in the hollow all the time by hisself and eat man cooking. "You just come to our house," I told him. And he took right off to coming. Come every Sunday. But he didn't give me any courting talk when he come. He just set and talked to Aunt Mayme about the witches, for he was having trouble with his hogs. And Aunt Mayme was forever having trouble with the sheep. So they set and talked about the crops and the weather and the witches.

Me and Aunt Mayme had some chairs there that we made out of hickory limbs—without skinning and dressing them. Just bowed and bent and twisted the hickory limbs around till we had them in the shape of chairs. With arms on them and fancy doings on the bottoms of them. There was one chair set on one end of the porch and one on tother end. And Jake, he would come over on Sunday by an hour before midday, before I could get ready to save my soul, and he would holler, "Hello."

"There's Old Man Gregg again," Aunt Mayme would say. "Dorthea, looks like you could spark a young man."

"Better an old man's darling than a young man's slave," I would tell her.

"You'd think it was me he was sparking," she would say: "if he means to be sparking—he may just crave woman cooking."

But Aunt Mayme would go to the door. "Howdy, Jake," she would say. "Come in and get you a cheer. Don't mind about the mud. The porch is done gormed up."

Jake would set down in the chair over on one end of the porch and Aunt Mayme, she would set down in the chair on tother end. And they would set there and hunt up in their heads for words to yell across to one another. For nigh two years they set and talked about the witches and Jake didn't name marrying to me. Nor anything much, not noticing even when I come to the door. Then I took to putting buttermilk and cow piles and cucumbers and mashed strawberries on my face to whiten it and made my dress—my Sunday one—low in the neck, and I crossed my legs and named the fire when I made it and broke mullein leaves and all else that I had heard tell of, even asking Gertie Cocke's ma if she knowed love root when she seed it. But Jake still kept his mind on the weather and the witches.

Till one day I thought on what Ma said. I heard her tell it before she died: when a girl wanted a man to marry her she should put a turkey gobbler's tail feather in his chair seat.

So, on a Sunday morning, when Aunt Mayme was gone to meeting, I caught up her old bronze gobbler and pulled out the biggest tail feather he had and put it in the chair Jake always set in, over on his end of the porch. And afterwards, somehow, I took to resting easy in my mind. And didn't bother about the cow piles and cucumbers any more.

That evening Jake come like general and set down and started talking to Aunt Mayme about potato bugs and kept on talking about the potato bugs until I come to the door, all dyked out in my red dress made out of Scotch flax spun up into fine threads and wove together right and colored with madder—the leaf and flower boiled together so that it was bright. And cut low in the neck.

I strutted out in my red dress, knowing I wasn't pretty, of course, with my long red nose and ears that flopped down at the top. But I was strong and healthy. I come to the door and stood there. "Howdy, Jake," I said to him.

"Howdy," he said back to me. I looked toward Aunt Mayme and giggled. I never had been a giggling girl and Aunt Mayme looked at me hard as a hornet. "Why don't you set down?" she said. And I went over and set by her. Just set there. And directly Aunt Mayme said: "How is your corn doing, Jake?"

"I've done laid it by," he said. "I think I'll have a yieldy crap this year." And he looked over at me and crossed his legs and uncrossed them and looked out across the hill and said, "Did your ewe get well, Mayme?"

"She got all right ater I cut the spell by biling milk in the skillet and pecking on it with a butcher's knife. But for a span I thought I was going to have to have Lige Bledso doctor her. Lige is counted the best witch doctor in these parts."

"I wouldn't have him as long as I could keep spells off myself," Jake said. "For they say he's turned roguish."

"I have heard a few things of late. Heard Old Lady Russell say his musket is big. Said it takes a whole dollar to make one bullet. But I always had faith in him."

"There are them that are dubious of him. Some say he don't use that dollar in the musket."

"Hit's getting to the place where you can't put any trust in anybody," Aunt Mayme said.

"Might as well have witches," I said, and giggled, "as to have doctors that are as bad."

"Never heard of sech," Aunt Mayme said. "He might well be in cahoots with them."

"I hain't had no trouble since I cast that spell off my old red sow," Jake said, "by getting in the branch up to my knees and elbows at midnight and praying."

"Seems like we can't never get shet of them," Aunt Mayme said, "and I knowed it would commence again when Dorthea started courting, for old Malissie Kling has ever had a spite on Dorthea's ma's folks."

I tucked my head and giggled, and Jake looked out into the yard not seeming to hear Aunt Mayme, and he said, "Your chickens are pretty, Mayme—are they laying much?"

"They are laying a right smart," Aunt Mayme said. "Dorthea has a sleight at chicken raising. I let her tend to them."

I giggled and looked at Jake and just set there. Till directly the sun started going down behind Lead Hill and Aunt Mayme said to me: "Hit's milk time, Dorthea." I got up and got the piggin. And started after Old Heif. I hung the piggin up on the gate post and started across the cow field without saying e'er a word to Jake, and he set there like a lump on a log, the way he did every Sunday evening. Aunt Mayme stared at him.

Jake, he set till I got halfway up the hill. "Believe I need some walking," he said to Aunt Mayme. The first time he ever said sech. Aunt Mayme didn't say anything. But told me afterwards, of course. So Jake got up and stretched his arms and yawned like a kitten—save he wasn't as easy and quiet about it. "Hit's getting away up into the shank of the evening," he said. "Don't seem like it ought to be that late." Aunt Mayme just set. Jake looked at her, then looked at me climbing the hill. "Believe I'll follow," he said. And he stretched and yawned again. Aunt Mayme said he was afeared to go across the hill for fear of spiling his Sunday shoes. For Aunt Mayme thought Jake was a tightwad. "So tight he squeaks when he walks," she said. And kept on saying it till I said I didn't like it and told her she was wasteful as a storm; and we had hard feelings at one another.

But Jake got up and started towards the gate. Sort of like a broke-legged snake, Aunt Mayme said. "Hey, Dorthea," he hollered, "wait a minute." I turned around and giggled. And waited for him. We went up the hill together—him walking

away over on one side of the ditch and me on tother side. Till
we got out of sight of Aunt Mayme. Then he sidled up close
to me. Sidled up close and I looked down at the ground and
giggled. He asked me if I liked to milk and I said I did, of
course. And about that time I run into a spider's web. I looked
at it close. And there it was, plain as the nose on my face, a *D*
wove in it. My initial in the spider's web. That meant good
luck.

"You are a good cook," Jake said.

I giggled and tried to stick my toes in the soft ground and
said: "Aunt Mayme says I learn right fast."

And I told him about the quilts I had pieced—the Lone Star
and the Log Cabin and the Tulip and the Lover's Knot. And
how I never got my belly wet when I was washing—I wouldn't
ever marry a drinking man. And I told him I could spin and
knit and weave, and about the Gentleman's Fancy kiverlit I
had wove and how warm they would be to sleep under at
nighttime. And he said, "You are strong and healthy." I stuck
my toes down into the ground and giggled and waited for
him to say more but he didn't say it, and we went on.

We drove Old Heif up to the gate and Jake stood and looked
on while I milked the milk out into the piggin. Then he followed me to the house. And he set in a chair on the back porch
while I strained the milk out into the crocks and holp to set
the table with supper victuals. Then I come to the door like
general and told Jake supper was on the table. "Come in and
fool your face," I told him.

He said he wasn't hungry, and he uncrossed his legs. "You
better come and eat," I said. "We don't have much. But if we
make out on it all the time you can once."

"I'll be heading toward home," he said. Then Aunt Mayme
come to the door. "Come on in and eat a snack, Jake," she
said.

"No, much obleeged to you," he said. "I wouldn't care for
any."

"Well, come and watch us then," Aunt Mayme said.

"I'll be getting over the hill soon."

"You better eat," Aunt Mayme said. "For you'll get hungry before midnight."

And Jake got up and come in the door and laughed like he did every Sunday night. I giggled, and Aunt Mayme's nose got redder. And her belly went up and down till I thought the house was going to fall with all the jolting.

Jake set for a spell after supper a-talking about the witches still and not naming e'er a thing about marrying. But I could tell he was restless, from the way he twisted and turned in his chair and grunted. And Aunt Mayme noted it too, saying he got the fidgets every time he set down; and she looked at me like an owl a-blinking.

The next Sunday evening it was raining like cats and dogs a-fighting and we had to set in the big house all evening for the rain was blowing in on the porch and the air was coolish. I brought Jake's chair in and left the gobbler's feather stuck under one of the cross pieces like I had it.

Jake was restless as a sick baby from the time he set down. He set awhile and told about Old Doll, the best horse he ever had, he said, a-getting bewitched and dancing. She couldn't eat nor sleep for dancing, first on her hind feet and then on her front feet; then on all four feet at once, he said. Then he got up and went to the window and looked out at the rain. He went out on the entry to get him a drink of water. Then he come back in again. And crossed his legs and uncrossed them. And scratched his head and rubbed his chin and kept on rubbing his chin till I feared he would rub all the skin off. But he still didn't get it out, and I had to use the feather again the next Sunday.

That Sunday it rained all day again. A cool rain, for it had frosted during the week. And was turning into fall. Aunt Mayme spoke of it when it come time to start dinner. "Jake shorely won't come out in this weather—with his suit and shoes," she said. I didn't say anything.

I dropped a glass on the floor kerwhollop. It rolled over and didn't break. "Good luck," I said and giggled. Aunt Mayme grunted. "All signs fail in dry weather," she said. And drawed a long breath like she was tired and wore out from waiting. I looked out at the rain.

And before we much more than got set down to the table there he come. Dripping like hot butter he was so wet. His clothes sticking to him like bark on a tree, a-showing up his long legs. It was a sight to see.

"Hello," he hollered.

"The fool," Aunt Mayme said.

I went to the door all dyked out in my red dress again. "Howdy, Jake," I said, "Are you wet?"

"Not much," he said.

"The rain has blowed in on the porch," I said. "Come on in here where it is dry."

"Hit is shorely a gully washer."

"We're eating dinner. Come in and eat with us."

"Much obleeged," he said. "But I went through the motion before I left home."

"You're wet plumb through and shaking like a leaf. Is it cold outside?"

"Hit is coolish—when a body's clothes are dank."

"I'll build a fire and thaw you out."

I bent and puffed and blowed and fanned. And I didn't even name the fire to see if he loved me. Maybe I didn't care to know. What I needed was a man to give me a house to live in. I didn't need sweet talking. And I knowed the shaking wasn't from cold. Or knowed in reason it wasn't.

"You better come and eat some more," I kept saying to him.

"Much obleeged, I wouldn't care for any more," he kept saying back to me.

He went to unlacing his shoes, and I went to the kitchen.

Aunt Mayme went into the big house to talk to him. "Anybody that hain't got any more sense than to get out in this rain ought to take the fever and die," she said.

"That's right," Jake said. "A body ought to, shore enough." For Jake could take teasing. He was tall and ugly. Because his pipestem legs were too long for the rest of his body and his nose was too long for the rest of his face. But he was a good man. And had a good house. And I wasn't ever sorry.

Jake stuck his feet nigh into the fire. He twisted and turned and fidgeted ever which a-way. First one way and then tother. But he was dried out pretty well when I come in. And was putting his shoes on. Of course I seed what he was doing. And I giggled. He was plagued red as a beet and twisted and turned some more. Then he said, "I gathered a whole pocket full of chestnuts as I come on. Let's play hull-gull."

"In the rain?" I said. "You stopped and picked them up?"

"Yeah," he said. "I guess I don't have any more sense than a loon. Sometimes I think old Malissie Kling's pestering me. Had sech a feeling last night, so that I wished I had somebody in the house with me. Hull gull?"

"Hand full," I said.

"How many?"

"Eleven," I guessed and got it right and he had to hand them all over to me. And said he had to hand things over to me the rest of his life. Laughed and told that to folks. Even towards the last, when folks come in to see him. Said when I come all the other witches left him alone, for when I got through with him there wasn't anything for the witches to bother. And I thought on the feather and giggled to myself. But I never did tell him about it.

He set in his chair for a short span. Crossed his right leg over his left leg. Then his left leg over his right one. Looked into the fire. Got up and stood with his back to it till I was afraid the seat of his britches was going to catch a-blaze, they were so hot and smoking. Then he got up and went to the door and watched the rain awhile. He grunted, and then started humming a tune:

Hey, boys, keep away from the girls, I say,
And give them plenty of room;
For when you are wed they will beat you till you're dead
With the bald-headed end of a broom.

"Hit's a bad day, hain't it?" I said.

Jake just stood. After a span he jumped and turned round, quick, like a partridge. "Did you say something?" he said and looked at Aunt Mayme. "No," Aunt Mayme said. "No, I didn't say anything."

"I reckon I'll be next for the witches," he said. "Old Doll— and last night I couldn't sleep, fidgeted all night long tossing and turning." He set down and rubbed his right hand over his cheeks awhile. And pulled at his beard. Then took his thumb and forefinger and pushed it up and down, his legs sprawled out. He got up and went out into the entry again. Aunt Mayme looked at me. And I looked at Aunt Mayme. Then Jake come back into the room. And I crossed my legs.

He stood up by the fireboard awhile and played with the string of peppers. Wropt them around a string of shuck beans. And got them so tangled they was worse to undo than a witch's knot. I thought he would never get the tangles out or that he would break the strings before he did. "Hit is a bad rainy day," he said.

"But Old Heif's bag fills rain or shine," Aune Mayme said.

"I'll go ater Old Heif," Jake said. "Hit's too bad for Dorthea."

"She'll have to do worse before she dies," Aunt Mayme said.

Jake looked at Aunt Mayme. I went and got the piggin. Pulled off my red dress and put on the gray one. I hung the piggin on the post and started, leaving the gate open. Jake looked at Aunt Mayme again. "Believe I need some more walking," he said. Aunt Mayme didn't say anything.

"Wait for me, Dorthea," Jake yelled. I giggled and yelled back at him:

"Last one through
Knows what to do—
Shut the gate
And latch it too."

I giggled again, and we went up the hill, me walking on one side of the ditch and him on tother side. As soon as we were out of sight of the house Jake held his arm out across the ditch. "Here, jump across to this side," he said. I held my hands behind my back and jumped. "You've got strong hands," he said.

"That comes from chopping out corn," I said.

"Look, they are nigh as big as mine, hain't they?"

"Uh huh," I said. And giggled. And kept my hands behind me.

"Where did you get that dress?" Jake said.

"I made it," I said and tried not to giggle.

"You look stout and workified in it," he said. "But I like to see you in the red one." And he looked at the sky. He hemmed and cleared his throat. And took a chew of tobacco and spit it out and took another chew. And spit the juice out in front of him. He looked up and the rain poured down in his face. He stopped still as a stone. And just stood there looking up. Like an old gander a-looking. I went on a pace. And turned and looked at him. "Hain't you a-coming?" I said.

"I want you to marry me," Jake said.

I stopped too. And stood. And giggled. And squshed the mud between my toes.

"You mean marry you?" I said.

"Go home with me and live with me and cook," he said.

I just stood, and he stood. The rain come harder. "I'm getting souzing wet," I said. "Why don't we hunt Old Heif?"

"Oh," Jake said. We started on. "Will you?" he said.

"Will I?" I said.

"Marry me," he said.

"I don't know," I said.

"Why?—" he said. "I'll make you a good living."

"Aunt Mayme would be took back," I said, and giggled.

"The rain is good on crops," he said.

"Uh huh," I said.

"If I could just get shet of the witches bothering the stock."

I giggled again at that.

"Look at the corns on my hands," he said.

"Uh huh," I said. And tucked my head and toes.

"Feel how hard the corns are," he said.

"Huh uh," I said and giggled and wouldn't tech the corns.

"My hand could mash yourn," he said.

I kept my hands behind my back. We walked on after Old Heif. Every time Jake got the least smidgin closter to me I sidled off. And I giggled when Old Heif stopped and shook one of her hind feet.

"She is putting bad weather behind her," Jake said. "So we'll have a good day for it."

"For what?" I said.

"For marrying," he said.

"When?" I said.

"Tomorrow," he said.

"Tomorrow?" I said and thought on the feather and I giggled and giggled.

But Jake never was pestered by the witches again. And I still giggle. Every time I think about the feather I take to giggling.

FOR LEAD

CRINGED as I felt Pony drawing his arm tighter around
my waist. "We could have plenty," he said. "Your ma
could live with us, Nettie. It would save her a lot of worry
about having enough to eat and sech."

I squirmed and didn't pay much mind to what Pony was
saying. That light! I had seed it before. Several times since Pa
died. At night. I had seed it start up over there in our lean-to
where Pa used to keep the lantern. The same light. It always
come on through the house. Hit looked for all the world just
like somebody—well, just like Pa, swinging a lantern along.
I had watched it several times. It had come through the woods
every time. Yeah, right towards that old gooseberry hill on
Pony Pangle's place.

I never had tried to follow it. Never had thought I ought to.
I never had wanted to go towards anything that belonged to
Pony Pangle. He used to try to spark Ma before Ma got married. But Grandma had put a stop to that. She had made Ma
go on and marry Pa. The old folks thought Pony was too
young for Ma anyhow. Cradle robbers, that was what girls
was called that married boys younger than theirselves. And,

more than that, Grandma knowed Pa had lead he could make things out of. Lead was heavy and added weight to things.

But that light over there. The same light. I was shore it was. Shore as a preacher. I wished Ma hadn't made me come on that old possum hunt with Pony Pangle. But Ma was sick and I couldn't afford to contrary her too much. Awful sick. Consumption taking her away by the littles. She couldn't hold out agin it much longer. Not much. It seemed that the old cyores like smoking dried jimpson leaves didn't do her any more good than drinking hot sassafras tea. So I thought I better come on with Pony just to pacify Ma. I kept wondering when the rest of the crowd was ever coming back and wished to Harry they would make haste.

"I'd about as soon try to hug a icicle, Nettie, as to try to hug you," I halfway heard Pony saying.

But I didn't care what he said. I wished he would keep his blamed hands to hisself. I couldn't halfway think with him pestering me that way. I wished he would just go to grass and eat mullein. I hated him anyhow—hated him worse than a chigger hates liniment. He had been running with them old Jarnigans most of his life. Just the same as sanctioning Pa's killing. He just acted like he was about half glad when Pa was buried. But then Ma acted that way too. Ma never did set anything a store by Pa. She just worked for him and slept with him and got a living for it and that was about all. But I reckon that was as much as any woman got. Maybe that was as much as they needed.

But I did wish the crowd would get together again. This was the way possum hunts turned out. One couple would get lost. Then another couple would get lost. And couples kept on getting lost till there wasn't but one couple left. But to have to be out with Pony Pangle. And on his own place too. He didn't have any more mind to hunting possums than a persimmon did. I knowed in reason he didn't. I knowed what he had in mind. He just thought he could treat me any old way while he was on his own place. His old whiskers and his old fishy grin. He put me in the mind of a groundhog that a pole-cat had stunk up. I had druther a-been by dung and forty miles from water than to be setting out there with him. I wished—but then I just couldn't keep my mind off that light. That was bound to be somebody toting it. Bound to be. A man. Setting the light down on the bank of that gulley. I could see him—good. As clear as day. He had a mattock in his hand. The light shining right on him. Oh, it was him. Pa! I hoped Pony didn't see him.

"Let's go, Pony," I said. "The rest hain't got any more idea of coming back than the sun has of raining."

"We need to set here and rest a span. I've got a hankering the dogs are going to tree a possum shortly."

"They won't. And I'm as cold as an icicle in the spring-house."

"Lay your head over here. I'll keep you warm a-plenty. You still think possum-hunting means hunting possums, don't you?"

"I've told you enough now. I'll slap the taste out of your mouth if you try to tech me again. You're nothing but an old stud horse, and I hain't your sort. You and the crowd can go to thunder. I'm going in."

He got up. "All right, I'll go along with you. Every time I look at you, you swell up like a toad frog. But you might need me to keep the boogers off. Maybe if I pulled you out of a bear's mouth you'd thaw up and marry me."

But it didn't matter a straw to me how much he talked about marrying. I couldn't tolerate him no more than a crow could tolerate a hawk. He stunk like kyarn. And his old hairy chest. But he sure thought he was something finer than silk. And—but I knowed Pa's secret now. I was as shore of it as snuff makes you sneeze. But me and Ma still wouldn't be any the better off. The lead was on Pony's place. And I wouldn't ask Pony Pangle for anything even if I was starving. I wouldn't want him giving me air if I was stopped up in a jug.

Me and Ma didn't have any land of our own. We just lived in that little old house on Uncle Bill's place. It was about as hard for us to keep up as it was for a crippled snail. Ma being sick and everything. And we just never had been used to doing without things. Pa always sold enough of what he made so we could have what we wanted. That was the reason Ma and him got along all right. That was the reason Grandma made her marry him. A girl had to marry somebody—just had to. And she had to sort of pick out somebody that could make her a living. Ma never had had to work in the field, and I never had neither. But it was making it go that much harder with us after Pa died.

Somehow or nother I had always had a sort of shaky feeling it might be on Pony Pangle's place. But I just never would let myself believe it. I just didn't want to. Hit had always made me wonder how Pa could be so nice to Pony when he knowed he used to try to spark Ma. But they always seemed to be about as thick as two in a bed. Pa always took up for him. He took up for him that time the stingy-gutted old scoundrel posted his gooseberry patch and wouldn't let folks pick. And Pa was the only one that took up for him. Other folks all thought it was a low-down trick. Everybody talked about him being so tight a tick couldn't get under his hide. And Pa taking up for him in a thing like that was one reason that made me think he must be beholden to him in some way.

I was glad Pony Pangle was able to move his legs without moving his blamed tongue. But I wouldn't mind if he would say something then. The night was so still and cold. No life anywhere. Everything dead as four o'clock. Made me feel like I was dead too. The moon and stars—but they was still too. As still as death. Not a single star had shot. I couldn't even hear the branch running. It might be froze over. The blood in my body might have been froze too. I felt like it was. I felt real funny after that light. Plumb quare. And I was proud

Pony come along with me, for I might have been afeared without him. We were in sight of the house now. I could see firelight in the room. Ma laying there in the bed with the window open. Everything about the place seemed lonesome and give-out.

I guess I jumped when Pony begun to talk. "I know what you've been thinking about tonight. I know all about it."

"You—you know what?" I said.

"I know all about your pa's lead. My own pa called me to his dying bed and told me there was lead on the place he was leaving to me. I was a youngon then. Just turned twelve year old. Well, your pa was older and about the only person I knowed I could depend on to be fair. So I told him. He said he would dig the lead and mould the bullets and give me half of what he sold them for. That was even before he started courting. But he come and got the lead and give me half of what he got—on up till he got married. Then he married the girl I wanted. But I told him after that he could have what he got for it. I didn't want your ma to ever have to want for antything no matter who got her. I knowed your pa wasn't much of a hand to tend crops, and I knowed within reason I could make a living for myself. Me and your pa just kept it between us. I didn't rightly want him to tell your ma. But I don't think she had to be told. I think she caught on. So I've been afeared to try to help her any since your pa got killed. I didn't want to make her feel beholden to me. Your pa wasn't the man she wanted to marry. She—"

"But she got along all right with Pa."

"And me and you could get along all right too. I could tend a crop. And you and your ma could mould lead and sell it. I would dig it for you. I guess I could be sneaking enough about it that nobody would track me on my own place and then steal it all. We could take care of your ma better. She is getting mighty feeble. She needs me."

"You still in love with Ma?"

"It's done too late now. But you look just like she used to look. You're just the spit and image of her."

I didn't know what to say. I had a quare feeling and almost felt sorry for Pony. I—but—what was that? A death bell ringing in my ear? Yeah. Two stars falling too. A worse sign. One member of the family was going to die. Soon. Me? Ma? But Ma just couldn't die yet. Not yet.

"I'll come around to see you and your ma tomorrow evening, maybe. You might decide to marry me. I can't get away from home in the morning. Got some churning and things like that to do."

"Churn—? You—!"

"Yeah, I'm my own old woman. But I hain't much of a good one."

"Me and Ma ought to help you. We—"

"I'm used to it. I get along. Such as it is. I don't blame you'ns for not coming around. I don't hardly know how to act around decent girls. Ain't kept company with none since your ma got married. Just didn't much care after that. But you're like your ma. That's the reason I'm coming back tomorrow. I'll have to be getting on home now."

I didn't like the way the room smelt. Quiet. Musky. Deadlike. I wished I had stayed out in the cold. I didn't reckon Ma was asleep, shorely. The room smelt smothery.

"Did you have a big time?" Ma asked. And I guess I jumped again. Her voice sounded hollow, like a ghost's voice. I reckon I was just nervous over that light. "Huh? Uh huh. I had a right big time." But I had barely tholed it and I didn't like Pony Pangle. And that light. On Pony's place too. I knowed that was what it meant. But I didn't any more think about seeing that light over there than a lamb thinks about being chased by a dog till one gets after it. I didn't know what to say to Ma. Pony said Ma knowed all about it. I thought I would just go on to bed and not say anything about it, for

I thought Ma didn't want to talk much that time of night. But I did wish Ma would get a little more strength.

It seemed to me that Pa was trying to tell Ma where he got the lead; then his breath give out before he could say anything. I guess Pa knowed Ma wouldn't feel like being beholden to Pony when she couldn't do anything to help him back. And Pa wanted her to understand. He couldn't rest satisfied in the grave till he come back and told her where it was. His spirit was walking with the lantern.

It was always a wonder to everybody in the country where Pa had got his lead. He always had a store of it ever since I could remember. Enough to make bullets for everybody in the whole country. And knucks too. And false teeth for everybody that would let him fool with them. He everly dabbed their mouths full of mud to see what size to make their gums. That was the reason we always had more to live on than anybody else in the country. Lead was high. It brought a right smart. We never had had to tend any crops. Folks traded Pa things to eat for the things he made. And we had always had everything in the world we needed. It brought good money but it brought trouble too. For years—ever since I could memorize —folks had watched Pa, trying to find out where he got it. But he managed to always keep it a secret. Several times some men had caught him out by hisself at night and tried to torment him into telling. But Pa would have walked barefooted through hot ashes before he'd a-told.

I remember Pa telling me once that when it come his time to die, he was going to tell me where he got the lead. He had learnt me how to make everything. And he wanted me and Ma to carry on. But Pa didn't know that he was going to get kilt by old Esco Jarnigan. That old whore-hopper was mad because he couldn't find out where Pa got his lead. Esco tried to be a blacksmith too. And he was jealous of Pa. He couldn't even shoe a horse. And I didn't believe that was the first time he had tried to kill Pa neither.

And to think Pa was doing him a favor too. Pa knowed Esco
was tired and needed sleep. So he went over there to set up
with that little old Jarnigan youngon. And Esco, he slipped
out like a cat and fastened a pole across the road. He fixed it
so it would catch Pa's neck when he rode under it. He knowed
Pa would come in home about midnight. And he knowed Pa
rid right pert too.

I knowed for shore it was old Esco. It couldn't a-been anybody else. His old woman pert nigh told it on him. Somebody
ought to have gone and cow-hided him. But nobody didn't
budge. Folks were as down on Pa as a starved hound. And
there never had been a man in the whole world that would
go as many miles out of his way to set up with the sick. Miles.
I knowed him to cut wood in the snow all day long for Esco
Jarnigan. He always went and holp cut wood when somebody was sick. And somebody was everlastingly sick at Jarnigans'. Then there wasn't anybody this side of creation that
could doctor stock like Pa neither. Many was the horse he
had drenched for Esco Jarnigan. And he had split many a
oxen's tail too. His was the kind of thanks considerate folks
always got.

People just turned agin Pa because he wouldn't tell where
he got his lead. Some folks tried to claim he found it over
there in Goldens' cave. So a bunch of folks got together and
went through the cave hunting for it. But they didn't find
anything save a flock of bats and a little old bear that might
nigh scared the stuffing out of them. They all took their heels
in their hands and run faster than a wild colt.

Hit has always made me shake all over like a leaf to even
think about that night Pa got kilt. His old horse come to the
door and nickered. Me and Ma jumped out like a frog to see
what was wrong. Old Doll was standing there at the front
door just a-panting. And Pa wasn't on her back. Doll acted
just like a person, with more sense than most folks. She pert
nigh told us what had took place. The night was awful. Hot

and sultry. Owls hollering everywhere. There wasn't a star in the sky. The moon not up. So dark you couldn't see your hand before you if you looked. Just the sort of night that things happened on. Just the sort that made a body feel like his own shadow was a black spirit. I can't ever forget that night, no more than a Melungeon can ever forget a grudge. It has stuck up in the front of my mind all the time. And when I saw Pa wasn't on the saddle I was scared worse than a shot deer.

But I told Ma to stay at the house and I would go find Pa. I got on old Doll and just set there for the poor old creature to take me everwhere she wanted to. And Doll knowed where to stop. She stopped and put her head down and smelt of something.

It was Pa Doll was smelling of. To see if he was dead. I didn't know what to do. I got as stiff as a hickory sapling, but knowed I had to get off. So I clum off and felt for Pa. And he tried to talk, tried to tell me something. I thought at the time I could about make out that it was something about Pony. And now I knowed. That was what he was trying to tell me. That was what the light meant. That.

And Pony Pangle was running after one of them Jarnigan girls that very night. That was one thing that made me hate Pony so bad—running with sech trash, an old whore, no matter who her Pa kilt. But I didn't reckon I ought to blame Pony too much. He said he wanted a decent woman, and it wasn't his fault that he didn't marry Ma. If he could have got Ma he wouldn't have taken to that old trash.

Pony might ought not to be held to account for running after them Jarnigan girls. All men run after whores. And folks can get along together if they have a mind to, even if they don't set anything of a store by one another. Ma got along all right with Pa and she didn't care any more for him than a jay bird does for a cat. I have heard her say she didn't. Ma got along with him because that lead brought them enough that she never did have to suffer for anything. Women folks have to marry somebody. They can't take care of theirselves. And they have to sort of get a man that won't let them starve to death. That was one thing about Pony. He would have plenty, I thought to myself. And the girl that married him never would have to go naked and hungry. I might not have to work so hard. But all women have to work some. I guess that's one thing they're put in the world for. Then Ma has to be cared for somehow.

And to think about Pony knowing about the lead all the time. On his place. And he never has cheeped it to a soul. Kept as quiet about it as a dumb man's ghost. He done that for Ma's good. He done it so Pa could take good care of Ma—so Ma wouldn't have sech a hard life to live. And he still wants to help Ma. He wants me to—but I don't want to think about it. I hate that old possum grin of hisn. Hate it like the scratch. He didn't even have any decency about him—trying to make me lay my head in his lap. He's nothing but an old whore-hopper—used to running after them Jarnigan girls.

He might not have meant any harm though. All men folks might do that way. I never have been anywhere alone with a boy and I don't know how they act. Pony might love me. But he never said he did. And I never did hear Pa say he set anything of a store by Ma neither. And they got along peaceable enough. He hardly ever did say a short word to Ma. That was all a woman was for anyhow, was to serve a man. It didn't matter much—just so it was somebody that wasn't mean. A woman has to work hard and raise youngons for all of them.

Pony said he set a heap a store by Ma. That might just have been his way of telling me he liked me. Ma used to say men never did come out and say just what they thought. I guess if he liked Ma he would set a heap of store by me too. He never has had a woman to do things for him. Then a girl has to marry. And nobody else never has asked me. I used to think about how somebody would someday. Somebody that didn't have whiskers on his face. Somebody that wore clean clothes all the time. But folks ain't able to go dyked up and work too.

But nobody else never has tried to spark me and I don't rightly know why. Ma said folks told around that Pa's mammy was a witch and they thought that was the reason he could get that lead. And they thought I might turn into a witch sometime too. Pony didn't believe any sech as that because he knowed better. But all that don't matter—a girl has to marry somebody. I reckon he'll ask me again. . . .

"Ma, are you asleep?" I said when I come in.

"Not yet. I'm not much sleepy tonight."

"Did you know Pony Pangle set a heap a store by you, Ma?"

"He used to, Nettie. But I've broke faster than him. It's not me now. Did he say anything about the—about—the—?"

"He told me where Pa got his lead. I guess you know?"

"Yeah, I know, Nettie. I didn't for a long time."

"He said he still wants to help you. He said—"

"I won't be needing much more help. It's you—did he say anything—?"

"He said me and him could have a-plenty. But, Ma—"

"I know, Nettie. But lead is heavy," Ma said.

THE LOOK

SHE didn't say e'er a word as she was dying, Ma didn't. She just looked at me, like a cat looking at a bird, setting its eye on it, making it set still where it is. And I come back home. I couldn't a-handily been blamed if I hadn't, I reckon, if I had stayed away and let the boys shift for theirselves. But after that last look, that morning, I couldn't do else but come.

Jamie I miss—the fiesty anticky little booger, spiled as a rotten apple. Always talking his baby talk and wanting me to wait on him. "Make me Job in his coffin," he'd say. "Me want pie. Tote me. My feet hurt—tote me—me like you tote me. Make me Jacob's ladder." Always thinking, I reckon, that I was hisn and nobody else's.

And Howard—him I miss, worse than water when the well runs dry. "What's that she's got tied around your neck, Jamie? What's she giving you now—pouring sheepball tea down you again?" I give Jamie sheepball tea to make the measles break out when he was two year old.

Howard, he said he wouldn't ever be pacified till me and him was married, told me that again tother day when I went for my things. "I knowed you would come back," he said.

"A daddy-long-legs come into the kitchen this morning bringing good luck. I knowed it would be you." Said that when I stepped up on the porch. "Jamie couldn't a-ever grown up without that tea." Then it was hard—more hard than I had aimed it would be—to tell him. He set mute for the whole evening; with a low-bent head, like mine, almost, when I get to thinking, like a weed broke down by rain. And Jamie, he commenced to bawling like a sick calf. "Me'll go too, can't me?" And I, somehow, couldn't get up my things that I had come for. Till it was nigh dark. And the old bobtail rooster, the one Jamie drove round with a stick, was crowing as he went to roost, and I knowed it would soon be raining. "I'll be back and forwards," I said, and nigh didn't get it up through my throat.

Howard, he didn't move a muscle—set there still as a stone and said it, come out plain as always he did, and said it: "I allowed maybe you would marry me now—thought it for shore." And there was that in his eyes he didn't say with his tongue—what has ever been there since the first time he set to talking—when we was chopping out corn. Ma was behind in her row, and Uncle Abe was ahead; and me and him, we was neck and neck together on the steepest part of the hill above the spring, me in the row below him. "If you should marry me," he said, "we'd always be like this."

"Like how?" I said.

"With not even the corn row between us."

I just stood then too. And tother day I stood till Old Bobtail crowed the second time. Then struck out through the cedar thicket a-thinking: Howard, he don't know. He may think. But thinking's not the same as knowing—not ever the same—and I heard him say it one time about the bent sapling making a crooked tree and about Sade Hyangton's girl, that she was wore out like an old dish clout. I thought on what he said. And Hubert's threats, I thought about them. And the look.

Howard, he never did talk pretty to me, he just said it plain, what he said with his mouth. There wasn't much for him to speak pretty of anyhow. Ma said I was the ugliest youngon she ever seed in her born days when I was little. "Ugly as homemade sin," she said I was when I was born, "and wrinkled as a dried up pomegranate." She was forever and eternally a-telling me I was ugly and awkward. "Awkward," she would say, "and blundersome as a blind buzzard." And she'd look at me and as much as tell me how pretty the boys were. It made me bashful to be so ugly, for I thought everwhat Ma said was so. She was pretty as a pink flower herself, or as a diamond, Ma was—with her long hair, down to her knees—reddish brown and curly, with waves on top of her head, three of them, and rolls when the hair hung down her back as she set combing it late in the evening—not ever fearing that dark might catch her and the witches would be mad. And her eyes.

She said I was a plague and Pa didn't want me before I was borned. He done had twelve boys already—ten by his first old woman and two by Ma—and he didn't want any more boys' long empty guts around to fill. But when I come I wasn't a boy.

She said she liked boys, and she didn't want a girl youngon. I reckon she meant it. Folks talk about the way she carried on with menfolks. And the way she could make them, always, do what she wanted them to do, Pa even, till after I was born. She started setting with boys when she was twelve year old, they say. I've heard that told. And married Pa when she was fourteen. Some of Pa's boys was as old as Ma—or older, maybe. Two of them at least. And folks talked as how she was happy with them, happy as a jay bird up to something.

But after I got big enough to walk, Ma said, Pa took a fancy to me; and he took to petting me like a sick pup. Every time she told it she looked at me and said as how she didn't ever want womenfolks around her. She hated them. Hated them like dogs hated snakes, she said, all of them.

I don't memorize Pa much. I had just turned three year old when he took sick. But I recollect how it was when Ma would throw it up to me about being as ugly as a mud pie. And I looked up to the boys too, because they was pretty. That is what she told me. I got in the habit of it, and somehow, I still think them pretty. But what scared me, and kept me scared, was the way she looked at me—like she maybe wanted to like me and couldn't. I don't know. Like she feared me maybe—feared some of the boys would pay me mind instead of her. Or held me to blame for something. Maybe that was it. I don't know. I reckon now it was. Anyway, when she looked at me I somehow did what I thought the look said to do.

And the way she said "the boys" when she went to brag on Lom and Hubert. I reckon she had set as much a store by some of Pa's boys by his first old woman as she did Lom and Hubert. But I don't recollect much about them, for they died early—all save Roy. Took the quick-going consumption and died. I recollect how two of them lingered for months and then passed on one day apart. Old Noah Knox, he made a twin coffin for them. I would sometimes bawl myself weak as a weasel on account of the way she said it—"the boys." She said it humble-like—like Old Man Simkins does when he is praying in meeting and calls the name of God. And I have shook all over, many's the time, like a wet dog, on account of the look—the way she looked at me always. Her eyes and the set mouth.

Ma cut a through when Roy upped and married Rosa, Uncle Abe's girl. He went over there to live because Uncle Abe didn't have any boys to help him work—none save Howard. And Howard, he was just turned ten year old then and not much more than knee-high to a tadpole, he was so slow a-growing. All at once he growed up big and tall and strong as an ox and crafty. Then he was just big enough to come to the field and

work half the day. Tother half he would come down here
and play with me, taking me to hunt heart leaves and sang
and black gum, running through the briars and bushes and
over rail fences after butterflies and bumblebees, catching them
—catching bumblebees when they lit on thistle blooms to suck
the sweet from them, claiming that if he held his breath and
spoke to the bumblebee

> Johnny Jizzer Jacket
> You can make your racket
> But you can't sting me
> Any more than the devil can count sixpence

then the bee wouldn't sting him. And I didn't catch on for
the longest time that it was just the yellow-tailed ones he
caught.

Or he would claim I was his bussy and say verses to me:

> The road is wide and full of ditches
> I hope some day you'll patch my britches.

And I would laugh, not thinking. He sometimes would try to
put his forefinger and little finger together but couldn't—
couldn't ever. "Shucks," he'd say, "I don't believe that sign
anyhow—I reckon I'll marry who I want." And he would
laugh, and I would laugh, and sometimes I would be plagued
a little. And once when I seed him coming I put a wasp's nest
in my dress bosom, for I've heard tell that would make a boy
fall in love with a girl. Of course it fell right out, nothing to
hold it there. "Where'd that come from?" Howard said. And
I hid in the weeds from him, I was so beat.

Ma said she didn't want Roy to get married, and she went
out of her head for two or three weeks. Sometimes she would
stay in bed all day and sometimes take the Bible with her
and hide off up in the woods. Stay hid the whole day long
and till we found her at night—under the old crooked pine
tree—with the Bible in her hands. We got Granny Norris to
come and make walnut-bark tea to clear up her mind. There

was a little talk. Not much. But folks talked some, saying that Rosa had better wear a silver dollar around her neck.

I was ten year old when Roy got married. I recollect how proud the boys was that he was gone. As proud to see him go as a lost faun to see its mammy coming. Lom said he was the head of the house now and he was going to run things as he damned pleased. And he did.

There was a hundred and fifty acres of land in the place. Good slate land—with oaks and locusts and black walnut on it—and four branches, running this way and that way and finally meeting to make a big one that we call Sycamore Creek. Fifty acres of it had belonged to Pa's first old woman. Roy said that fifty acres was all he wanted, ever. Ma, she fixed that up all right so's he could have it. That left us a hundred acres—still more than anybody else had in Cocke County—anybody we knowed. Lom, he said he was selling that and putting it in something he could make some money out of; he needed money, and he tried to sell it off as hard as a caged bird tries to get free. But nobody would buy it. Uncle Abe norrated it around that he didn't want it bought, for we wouldn't have any place to live if the boys should throw that to the wide winds. There wouldn't be anybody to take us in. Ma, she said she could sell it if it wasn't for me, and I thought maybe I was to blame for every thing bad that come. And was, I reckon.

Me and Ma, we did all the work and took the beatings and the cussings when the boys was mad. Hubert was forever mad. When Roy left we still had a plenty to live on. We had six hogs and a yoke of oxen, Old Nick and Neb, and two cows, Old Bess and Old Beauty, and Jerse, the little yellow calf that Ma set so much a store by—the only one she seemed to like—because it was the last calf from the cow she brought with her when she married. She raised the cow herself. And several chickens a-running about all over the place foraging for theirselves, and singing and laying and stealing out their nests for me to hunt. Or hatching off a bunch of little ones and strutting up with them saying, "Uh, huh, you didn't find this one, did you?" And cackling and cackling till I was right plagued by their uppish cackling.

But inside of a year the boys had kilt both of the oxen. They beat Old Nick and Old Neb till they got overheated, trying to show off in front of Old Erve Tompkins. He was the man they rented the place out to so they wouldn't have to tend it, claiming he would make enough for us to live on. They sold the chickens and hogs—every lasted one of them—took off first the hogs and the chickens—a bunch every Saturday, till the last old dominacker hen was gone, and we were out. I had raised the chickens, and I begged Ma not to make me catch them up to sell. But she wouldn't ever answer me, not e'er a word, no more than a dumb man's ghost. Just looked at me. And I went and tolled Old Cackly—the old dominacker hen—into the stable and caught her up. She was the last and seemed to know, for she stuck tight as a tick to my hands.

Then the cows. They sold Jerse to Uncle Abe, and as he was leading her away she turned around and looked at Ma and bawled. Ma turned into the house and was so weak she fell into the floor. She crossed her hands across her breast and just laid their for a spell. And the tools, they went—every tool on the place, down even to the axe, it went. Lom was the one that did nigh all the selling. He give them to men for drams of liquor, or sold them for money to pay Bell Hearst that lived up on Slop Creek and was a whore. I learnt, after a short while, not to say e'er a word against it. Seemed like it made Ma hate me worse, if she hated me. I don't know.

Hubert, he wasn't so bad for selling things. He was just lazy and ill as a hornet and was forever throwing things. Me or Ma one had always to scratch his head for him and bring him a drink of water when he wanted it, no matter where he was setting or laying—even when he was in arm's reach of the bucket. He would fly off the handle at the table and throw the dishes at me and Ma. And when I started to fuss back, Ma, she would look at me and I would shet my mouth up as tight as a corn shuck and fear to open it again.

Then Lom, he took to giving the bed quilts and furniture away to Bell. Took my dulcimer that Howard give me and let her have it too. Howard give it to me when I was nigh eleven year old, for he said he didn't have a turn for music. Uncle Abe just got it for him. Said he would give it to me if I would play,

> Come rede us, fathers, come rede us, mothers,
> Come riddle us two in one
> Say, shall I marry fair Eleandor,
> Or bring the brown girl home?

He liked that song better than any other when he was growing up and always called for it. Sometimes I thought he meant something by it, after he was bigger, I didn't know. Me being so dark—"black as a burnt log," Ma said—and I had heard some men talking that Howard had a blond-haired girl somewheres in Hamblen County. I don't know. But I can't help but think.

It wasn't so powerful long till the only thing left was the bed that Lom and Hubert slept on. Just one. Then, one day, a drizzly day and bad, and Ma was acting quare, they swapped the bed to Old Man Hays, from up in King's Hollow, for a copper still—a fine forty-gallon copper still. And said they would sleep on a pallet. It was pretty, the still was. Me and Ma shined it up with ashes till it glittered like a diamond in the sunshine, it was so clean and pretty.

Aunt Maude, who was Ma's only sister, she come up here one day and seed how things were. The next day she come back and brought a bed with her, saying for me and Ma to sleep on it. But when the boys come in Ma told them Aunt Maude had brought them a bed. "A bed for you," she said, "to sleep on."

The boys claimed they needed a still. Lom didn't have ne'er other thing on the place to trade off. And couldn't get things on the credit. Belle Hearst, she wouldn't let him fool around her any more. He come home and told it hisself about the time he waited out in the woods till she come for an armful of limbs. He told her what he wanted. She said for him to wait till she could tote the wood into the house—it wouldn't take her a blink of a frog's eye, she said. She come back—fetching a shotgun—and told Lom to light a blue streak for home. He took his heels in his hand. And Bell, she shot a hole in the ground behind him, and the dirt nigh covered him up. Ma, she got mad at Bell—got mad at her as a fighting bull does at a pitchfork. And looked at me. And there was knowing in her eyes.

Directly Lom, he said he had to go to the barn ater a piece of rope. And he told me to come and go with him. I told him I didn't have any need to go to the barn; but he give Ma a look, and she looked at me, and somehow I got up and went. I give into her. And to him.

One day a bird—it was a little chickadee—got in the house, and I chased it with a broom. It flew from corner to corner and back again and butted its head into everything in the house saving the door. Ma looked at it. "Somebody is going to die," she said. "Hit might be your granny." I never had been to see Granny—Pa's ma. And soon the next morning Ike Howington, the man that lived on Granny's place, come over here to bring word she died the night before. Said she took to getting her breath hard and claimed there was a witch woman setting on her chest smothering her to death. Ike said Granny told him on her deathbed she wanted everything to go to me, everything she owned.

Ma told Ike she didn't reckon she could go to the burying. Told him I took a duck fit everytime she started anywheres. She didn't go neither. She didn't have any clothes to wear. That was one reason. And somehow it seemed like she didn't

care to ever see anybody save the boys. Folks talked about her
not going. Whispered things around about it. Ike come over
here one day and told her how folks talked. And she just set.
"Talk don't hurt me and mine," was all she said.

I never did see the cows nor the quilts, nor any of the things
Granny left me. The boys, they both went. And I reckon, if a
body can judge by hear-tell, they had nigh about everything
sold before Granny was covered up in the grave. I don't know
what they got for things nor what things there were—save
the land, and Ma had to go to town and do some signing for
that to be sold. I got it by hear-tell that there were quilts—
an Indian's Hatchet pattern and a Mill Wheel and a Snake
Fence—and all sorts of coverlets—Rose of Sharon and Snow
Drop ones that I wished for; and kiln-made jugs and crocks
and dishes. But I don't know. I know I didn't get to go to
the burying. Ike said his woman told him to bring me home
with him. She would fix me up to go. I said I would, but
Ma looked at me, and I took it back and told him I reckoned
I couldn't go.

They did bring one thing home from Granny's. The little
piedy calf with her right front leg broke. Rose. They were
trying to get her into the stable for the man they had sold her
to, and Hubert broke her leg with a rock he throwed. The
man wouldn't take her then. But Rose was gentle and pretty.
Piedy all over—red and white. And she had brown eyes, with
water sometimes in them. Rose loved me better than she loved
clover. She liked it when I rubbed her head with my hands.
I set her leg, and she stood still as a rock while I did it, knowing it was for her own good, I reckon, for she was a knowing
calf. Once she turned her head and licked my shoulder, getting
my dress wet and sticky. Before two weeks she could walk nigh
without it being told she was a cripple. We liked to play together, me and her did. Every time I got a chance I went with
her when she wanted out of sight of the house to pick. And
she would go with me when I went to play in that patch of

wild sweet williams down on the new ground hill. She liked
to lay down and let me gather blooms and cover her up with
them, from head to tail. Sometimes Ma would come hunting
us. We started running when we seed her coming. Rose was
afeared of Ma.

Times when the boys were mad at me they would make
me watch them while they helt Rose and beat her, for nothing
she had done. They would laugh fitten to kill when Rose
started shaking and bawling and going on. Once they rubbed
her red with a corn cob and put turpentine on her. They
laughed all over theirselves, the both of them, and I shook
and cried and hurt. Lom, he said I was too hot and needed
cooling off a little.

Roy paid the taxes on the place every year till he got married. After that he took to leaving our part not paid. The first
year I raised enough turkeys to pay them; but the boys, they
took the money, and I never did see hide nor sole leather of it.
I made mention of the taxes when they told me to catch the
turkeys up. But Ma, she sided against me. And the taxes, they
didn't get paid.

Me and Ma stole corn out of Old Man Worthington's corn
crib to make liquor. At first the boys made it. Then they got
so they stayed in and slept at night, and me and Ma, we went
and made the liquor. We got to be right good at making it.
The nights were dark, and everything around was quiet—save
for the owls. They kept a-hollering. The fire in the furnace
made a little light; and Ma, she set there in the light and I
could see her eyes and the waves of reddish hair like the copper.

For four years we didn't put out any crop. We didn't have
any more tools, and the boys said the renters would do enough.
But they were cheating, lying folks, the Tompkinses were, who
didn't do anything but ruin the land they worked. And steal.
Uncle Abe said they would steal the stink out of stink ball,
they were so roguish. And that winter—that second winter—
we didn't have anything to eat save wild things. I don't know

what kept us from drying up and falling to staves. Three times we had mush—twice when I went down to Nona's—Nona was the woman that lived on the place, Old Man Tompkins's woman—and borrowed the meal, and once when Howard brought us some—a little in a poke, not much. Some he had ground hisself, and Ma said it was fine as fiddle dust. She liked Howard, she couldn't help but show it.

Old Man White, at the Cedar Hill store, he got to the place he wouldn't let us have anything more on credit. Said we owed him a hundred dollars for shotgun shells and sardines and cheese and crackers. And he wanted pay for them, he had to have it. Me and Ma didn't can much. The few blackberries we did can had to be emptied out so's the boys could have the jars for liquor, giving the liquor away, always, free of charge. When they come to the table and found me and Ma didn't have anything cooked to eat they throwed the dishes against the wall— till we didn't have any dishes.

Once they both come in drunk and said they was going to kill Ma. Hubert took the pistol and beat her with the butt end of it, while Lom, he was kicking her. I took to kicking Hubert, and Ma took to clawing at me with her fingernails and looking at me. And I got stiff as a poker and couldn't move a smidgin.

They tore the skin plum loose on Ma's head and she nigh fainted, but nobody didn't see her while she was in such shape. And nobody never did know about it. Once I asked her if she was hurt and she didn't answer me no more than a log would. Just looked at me. I didn't ever name it to her again.

Howard give me two rabbit boxes. I was lucky as a rusty nail and caught twenty-five rabbits during the winter, and seven muskrats with the steel trap he let me have—just loaned to me, he said, but never did ask for it and never would take it when I named it. The boys sold the muskrat hides to Dewey Fawver to ship; and the rabbits they took to the store and set folks up to cheese and crackers, them blackgyuardish men that set up there by the stove spitting and joking without anything to do at home. Me and Ma, we stayed close in, and we nigh starved to death. I named it to Ma, but she just looked. Once she said it was the Lord punishing me for my sins. "Your many sins," she said. She never would own that she was hungry.

I took to keeping out some of the rabbits and roasting them in the fire when the boys went off to loaf at the Cedar Grove store house. I eat all I could hold. But Ma, she said it wasn't right for her to eat when the boys weren't there. Said she couldn't eat for thinking about them a-being hungry. And the way she said "the boys." Like Bogus Hyder did when he prayed for the Lord not to let his girl die—one time I heard him up on top of King's mountain a-praying.

Nights when the boys brought some old man home to stay the night with them they sent me down to Nona's or to Uncle Abe's to borrow something—anything—to eat. Soon they got so, both of them did, they didn't want to let me have it. And the boys, they would kick me and call me a whore in front of them old men—nigh all of them whorehoppers, the men were, or having the name of being. When I cooked up what I borrowed Ma didn't like for me to eat it. If there was a bite left after the men got through—but there wasn't ever much, for they had bellies like rat holes they was so hard to fill—it had to be saved for the boys the next day. If I started to take a bite Ma would look at me and I would put it back, generally always, unless I was so hungry I swallowed it before I looked up. Sometimes I did.

Uncle Abe and Nona both, after a while, got to where they wouldn't loan me anything when I went for it, saying it wasn't right to uphold the boys any longer in their shifty ways and devilment. The first time, and the next, when I come back and told Ma what Uncle Abe and Nona said she just looked at me; and Hubert, he slapped me on the mouth and told me to go back.

One day Ma heard Uncle Abe and Roy up in the thicket above the house chopping wood. Lom told her now was her chance to prove I had been lying. When they had stopped and gone in for dinner she left the house. I knowed where she had gone. I heard Lom tell her to hide behind a log or tree one so she could hear what was said. He would send me to ask for money when he heard the chopping start up again.

I went and told Uncle Abe what Lom said for me to tell him, that Ma was sick and would he loan us a little money for a few days, that we would pay it back. He went over the same thing, Uncle Abe did, saying what he always said. He was willing to help me and Ma all he could. But he wouldn't give the boys the spit off his tongue if they was parched with thirst.

When he said that Ma stepped from behind a tree and stood and didn't say anything, but she fell down on the ground and crossed her hands across her breast. I went to trying to pick her up. She opened her mouth and gaped like a dying chicken. "She's dead," I said. But Uncle Abe, he laughed. And told her, God damn her, to get herself up from there and get on to the house where she belonged. She got up, and me and her started. And she didn't take her eyes off me all the way.

Ma told the boys Uncle Abe said he wasn't going to help anybody that kept a whore like me laying around the house. Looking at me all the while she talked. Then Hubert, he set in on me. He kicked at me and missed and fell down on the floor he kicked so hard. And just laid there and kept a-kicking.

In the summertime we managed, somehow. There were blackberries and huckleberries and strawberries and wild potatoes a-plenty, and folks didn't mind giving things from their gardens in times of plenty. Uncle Abe and Roy and Howard, they all tended a crop together, and me and Ma took to working out for them. We worked nigh every day, dropped the corn— I dropped it for Howard to cover. "Four grains to a hill," he said. "One for the cutworm, one for the crow, one for the witches, and one for to grow." We chopped it out and holp them cut it and shock it and pull it. We got one good meal of victuals a day. But Ma, she wouldn't eat much. And Howard once asked me if she stayed at home all night. He seed it took me back, so he was quick to say, "I just allowed she might hunt something to eat at night; but I reckon not—she seems so dauncy about her eating." We handed our money over to whichever one of the boys we seed first, generally Lom; for Hubert, he just set in the house and fussed and fussed and never tired from fussing. I don't know what about and don't reckon he did either.

Me and her didn't have any clothes save what Nona and Aunt Maude give us. And of course no spinning wheel or warping bars or anything. They sold them at the start.

Hubert kilt Rose one day—just beat her till she fell over wet with sweat, the slobber running out her mouth, and died. Done it because he was mad at me—for something, I never did rightly know what. Him and Lom made me get Uncle Abe to bring a team and drag her off—over to the back side of the well field—and throw her in the big gulley there, after they had skint her. Uncle Abe didn't dig the dirt in on top of her. Just left her laying there. And the buzzards, they swarmed all around, and the dogs, they come to eat her. Midge even, Howard's dog, that had played with her. And the smell of her was on Midge and in the air for a whole week and more.

Things went that way till the day Ma told the boys Howard talked to me a heap, and me to him, she told them. Said every time he stopped to let the horses blow a spell he set down and talked to me the whole while that he was stopped. Low talk, she told them. Hubert, he flew off the handle and he cut gashes on both my legs with the whip made from Rose's hide. He whipped Ma too, Hubert did, because he said she hadn't told him before about me and Howard. I told her I would go to the branch with her and wash the blood off her legs, if she could stand the walking. But she looked at me, and it was worse than ever before, the way she looked. And the blood dried.

I quit working. I don't know what Ma told Uncle Abe was the reason for it. On rainy days—might nigh every rainy day —Howard would come to the house. If I seed him coming in time I crawled up in the loft and hid, listening to hear him ask about me. Two times he seed me afore I could get out of sight, and he hollered, "Hi, Rabbit. I nigh trapped you this time." Rabbit was what he called me, because I was so quare, he said, and always running from him. He was the only one I ever played with save the boys. We made mud houses and mud pies together, me and Howard did, when I wasn't any more than knee-high to a tadpole, when he come to the field with Uncle Abe. It was good to play with Howard, for he was mannerable. "You take this mud, it's done worked up. Can you jump that? Give me your hand. I'll go first to mash the weeds for you." He was about the only boy person I ever seed, save them old men the boys had to come here.

Ma went on and hired out for all the summer. And the next winter, it started out like the one before till we took some kind of breaking out. We had little red bumps all over and itched like mangey dogs, all of us did. And Ma was weakened by hers and never did get stout again. About the middle of the winter she got sick—bad sick. It was during the time of the cold snowy spell. Me and her had borrowed Howard's axe and had been cutting wood during the cold days. One of us cut while tothern tended the still. I was proud they was letting us make the runs in daytime. The look wasn't so bad when it wasn't dark; and the trees was bare, so that we could see. All was quiet save sometimes a rabbit hopping or a fox slipping through the cedar bushes. And we knowed them sounds. The boys sold six cords of wood to Grady Jenkins over in Hawkins County.

Ma laid there sick, and the water poured in on her when the snow melted. A heap of the boards had blowed off the top of the house; so the water poured down as she laid there. And

I took a broom and kept it swept out from under her bed as best I could. Folks come in and brought things to eat and things to put on her bed. None of us had enough cover to keep us warm, since Lom took it off and give it to Bell. But it was easy on me, Ma being sick. I got my part of what folks brought to eat. And after a while the boys stopped bringing them old men home with them. At first it had just made a chance for them to come. Made out that they was coming to set up with Ma. They set and told tales and asked riddles and folks norrated it around that I was sleeping with any of them that asked me to. Uncle Abe and Aunt Maude, they come every day and brought lard and meal and canned stuff to eat. Nona and Rosa, they did too. But at first they didn't stay to set up, for the boys made it knowing to them that they weren't wanted.

Then it got out that Ma was out of her head and couldn't live any longer than three days more. When it did, Howard and Uncle Abe and all of them, they took to coming to set up. And Howard named it that Old Jerse was sick too—had the hollow horn, he said, and Uncle Abe split her tail and put salt and pepper in it to cyore her. Aunt Maude, she said there was need for her here and she didn't care if the boys didn't want her. Every time she come they went traipsing off somewheres, I don't know where. And don't care to know, don't have any reason for knowing. Ma, she would sometimes take spells of holloing for them, and she would cry and scream and say she knowed her boys were kilt. If they was here when she took a spell they would cuss her and threaten her, and she would shet up like a scared hound.

One time Uncle Abe was here and the boys went off early in the night. They hadn't been gone but a short span of time till Howard come. He said me and him could set up with Ma, and Uncle Abe could go back home. So me and Howard, we got to set up by ourselves. Set and talk. And he said he wanted to marry me, it didn't matter if we was first cousins. That didn't matter a whit. Said I ought to marry somebody. Said there was a buck rabbit for every she rabbit in the whole world and he was my buck rabbit, and grinned about it. I thought on things—on going to the loft with Lom, and what Hubert had said, for he said it over and over a blue million times that if I ever tried to get married he would kill me. And the man too, he said. I told Howard I didn't want to ever get married. But we talked on, and he took to asking me riddles. "Why is a man like biscuit dough?" he said, and answered it hisself: "Not because a woman needs him but because he is hard to get off her hands." And laughed and looked at me and kept on laughing. And I laughed too. "I'll keep on pestering you," he said. "I hain't never going to stop asking." Directly he put two apple seeds in the shovel and helt the shovel over the fire. "Look," he said, "the apple seeds move towards one another. Bet you can't guess who I named them?"

Ma took one of her spells that night. She raised up in the bed and prayed for the Lord not to let her die. Told Him she would live right if He wouldn't. And not hold any grudgement agin Him, ever. Said she smelt sulphur a-burning and that her straw tick was on fire. "The fire!" she said. "Don't let it burn me. My legs are scorching!" She jumped out of the bed and hit the floor kerwhollop; and we had to nigh buckle her to get her back in again. Then she cried and said God had forgive her sins and she was ready to go. She crossed her hands on her chest, saying she was ready to face her Lord, and she knowed the boys would meet her there some day. She took to singing:

> Glory, Glory, Glory,
> Glory to the Lamb
> Hallelujah, I am saved,
> And I'm so glad I am.
>
> Mother's gone to Glory
> And don't you want to go
> To see the shining angels?
> And don't you want to go?

Yes, we'll all go,
Yes, we'll all go
To see the shining angels,
And don't you want to go?

Both with one tune. Her boys were saved too, she said. Her and
them, they would have a big time up there in heaven together.

The boys come in as the roosters was crowing for midnight.
Lom was drunk as a lord, and Hubert, he looked bleary-eyed
and quare as a white eagle. They seemed quiet, and I thought
they looked like something more than liquor was the matter
with them, both of them. They told it later. A whole passel
of men had gathered themselves together and followed them,
just to let them know they didn't have any use for their ways.
And that night while they was gone somebody stole the still
out from under the feedway where it was hid.

But me and Howard, we had a good time talking to one
another before they come. "Got any popcorn to pop?" he said.
And it plagued me to have to tell him we didn't have, as it
always plagued me to have folks come when we didn't have
anything to eat. Or when we didn't have wood. He told me
he was going to give me some little chickens and turkeys when
it come grass, or as soon afterwards as he had any hatched off.
"For you've got a sleight at chicken raising," he said.

And he did—he give me fifteen turkeys and twenty-five
chickens the next spring. I raised them—not letting e'er a one
die. One took the gapes but I twisted up a hair and put down
its throat and pulled the gapeworm out. And it lived and was
a pet and not much littler than the rest. But I had to catch my
chickens all up—every last one of them—before they weighed
a pound a piece and the boys took them to Cedar Hill store. I
don't know what become of the money. And the turkeys. They
was pretty—slick and glittering like a copper still when the sun
was on them. They loved me like a faun loves music too. Didn't
ever give me any bother. Used over in the back side of the well
field and come up early nights as regular as a fox feeds her

young. When I was out in the fields or in the woods sometimes
they would see me and here they would come, gobbling and
stretching their necks and yalk-yalking as best they could, and
pecking, sometimes at my toes. At times they come to the house
during the daytime. Stood at the door and yalked and yalked
till I went out and spoke to them. They stretched their necks
and turned their heads and were pacified. But I tolled them into
the stable and caught them and tied their legs and the boys sold
them on the Thanksgiving market as soon as it was open. And
the money didn't go for the taxes as I had aimed it should.

But the boys were mad because Howard was there setting
up that night, and Hubert hit me over the head with a plate,
one Aunt Maude had brought, the next morning.

Ma, she never did take any more spells after that night, and
she begun to get better by the littles, like a wilted plant when
it's been put in water. And we kept the kivers and things that
folks had brought—even the other bed that Uncle Abe brought
in the wagon one day; so that we had two beds, and they laid
soft at night time.

Then I come a woman, and I took to getting contrarious with
the boys. One day I got the shotgun after Lom. I couldn't a-hit
the side of a barn but I got it after him. He went sneaking off
like a sheep-killing dog and didn't bother me so much after that.
Aunt Maude give me seeds to plant a garden, and Howard, he
give me two hoes with cedar handles in them and some jars to
put up fruit in. Every time anybody made mention that the
garden was pretty the boys kicked; and Ma, she looked at me.
But I got to the place where I didn't care any more for a beating than a balky ox does.

We had enough to sort of make out on the next winter, but
the boys stayed huffy and contrarious all the time, and Ma was
ever sullen like a caught possum. One day she went over in the
woods by herself to hunt dead limbs, and whilst she was gone
Howard come down into the lower field to feed the sheep. He
come to the house and stayed a right sharp whet of time—save

it didn't seem long. He said if he was me he would leave home
and go stay with somebody else, if I was set on not ever marrying. "Why won't you, Rabbit?" he said. I didn't make him
any answer. And he set in to talking about queer things, about
Old Jerse, and about witch women a-losing their power with
menfolks when a girl youngon was born to them. And I just
set. He said lots of folks over in Hamblen County would give
me my board and clothes for the work I done. Ma come back
to the house before Howard got out of sight. I could tell she
was mad as a wet hen; but she didn't open her mouth to
speak a word.

All during the time the sheep was lambing some of Uncle
Abe's folks stayed down in the field to sort of take care of
them and keep them from freezing. Everwhich one come nigh
always come down to the house and stayed full half the night.
One night when it was spitting snow, along about dusk time,
I heard Howard up there a-singing. He was just singing away
like a mocking bird on,

> I'll give to you a dress of red
> Stitched all around in golden thread
> If you will marry, if you will marry,
> If you will marry me.

I just said it sort of halfway to myself that I guessed maybe
he would come down to the house after while. Hubert, he flew
off the handle and said he would slap the silliness out of my
head. He said for me to get in the bed and stay there. That
I was in love with Howard and if ever I spoke to the God-
damned son of a bitch again he was going to send us both to
the middle of hell even if he had to follow us there for doing
it. He said I didn't need to be hossing for Howard and not to
think I could ever marry him either, that he would kill the
flop-eared son of bitch. I crawled into the bed, and he said
for me not to speak to Howard if he did come. And Ma, she
stood at the foot of the bed and looked at me for a long span
of time.

In a short while I heard Howard holler "Hello." Hubert told me now, damned me, to lay over there and keep my mouth shut. "Where's Rabbit?" Howard said, the first thing. Ma told him I was piled up over there in bed, and he said, "Hop out of there, Rabbit. I allowed maybe you heard me a-calling the sheep." I didn't say anything—just laid there and trembled all over like a shot bird.

Ma told him I was on a high horse. "I allowed she was mad at me," he said.

Howard come over close to the bed, and he said, soft as the wind almost, "You wouldn't be mad at me, would you, Rabbit?" I just busted out and went to bawling like a lost lamb. Something down inside of me stung like a snake had bit it, and I laid and shook.

Howard, he went on talking to Ma and Hubert. And I thought from the way he sounded that maybe he knowed—I wanted him to. And it made me content, like a pet faun, to think he did. Then I took to wondering again. I wanted to get up and talk to him. I heard him say there wasn't any need of going back over in the field till round about midnight. Ma told him to lay down by the side of Hubert, that Lom would be in about that time.

Ma come back to bed. I felt quare—him over there asleep, or maybe thinking about me. I didn't cry out loud and soon went off to sleep and didn't know any more till Lom called me, about chicken crow, and said it was time for me to get in the bed with him, said Hubert had gone up in the field with Howard, said some of the lambs was about to freeze. I got up and got in the bed with him. And somehow I hated him worse than I had ever hated him before and wondered if Howard helt any grudgment against me for not speaking to him.

Two weeks after that it was that Lom come in one night and said Howard was married. I kivered my head up and nigh choked—felt like my lungs was going to burst open, they were so big, like a blowed-up hog's bladder. Then I got to think-

ing maybe Hubert would let me speak to Howard now that
he was married, if ever I should see him again. Lom said his
old woman was from over in Hamblen County, and I took
to wondering what sort of a woman she was—if she would
make him a good woman and if she would help him work
and do things he wanted to do and thought in my mind of
course about Fair Eleandor. Lom said Uncle Abe give Howard
a feather bed and a cow—Old Jerse, he said, and eight hens to
start out on. Said Howard had bought a place over in Hamblen
County close to where his woman was from; done had part of
it paid for. The stingy devil, Lom called him, saying he was
too stingy to blow his nose, and I hated Lom. I hated Howard's woman too. She wouldn't know how to do for him like
I did, and she might not even set anything a store by him.
Might not even raise chickens and feed them. Or know what
to do if they took the gapes.

Of course, Howard never did exactly tell me he set anything
a store by me, but I could tell it in his eyes—the way they
looked—and by the way his voice sounded—soft as a kitten
purring and not like it come from just off the tip of his tongue,
but from way down deep in him somewheres—when he talked
to me. I wished I could see him or hear him say something.
I wondered if he had ever named me to his woman. I couldn't
handily be blamed for hating her. I hated everybody in the
world save Howard—everybody I knowed. I tried hard as
a hurt dog not to show it—that I was bothered in my mind—
but for two whole days Ma didn't do anything save to stare
at me with that look in her eyes, not ever saying anything,
just looking.

Howard hadn't been married but nigh on to six months till
Lom told it at the supper table one night that he heard Howard's old woman had the consumption. Said he heard she was
right bad off with it, besides being called to straw too. I didn't
know how much of it to believe or not to believe, knowing
as how Lom always measured things by a coon's skin with

the tail throwed in; so I just let it stay on the outside of my ears for the whiles.

But four nights it was after that when Lom come in and said he was going to hire me out. He said Howard wanted somebody to stay with him. Hubert riz up and said I shouldn't go. But Lom told him to keep his mouth out of this, that Howard had all the woman he could take care of and they needed the money. Said he had done told Howard I could come and do the work for fifty cents a day. But said I would have to come on back home Saturday evenings and stay Sunday.

It wasn't but a little more than a whoop and a holler across the county line and through the cedar thicket. Lom, he generally met me before I got halfway home. Like he couldn't wait to get his hands on the money. Or me. When he was through with me I would go on home and go to work, with Hubert setting around fussing and cussing always, first about one thing and then about another. It didn't matter what. I never did know. And I thought all the while on Monday morning. And Howard.

Before I went I just knowed that Howard's woman was named Sarah, and that is all I knowed. But she was good to work for. Howard, he did nigh all the outside work. All save milking and gathering up the eggs. All I had to do, save to wait on Sarah, was to do the cooking and washing and ironing, and make up the beds. Then I milked the two cows—Old Jerse and Old Heif, the one Sarah's pa had give her when she married. The first time I went to milk Old Jerse she walled her eyes around at me in a quare sort of way but I didn't pay her any heed. She let me get nigh through, and then she set to kicking every time I touched one of her back tits. Then I gathered up the eggs to help Howard out, for he was forever busy as a sow with pigs he had so much to do. And things was fixed handy so that work wasn't hard. I liked to take the clabber and make gobs of yellow butter, with Sarah's white-ash dasher, and her churn had a horseshoe nailed to the bottom to keep the witches off. The milk always turned good over there and the butter stayed together. Sarah had pretty moulds too, with pictures of little acorns cut into them—three bunches— and they left the prints of the acorns on the butter. Me and Howard and Sarah, we all got along like a den of young foxes. Nobody ever was contrarious with anybody else, and it was restful there.

We had good eating. I took Sarah's plate to her first. Then me and Howard, we set down at the table together and eat. We didn't talk much. We didn't have need for talking. But sometimes I would glance up—and catch him looking at me. And we would set and set, till directly he would say, "Setting here hain't buying the baby a new dress nor paying for the one hit's got." Then he would get up and go and I would just set there.

Sarah was easy to wait on—never did speak a short word to me, ne'er a one the whole time. When Howard was in the house she asked him to bring her a drink of water or an apple to eat, instead of calling on me to get it. I was content when I was in the house with her—save when I looked at her light hair and skin and her blue eyes; but I tried to raz things from my mind—and I was content when I was out helping Howard do up the work. Sometimes when I was done milking and went up in the loft to gather up the eggs Howard was up there throwing down hay, and I would think; or I would look at him and know what he was thinking. Then I would hurry down the ladder. It would have been different from Lom; but I feared Howard might could tell. I don't know.

Sarah sent by Howard for me some shoes—brown shiny ox- ford slippers with strings in them that laced and tied in a bow. And cloth for a dress. She said she didn't think the boys treated me right. But I didn't say anything to her about them one way or tother. Nor about Ma neither when she asked me if Ma seemed to hold any grudgment against me for anything. And I never told her any more when Old Jerse kicked, for that first time she seemed upset and said, "She never did kick Howard. That's quare why she didn't."

Howard, he took notice that I looked more better in pretty things. "What color of red is that you've got on?" he said. "Hit suits you, like in the song. But I couldn't find any gold thread." Sarah showed me how to make my dress. It was red with tiny white roses in it—with gray leaves onto them, and black dots scattered around between the roses. Made with a flared-out skirt and wide, like girls in Hamblen County wore. I wore it home on Saturday, and Ma looked at me with that look—only it was different from what it had ever been before and was worse, for seemed like it had pity in it. I don't know.

Hubert cut a through about my dress, saying Howard had bought it for me and that I shouldn't ever set foot over there again, and he hit me on the shoulder with his knucks. Ma took to crying, and somehow I did too. Lom told Hubert he would just have to quile down a bit, that they had to have the money. And come Monday morning nothing was said against my going.

One day when Howard come in from dinner he said he had seed Uncle Abe and Uncle Abe said our place was being sold soon and nobody was doing anything about it. Said the county was selling it for the taxes that hadn't been paid. He said the back taxes for the past nine years come to two hundred dollars. I thought about Ma—without even four walls to live inside of —no more than a wild dog. And I set in to bawling right in front of Howard and Sarah. They looked at one another and both of them looked at me and I bawled on. "You'll get your eyes wet a-crying," Howard said. "A rabbit don't give up so easy." But I bawled on, till Howard said he would go to New Port and pay the money. Said he would get a soon start the next morning and put the bid in my name so nobody else would bid against it. Then one day he brought the deed and give it to me. All in my name, the place—the whole hundred acres.

I thought Ma and the boys would be proud when I told

them what Howard had done. But they, the boys did, both of them together, lit in to cussing me. They said I had to sell it and pay them what I owed them. That they had had to keep me up for seventeen years and they was going to have their pay for it. Ma, she stood there mute. She didn't say a word to me during all the day Sunday. Just looked at me. And something inside of me was afeared. I don't know what.

I thought quick as a fox and told the boys the deed wasn't in my name yet, that Howard had it in his name and was going to keep it in hisn till I was thirty year old. They don't know any better yet. And needn't. It's two year more. They said if Howard owned the place, by God, he could pay the taxes and I could make him put a top on the house. They didn't aim to live in it as it was, with the top like a sifter. I flared up and told them they ought to be proud somebody kept them from being throwed out into the middle of the big road. And Ma just stood. And Hubert, he kicked her on the shin on account of me, and she bent double with hurting. I got her to the bed. "The boys are hungry," she said. "Fix them something to eat —they're hungry boys." She put her hands across her breast and laid there on the bed and frowned from hurting and stared at me with her eyes, like a snake trying to charm a gopher.

Then Ma took sick again, and I come home to stay the while and wait on her. Folks around give all sorts of reasons for her being sick. But I don't know, nor care to know; for it is better not to know than to know what a body don't want to know. Some said she was called to straw. At her age they told it. Folks always talk. Some can't breathe without talking. But she was sick and something went up to her head again. She laid there in the bed and prayed nigh all the time—out loud. She screampt and yelt and talked about sin and the Lord a-punishing her. Then set in on me. Said she wished she had dried up her breasts when I was little and starved me to death. That I was a plague to her. I was with her by myself then, nigh all the time. Hubert, he looked sheepish and didn't stay around. She kept looking at me; it seemed as if I moved the way she wanted me to move, without any mind of my own—like a feather blowed here and yon by the wind.

I waited on her till she was stout again. Howard done all the work over there and tended to Sarah. And Sarah, she was ready to have her youngon any time. Howard kept on paying the taxes and paying me, and I ne'er spent a copper of it on myself. Sarah's baby did come, as I knowed it would, while I was with Ma. The baby lived but Sarah, she died about her next breath. The boys come in and told it and Ma, she looked at me and I could tell what was in the look. Or thought I could—almost.

Howard, he lived on there, saying he couldn't bear it to move back to Cocke County and live with Uncle Abe. So Uncle Abe moved to Hamblen County with Howard and left his place in the hands of Roy and Rosa. Still there wasn't any woman person to tend to the baby. So as soon as Ma was up and strong enough to wait on herself again Howard come and asked if I could stay with him and Uncle Abe and care for the big boy. It was while he was standing out in the yard talking to Lom and Hubert that I heard a dove holloing on top of the house. I run out into the yard, aiming to throw a rock at it; but it was done gone; so I didn't give it much more heed than I would a rat's tail in a meal box. Save the morning I left, it seemed like Ma was a little shakey. And once or twice on Sundays I took note that she had nigh about stopped talking, even to the boys, but just set; and it made me, somehow, think on the dove. But I didn't name it to the boys. Nor think too much on it.

And I stayed on with Howard. He said Sarah told it on her dying bed that she wanted me to name the baby. And I named him Jamie. The little dirty booger, it suits him right well. "My Abbit, me can't sleep with Pa. Pa kicks. My Abbit don't kick." And I would never make him, for he sets as much store by me as a sheep does by clover. And nobody has done a whit for him the whole three years save me. Till now.

Howard, he would ever watch me as I fixed the milk, being careful always not to give Jamie Old Jerse's milk, for Howard said Sarah named it on her dying bed she wanted Jamie brought up from her own cow. And Howard, he would accuse me of stealing Jamie's dinner when I tested the milk on my lip to know if it was warm enough and not too warm. Sometimes I got fretted with him, poking fun at me about the things I did for Jamie—the time I made sheep-ball tea for him when the measles wouldn't break out, or when Jamie was cutting his first tooth. I dug the best part of three days in the hot sunshine to find the mole. "What's she got tied to you now, Jamie?" he said first thing when he come in. And kept on asking till I had to tell him to have any peace.

"Hit's the left front leg of a mole," I said.

"What does hit do to him?"

"Makes tooth-cutting more easier—that's what Granny Norris does."

"Hain't you ashamed to treat a little mole such way?"

"I kilt it first."

"Hain't you never heard Preacher Lavrin read the Bible?"

"That means a man."

"Don't you reckon the little mole had feelings same as a man?"

Till I was nigh sick for pity of the mole. And was mad too, at Howard. I got peeved again that evening when Jamie was fretful and whiney as a sick pup and Howard set down with him on the back steps to try to pacify him whilst I washed up the dishes. But Jamie, he twisted and turned like a fly in hot milk and whined till I come out and took him. "My Abbit," he said and put his hand on my face and his head tight up against me. "Pa's lap hard. My Abbit sets good." And soon was quiet as a full kitten.

"Hit ain't right for you not to have one of your own,"

Howard said. I didn't make him any answer. "Recollect what I told you that night?"

"What night?"

"Setting up with your ma."

"Huh uh."

"About the buck rabbit?"

"Oh."

"Hit's so."

He set there for a right smart whet of time. Then got up and walked out into the yard. It was getting dark. The frogs down the branch a piece was calling to one another:

> Come across, come across, come across.
> *Too deep, too deep, too deep.*
> Roll up your britches, *roll up your britches,*
> roll up your britches.

Coarse voices, and little voices, and whiney voices like Jamie's, and some deep like Howard's, almost; and gentle. I couldn't help but think about Howard's riddle:

> Three bull frogs
> Sitting on a log.
> One took a notion
> To jump in the ocean
> And leave the others on the drift.
> How many frogs were left?

and always his answer before I had a chance to rede it: "Three —he changed his notion before he jumped."

In between the frogs' hollos was the noise from the water-fall—just down below the pippin apple tree. The moon through the leaves of the old oak. And two stars in the sky. Seemed like I couldn't move, got stiff all over my body, and when Howard come back to the steps he said it again, that it would be better if he didn't have to leave me alone at nights. A sort of aching feeling went over me; and my mouth got dry as powder, so that I couldn't speak.

"Why won't you ever marry me?" he said, and stood up.

"I reckon you know me so well you just can't thole me." Then he went on into the house.

I set on the steps a-hating the boys and thinking—it was one thing with one breath and another thing with the next: that I would tell him I would, that I wouldn't, that I would tell him, that I wouldn't tell him—set there with Jamie in my lap till the roosters crowed for midnight. Old Bobtail first, then Old Smart Smarty and Old Popeye—and two from across the hill somewheres, Howingtons' I reckon; and the roosters' crows and the frogs' hollos and the owls and the night jars— the noises from them—they all went around in my head like a whirlwind and got mixed with what I was thinking. Till I got to fearing again and thinkng on what Howard said about the sapling; and seemed like the face of the moon was Ma's face with her eyes looking at me; and a cloud covered one of the stars so that there was just one left, and I somehow got up and got to bed.

Howard seed I was bothered in my mind next day, and he didn't name it to me more, and I was content taking care of Jamie—that morning.

I was squeezing and pulling away, like always, on Old Jerse when I looked down and noted the milk in the bucket. It was a pinkish color. I tried each tit, watching the color of the stream. The left hind one. Blood streamed from it. I jerked back my hand, to not strip it, and poured the milk quick on the ground.

I wasn't much more than to the house when I heard Lom's voice. "She's needed at home. And will be." And then I started running. And thinking: I just couldn't stay, Howard. I couldn't. But somehow—. Then there she was, Ma was, in the bed at home pretty as a diamond, with her hair loose and curly and shining like the moon on the pillow. And her eyes.

"Ma," I said. But she didn't say anything. She just looked at me. She was just giving me that look and not breathing.

DAVE COCKE'S MOTION

I NEVER have heard such singing. Malissie started playing, and everybody in the church house started singing till the roof nigh raised from the singing. It was the protracted meeting, or Dave Cocke's motion, I don't know which, that made the change in folks. Seems like, ever since then, it's no big matter if a body is a Democrat or a Republican. Folks just want to sing. They all started up, and they kept on at it—all save Abel Sneed. I never have heard him singing.

But early in the morning—nigh every morning still—I hear Levi Graham singing. "Glory, Glory, Glory," he yells out as he goes to feed his hogs. "Glory to the Lamb—piggy whoo pig—Hallelujah, I am—pigg-ee—saved, And I'm so—piggy whoo pig pigg-ee—glad I am." Even Albert Benton has took to the guitar and sings over at McMinns' on Saturday nights. It's been told—Agnes Maclin told it to me—that Albert put a new verse to "The Old Time Religion" one night and sung "Makes the Democrats love the Republicans," not seeming to recollect the time he knocked two teeth out of Ray Tom's mouth for saying fried rats and stewed cats are good enough for Democrats.

Preacher Bradley makes out like it was all from his preaching.

He said from the way folks looked, the first week of the meeting, he thought them ready to fall to staves. They all just set, stuck to their seats, not taking any more interest than a terrapin would and not offering to stir themselves about any till that Sunday morning—five years ago it's been—when the organ was back.

Folks all wondered and stared at the organ—just stared and didn't say e'er a word. Soon they set into singing like they hadn't sung since the organ left. And it's been the wonderment ever since, and will always be, I reckon, of everybody in Sarananny District how the organ got back into the church house. Some think—Agnes Maclin does and Eudora Claiborn does, and they are both Republicans—that the piano did, of a certain, fall through the floor, on down into Hell, where it rightly belonged, as Dave Cocke motioned. But I don't know. All I know is that it was gone, the piano was; and the organ—the same organ, for there was the split place made by the Yankee's maul—it was back, just setting there natural as a leaf on a tree. And Malissie Hayworth was back to play it, already on the organ stool when I went in, seeming herself. Folks claim it made her well, or something did at that time, and she went on through school and got a good paying job in town and can't now be stopped from playing and singing, no more than her grandma could.

I didn't see Abel Sneed when he come, but Agnes, she seed him. She said the first thing he done when he got to the door was stretch his eyes at the organ. Then he tucked his tail between his legs and took hisself to that back seat, for he was late; and Malissie was playing "Bringing in the Sheaves." She was down to the line that says "We shall come rejoicing" when Abel come in, and Agnes said he was the only one in the whole crowd that didn't seem much to be rejoicing.

It all started, the trouble did, about the organ, when Abel was Assistant Superintendent and got up one Sunday, after Belle, his youngest girl and the ugliest, had been taking music lessons in Smithtown for about six months. Well, I reckon, rightly speaking, it started sooner than that—when Malissie Hayworth was born maybe, or maybe when it got out that she could learn fast and was a born music-maker like all her folks before her; or it might shore enough had its start when the Civil War was fit. Abel Sneed's and Dave Cocke's pas fit against one another in the war. Abel's pa was a Yankee and Dave's was a Rebel. Malissie Hayworth's grandpa was a Rebel too, but I don't reckon it made much dent in Malissie's forehead. Abel, he claimed he hated all Democrats, saying they hatched from Rebels. But I don't know. It might a just been he was jealous of Malissie and took the spite out on Dave because Dave had been good to help Malissie and her ma. Anyhow, he needed backing to get rid of the organ; and he had to bring up something that would make the Republicans stick to him, for Boone County is thick with Republicans and it was Annie Hayworth, Malissie's grandma on her pa's side, that saved the organ from the Yankees. She was seven year old and was living close by in the old Hayworth house over there when the Yankees slept in the church house for a week. One morning, shortly after the crack of day, she heard a noise loud as thunder and she run over to the church house, not thinking to be afeared. There was a soldier man in there a-splitting up the organ with a maul. "I play on that organ," she told him. Just walked up in front of him and spoke it out. "Sometimes I waste my whole day a-playing on hit." He looked at her and laughed to hisself and didn't say e'er a word and went on beating with his maul. Annie pushed herself by him and set herself down on the stool, cool as a cucumber, and started in to playing:

> And it's O, dear John, and it's O, dear John,
> And I know you'll marry me now.
> O, how could I marry such a pretty girl as you
> When I got no shoes to wear?
> Up she jumped and away she ran
> Down on the Market Square.

The soldier man, he acted like the lightning had struck him. He stood there and rubbed his chin and pulled at his whiskers and blinked his eyes like a toad frog in a hail storm and made Annie play every song she knowed. She played "Black Jack David" till her arms ached from the playing, and the soldier man stayed and kept on a-staying—till he feared to stay longer. Then he throwed his maul over his shoulder and went on off without saying e'er a word and without so much as turning his head to look back.

But nobody had ever made complaint about the organ being a Rebel organ till that Sunday. It was on a preaching Sunday, just before Preacher Bradley commenced to get started good, when Abel got up and told the congregation how backwards they all were for being content with music made on that old broke-down organ, not naming anything about the split. Said every church house in Boone County had a piano save Sarananny, and he thought they should swap the old organ in for a piano and pay the boot and would somebody make a motion to that effect. "Let's hear the motion," he said. He stood up there holding his neck like a board, waiting for the motion; but everybody just stuck to his seat like a leech, and nobody offered to make it. "We've got money in the treasury to pay the boot," he said.

Still folks all just stuck to their seats. They took to whispering amongst themselves, and I heard Albert Benton say: "His gal's a-learning pissanner in town." And Agnes Maclin, she said to me: "Huh, trying to keep Malissie from making the music." And everybody just kept a-whispering and whispering and shaking their heads and naming it about the organ being there so long a time and saying what they wanted was music like Malissie could make and her pa and grandma before her, and nobody made the motion. Abel's eyes took to blinking like a hoot owl's he was so took back, and he hunted around in his head for something to say. And then he said it: "This here old organ is the very one Noah took into the ark with him anyhow.''

Dave Cocke, he riz up at that, and he said: "Hit don't make no difference if hit's the one the Devil took into Hell with him, hit makes good music, and we like it." Dave Cocke was a hard-working, honest-living man that had give Malissie and her ma a house to live in and had bought them flour and clothes and such. His pa and Malissie's grandpa went off together and stayed together through the whole war.

So, of course Abel was mad. He grinned that grin and said, "Well, Brother Cocke, this hain't a time for sharp-shooting, even if you do roost on the grindstone. This is business brung up before the congregation." So Dave set hisself down and riz back up again and he said: "Mr. Chairman, or everwhat you are, I'm going to talk and say what I want to say." And he set in to say it. He said he thought folks ought to bear a heap of things in mind before they went running out to buy a new piano. The first was that everybody in Sarananny District liked the music they had there. It was noted that they had the best music and the best singing in all of Boone County, he said. And next, there were things they could do with any extra money they had. Said there was a widow woman living close by with eleven youngons to buy shoes for. Her man had been killed, he said, and the varmints—some two-legged pole cats—had caught all her chickens at night. That was a right techy thing to say to Abel, of course. Everybody knowed he meant Hannah Mills, and it was Abel's hired man, Ray Toms, that was nigh caught a-stealing Hannah's chickens.

"Well," Abel said, grinning that grin again, "I've heard tell that some old men buy shoes for young gals. I'm not so rich myself; but I could buy some shoes, if need be, out of my own pocket."

Dave Cocke still stood. "I know what you're throwing up," he said. "But there hain't nobody but'll tell you Malissie is the best music maker in these here parts. Takes it after her grandma. And she hain't never failed to play for Sarananny day or night, nor rain or shine."

Abel's hair riz up, and he looked like a mad tom cat as he yelled out. "We hain't beholden to Malissie Hayworth for nothing. She don't even know one note from anothern."

"She knows how to play the organ the way Sarananny folks like the organ played," Dave Cocke said. Everybody in the church house showed it in their faces that he spoke their minds too. But nobody said e'er a word. They all just set like scared rabbits and listened to Dave and Abel argufy back and forth till Abel said, "If a Rebel youngon had tended to her own business that organ wouldn't be here now; and hit won't be long."

Dave come back with, "That organ will be here when Hell's froze over, making a covering for the Yankee that tried to bust it up." Still the motion wasn't made.

But Abel, of course, he was bound and set on it, and folks, them that were against him, took to jesting about him bringing it up every Sunday. They laughed about the weeds taking his corn crop whilst he went backing and forthing to town looking at second-hand pianos. Albert Benton said he was down there one day in Anderson's store and said when Abel come in the door all the pianos upped and started playing "Jesus Loves Me." That was the song Belle had learned to play. But still nobody ever made the motion.

Abel told it around that he was going to have Dave Cocke churched, claiming he was carrying on with Malissie. He nigh said it out in church one Sunday. "Well, hit hain't for nothing that an old rooster crows over the slick feathers of a pullet," he said, when Dave was arguing that Sarananny had good music. Nobody paid Abel any mind about that, but they all did get mixed up in their thinking about the Yankees and the Rebels; and Dave said even the Devil out of Hell couldn't make Abel see anything, he was so new-fangled since his girl had become a town lady.

So the arguing kept on. Folks from all around come just to hear it, and Sunday School got twice as big as it ever had before—till the benches all were full. And one broke down one night with Dave Cocke on it. And Abel, he laughed all over hisself, of course.

At first folks didn't think much nor take sides; they just come to hear the racket. Then they took to going back into their lives, thinking how their pas and grandpas had fit in the war. And some didn't know and nigh got on the wrong side. The Republicans all felt they should side with Abel, but none wanted to get rid of the organ. Then the Democrats started setting on one side of the church house and the Republicans, of course, took to setting on tother side.

All sorts of rumors went floating around in the air about what Dave and Abel did and said outside the church house. They had been at outs all their lives, of course, but just never had started arguing. The way Dave run Abel off was the funniest of all. Dave's woman, Gertie, told it. One day Abel took his hired man Ray Toms, who was as big as the side of a barn, with him and went to Cockes' house while Dave was out in the yard a-cutting stove wood. Abel said to Dave, "Howdy, slave owner, you wouldn't want to know what's being said about you and Malissie Hayworth, would you?" Dave, he just looked Abel square-dab in the eye. "You see that road out there," he said and waited for answer. Abel just stood. "You see that road?" Dave said again, taking a step towards him.

"Ye-yeah," Abel said, jerking his head.

"If you don't want to hit Hell, and that right soon, you better hit the road," Dave said. And Gertie said she knowed a cat couldn't a-winked its eye as quick as Abel got into the road—with Ray Toms stepping on his shadow. Abel didn't even look back—just kept a-cutting the grass. Gertie said she reckoned he thought Dave was behind him. Ada Carouthers said he was still running when he passed her house, with Ray at his heels; and Ada called her man from the field, thinking

Ray was out to harm Abel. And he took to running too. And
they all kept on a-running. One behind tothern.

After that, Abel didn't come back to Sarananny. He did all
his talking outside the church, and right when he was cutting
his biggest through about Dave and Malissie, poor Dave, he
upped and breathed hard and died. Just fell dead out in the
cornfield one day. There were some that wondered about it; but
I don't know. Abel come to the burying, and folks talked about
the pleased look on his face when he marched around the coffin.
Said he stood for a right smart whet of time staring at the
corpse. Then walked away grinning.

Malissie, she, of course, stayed home from school the day
of the burying and played the organ for the singing—the best
playing she ever did and the last till that Sunday when the
organ come back, if it come back. The last song they sung was
"Till We Meet Again," and I recollected what I heard Dave
say one time, right after the arguing about the organ started,
that when he got down to Hell he expected to meet up with
several Sarananny folks down there—Democrats and Republicans, he said. Then seemed like folks just got so they couldn't
sing.

Right after the burying—it was a soaking-wet Sunday,
drizzling rain all day long—Abel was at Sunday School, big
as a king. He didn't ask for any motion. When he riz to dis-
miss he told that he was giving fifty dollars on the piano and
that it would be there the next Sunday. "I've done picked it
out," he said and grinned. "Hit hain't never heard tell of the
war."

The next Sunday everybody in the District was at Sarananny. Some come from up in Crockett County—folks I never
had heard of. And there, the first thing I seed when I went in
the door, there by the side of the pulpit, was the piano, not
facing the congregation as the organ had, but setting sideways
so that everwho played it could see and be seed by everybody
in the church. When Abel got up to call out the numbers he

said, "Malissie, you can't play the piano, can you?" and grinned
that grin.

"I've not had a lot of lessons like Belle has," Malissie said.
And Abel looked out over the folks and grinned again.

So Belle, she twisted herself up to the piano like she thought
she was something specially screwed together, all dyked out
in a brand fired new dress—blue silk—bought just for the
show off. And it did show off her hind end.

"Number twenty-six," Abel said. That was "Jesus Loves
Me." "I've been giving Belle piano lessons for seven months.
Young gals shore are dear costs to their pas." He grinned again.
And I thought of his ma's pension from the Yankees that Abel
used to take.

Belle, she opened the book and got up and pulled at her dress
tail and set down again on the bench and turned and twisted
her hind end around and nodded her head and held her hands
up in the air like a sailing buzzard's wings and started pecking
at the keys like a buzzard pecking at kyarn. Hal Cumberland
—he had been used to leading the singing and was a Republican, and some thought it was to get thick with him that Abel
wanted Belle to do the playing instead of to get even with a
dead Rebel girl—Hal, he started out; but he seed it was too
slow and he asked Belle to go a little faster.

"The music hisn't written to go faster," Belle said out loud
and turned her head up sideways and stuck her chin out. She
started leading the song herself and Hal, he set down, for that
was all he could do of course. A few folks—Old Man Jefferson
and Louise Meigs and Van Garnes was all—droned along with
Belle; but her and Abel, they did most of the singing by theirselves, and kept on doing it every Sunday. Others all seemed
not to want to sing or even to feel like it. The bunch of boys
that set in the back and were too young and blank-minded to
know whether they were Democrats or Republicans, they
laughed and made fun of Belle's "Pissanner" and Abel's "music
pecker" and Belle's and Abel's "duet so sweet." "The two, they

do duet so sweet," the boys said, for seemed like Abel left a
bad taste in everybody's mouth even if some did feel bounded
to side with him.

He was Malissie's uncle, being her ma's brother. Him and
Malissie's ma, Eppie, were Eli Sneed's only two youngons,
and they were left, when Eli got killed off with the Yankees,
with that big old place up there on Salt Creek. Abel beat Eppie
out of her part of the land before she ever married Ethan Hayworth. Then when Malissie was five year old Ethan died of
blood poisoning from a cut on his shoulder. Nobody ever did
know how he got the cut. And Eppie never was right in the
head afterwards. Soon Abel had the land Ethan left Eppie too,
claiming she owed it to him for paying the taxes and loaning
her money. Eppie and Malissie had to get out. Dave Cocke let
them live in that house down there on his place where he had
been keeping his sheep.

Malisse held grudgment against Abel, of course, recollecting
as she did what he said to her the day her pa was buried. Told
her he wasn't in heaven, that Democrats couldn't get to heaven
"for carrying on with Negro women," he told her. She
wouldn't talk to him save when she seed him out in a crowd
at meeting or at the store house; and then he was forever
throwing up something to her to plague her. Once he caught
her in front of a big crowd up there at Golden Gate store and
he said: "They tell me you've mended your ways and become
a Republican."

"I hain't no sech a-thing," Malissie said.

"Well, Democrats believe in making slaves of the folks they
have to keep up. How'd you like it if I made slaves out of you
and your ma?"

"We hain't never been beholden to you," she said.

"Look out how you talk to me," he said, and grinned his
grin. "Your ma could be put somewheres."

And when Malissie started to school at Pine Grove, Abel
took Belle out and sent her to Miss Teelie Monroe's subscrip-

tion school because Miss Jennie—Miss Jennie Garnes was the teacher at Pine Grove—skipped Malissie up to the third grade, putting her ahead of Belle. Then after she got bigger, one time Abel hid down there in the hollow and tried to scare the daylights out of her as she went home through the fields. She run back up to Cockes' house and Gertie Cocke went the rest of the way home with her. Dave headed Abel off down there in the sedge grass field and give him a good briar whipping. But after that the other scholars—they were nigh all Republicans that went to Pine Grove—they wouldn't let Malissie play ball with them and wouldn't walk along the road with her coming or going. Every time she went nigh Bertha Hamilton, Bertha would say, "Malissie is a rose with a broke stem. Her grandma loved a yankee and married a Rebel." Or she would snigger out, "She may have a baby." And Rachel Claiborn took to singing:

> I've been a-wondering all my life
> Where Dave Cocke could get another wife.
> Down to Eppie Hayworth's he will go
> To see Malissie you might know.

Bertha moved when Malissie set down beside her on the recitation bench one day, and Rachel held her nose and whispered, "Sheep smell, phew, phew, sheep smell." Malissie just give up and stayed at home or up at Cockes' working like a horse.

Till right before the last war started, the one with the Germans, when the bus from town started coming out this way, passing in front of Cockes' house—Malissie started going to school again. She hadn't been to Pine Grove enough to get in the high school at town; but Miss Jennie got it fixed somehow so that she could go. Belle was down there at the same school, of course. Abel boarded her in town and paid a woman to show her how to play the piano. But she was in a class ahead of Malissie, and the boys and girls down there hadn't heard any of Abel's tales, so everything went all right till Malissie made friends with a girl that knowed a heap about playing the piano. The girl showed Malissie at recess till Malissie caught on and took to playing by ear for the school to sing by every morning. And the teachers asked her to play the guitar when they had big programs.

That didn't set well with Abel, of course, and he went to the head man and told him tales on Malissie and claimed he couldn't have his girl in a school with such. The principal told Abel he might as well take Belle out, she wouldn't get out any other way. Abel flew off the handle and went to Square McMinn and Square Lunt. They were Republicans, and they threatened the head man with not giving the school any money, or some such threat, till he had to come under to Abel and promise he wouldn't put Malissie forward. Miss Jennie told me about it, and I set and thought: Hit just looked like Abel could run everything and there wasn't any need for God being in Boone County—or the Devil either, as Dave Cocke said. Dave said Sarananny District was a few acres of Hell with the Assistant Devil a-running it.

The things Abel stirred up all got so bad the teachers wouldn't let Malissie play the school piano any more. And Abel kept running to Eppie with a lot of stuff till she took to fussing, claiming Malissie was trying to get above her raising and was putting on airs and all such, till Malissie quit again. Seemed like she just dried up and folks around in the District nigh dried up too for want of singing.

When anybody went to see Hayworths, Malissie hid out in the weeds and wouldn't come in, till folks told it she had consumption and was wrong in her head like Eppie or worse. She kept on acting that way, at least.

If it hadn't been for the turn during the meeting, after the motion, Abel might a-been running the whole world by now —there hain't no telling—and I reckon folks in Sarananny District would have all been like rotten apples, for the preacher man was dumbfounded that first week when all the old folks set like rocks and the young ones giggled. Every time Belle went to play somebody would start giggling. If it wasn't Albert Benton it was Katy Hawks, and somebody else would take it up, and the giggling would go over the whole church just like giggling was catching. "The two they do duet so sweet," the boys in the back tried to sing to the tune of "Jesus Loves Me." "Jesus loves me," Tob Sevier would say, and Albert Benton would say back, "He loves me too—He just don't show it." And the giggling would start again, till some folks called the meeting a protracted giggling.

But Belle, she strutted just the same, lifting her hands up and letting them down again, like she was pushing the dust out of the air, and nobody sung and nobody made any profession. I reckon they all got to wondering if they were Christians, or whether they were just Democrats and Republicans, for they all set like dead lice were dropping off their coattails.

The second Sunday morning was experience-telling morning and nigh everybody felt it was time to stir, for they had all set still for a week. Old Lady Greene (who was a Democrat) talked first—about starting lies on Nancy Bean (who was a Republican). Then Picken Sevier told of having a liquor still when he lived over in Cowbird District and of keeping it hid under the feedway. (It give some folks notions.) Then Preacher Bradley, he told about hisself, how he used to be a jockey and how he sharpened the teeth of horses and pasted false tails onto them and dyed scarred spots with black shoe polish and all sech, till he got a mule put off on him at Jockey Town one Monday that didn't have anything real save the bridle; and when the mule all come to pieces and fell apart he asked the Lord to forgive him. The Lord, He did forgive him and what's more He called on him to tend to the sins of others, and Preacher Bradley hadn't ever seed Jockey Town since and hoped he never would, though at times his legs did get tired from walking.

Then Abel, he riz. Everybody in the church got as still as night and set tight on their seats, thinking as how he was going to tell about his fight with Dave Cocke, or maybe tell he killed him. But Abel didn't aim to tell any sech. He told as how there had been some lies—he didn't name what they were— told on him in the country and how the Lord, because he was close to the Lord and had been ever since he give hisself to the Lord when his pa got killed off fighting the Rebels, the good Lord had lent him strength to forgive them that started the lies and not hold e'er a bit of grudgment against them. Just like he didn't hold any grudgment against Democrats in Sarananny District for what their pas had done wrong. Said God made him a forgiving man when he give hisself to Him. And he grinned.

Everybody else just set. Even the preacher man set for a right smart whet of time, without blinking his eyes. Finally, after what seemed half of forever and nigh on to milking time, he riz up and prayed a prayer and said there would be preaching that night and Monday night and if they didn't do any good they would have to close the meeting.

It was then that things took the turn, I reckon—that night. Abel was taking Preacher Bradley home with him to spend the night, and of course he had to wait till the preacher man shook hands and talked with them that wanted to say anything to him. That made him and Belle and Preacher Bradley the last ones to leave. Abel started to blowing out the lamps. When he got to the one over there away from the piano, Preacher Bradley told it afterwards, Abel stopped dead still and stared like a scared hound at the window. "Who—what—O," he yelled. "What's a matter?" Preacher Bradley asked him. Abel turned around. "The window," he said, "There's somethi— somebody—" and he was shaking so he couldn't get any more words out his mouth. Preacher Bradley went over and raised up the window and stuck his head out, but he couldn't see hide nor sole leather of anybody or anything. They blew out the rest of the lamps and went on home.

There wasn't any meeting in daytime, save on Sundays, so

Preacher Bradley and Abel and Belle, they all come together the next night. Abel, he stood up at the piano and yelled out: "Number twenty-six. Now let's all sing this song. What's a matter with you folkses—afeared you'll suck bugs down your throats?" and he grinned. Belle, she lifted her hands up and started letting them down. And about that time Abel turned as ashy as a ghost. He didn't say anything; but a quare, white look went over his face. Folks noticed everything was as still as death. Belle's hands never did tech the piano. She jumped up. "Pa," she yelt. "What's the—" Then she stood stiff too. Everybody with a pair of eyes gaped toward the window. And there it was—greenish white at first and by the littles forming into a shape. A man. Everybody just set—them that were setting did. Abel and Belle, they stood, and the preacher man.

"Hit is Brother Cocke," Preacher Bradley said. "Come in, Brother—" but he bit his tongue and couldn't say more.

"No, much obleege to you," Dave Cocke's voice said, as plain as daybreak. "The noise from that thing's worse than Hell. I make a motion to send it there, where it rightly belongs, with all them windy Republicans." He said it plain, so everybody in the church house heard it. And then he wasn't there any more. Gone up in smoke like grease on a hot skillet.

Nigh everybody—Democrats and Republicans—in the whole country made professions that week. Even Albert Benton renewed up, and Old Man Hancock got through, though some say he never took the fire out from under his still. And the next Sunday was what set everybody to wondering and has made them wonder all five years and will always I reckon—I just don't know. Of course everybody knowed the meeting would close that day and a big crowd come. The house was so full that folks couldn't be choicey about seats, and Democrats and Republicans got all mixed up together. I don't know who was the first one to get there. Nobody has ever owned up to being first; but when I walked in the door, there it set—natural as the nose on my face—the organ; and Malissie on the stool with her back to folks—just like she used to be. Directly she started playing, and folks all commenced singing to the tops of their voices:

> Bringing in the sheaves
> Bringing in the sheaves
> We shall come rejoicing
> Bringing in the sheaves

And Abel, there he was on the back seat, not grinning, and Belle, and Democrats scooting over to look on the book with Republicans, and everybody a-wondering, I reckon, and nobody asking; and Malissie playing, and everybody just a-singing and singing. I never have heard such singing.